The Lost Roller

The Autobiography of Nobby Clark

Strategic Book Publishing and Rights Co.

Strategic Book Publishing and Rights Co.
12620 FM 1960, Suite A4-507
Houston, TX 77065
www.sbpra.com

ISBN: 978-1-62857-822-5

Book Design: Suzanne Kelly

My sincerest thanks and gratitude to:

My daughter, Sarah, and my ex-wife, Sheila,
for allowing me to write this book.

Geraldine, for your patience and understanding.

Flora Harrold, I couldn't have completed this book without
your encouragement, support and hard work
and the precious time you put in sorting my mistakes.

My family and friends.

Acknowledgements

Front cover design by Kenny Herbert.

Cover photograph and statue photograph by Stuart Stott.

Proof reading by Sandy Mcnair.

Final editing by Tricia Corney.

Edinphoto for photograph of Clermiston House.

Corstorphine trust.

Contents

Preface

I woke up flinching from a sharp pain in my side. It was dark, and I could feel the rough hairs of a blanket over my head. My right arm and leg were completely numb, and the side of my face was pressed hard against a concrete floor. I slowly pulled back the blanket and screwed up my eyes against the light—I could just make out the words "Ernie was here" scratched into the surface of grey-painted brickwork. A plank of wood ran along the full length of the wall, sloping down towards the floor to make it uncomfortable to sit on for any length of time, and I recognized the small, barred window that was too high up the wall to see out of. I muttered to myself, disgusted and defeated, "Oh no, not again… police cells."

What had I done this time? I had no memory of how I got there, nor why, and had no idea of the time, day or night. The blue, padded jacket I had on was filthy and my trousers were wet. When I exposed my feet I was wearing old, worn sandals with no socks. I was cold, very cold, and started shaking uncontrollably.

I crawled over to the door, hardly noticing the other two bodies in the cell: one was propped up against the wall, beside the exposed toilet bowl splattered with vomit; the other was lying comatose in the corner, wrapped in the familiar grey, horsehair blanket. I reached the door and banged as hard as I could, but no one came. A loud voice was shouting down the corridor, "Turnkey, turnkey!" over and over again, interlaced with, "You fucking bastards!" and deep, resonating thuds that sounded like a boot against a door. I found a button on the wall to the right-hand side of the steel door, and I pressed it repeatedly. There was a distant ringing but it got no response.

My shaking was getting so bad that I couldn't control my hands, and my clothes were already soaked through with sweat that stank of body odour and alcohol. I kept banging the door and ringing the bell for what seemed like eternity until, eventually, a small sliding panel opened at eyelevel and a face appeared. I could see a white shirt and black epaulettes with raised silver numbers across the top of his uniform. He looked angry at being disturbed and growled impatiently, "Yes?" "I'm an alcoholic," I said begging for sympathy, "I've got to have a drink... Please... I need to have a drink." The panel slammed shut in my face.

How my life had deteriorated so quickly. It didn't seem very long ago that I was singing in front of thousands of fans and making hit records with The Bay City Rollers, appearing on Top Of The Pops and other television shows, touring all over Europe, doing radio interviews, photo shoots and taking part in recording sessions with world-class musicians.

I've searched for reasons why I've been tormented all my life by obsessive and addictive behaviour. Was it hereditary? Was it mental illness? I knew only too well that I had suffered from bouts of depression for most of my adult life, but was it brought on by my low evaluation of self worth or a genuine chemical imbalance?

I seemed to go into self-destruct mode often just when I was on the brink of a breakthrough. After a prolonged, determined effort to achieve an important personal goal I would sabotage it right at the last minute. Was it fear of failure or fear of success? Did I not deserve to be happy or feel important? Was I punishing myself? I've felt fear, fear that is indescribable, an unknown terror that exists in my head and scares the hell out of me. To see things coming out of the walls and to feel something moving on my skin that appears so real, but has no basis in reality.

As I've grown older I have become more and more aware of my fears and insecurities. The phobias, values and emotions that are the consequences relating back to events in my childhood. Even after years of fighting with my alcoholism, denying its existence, and living with its destruction, long spells in psychiatric units and many therapy sessions, I am still searching for the answers to many questions.

I have decided to face my demons and expose them for what they are worth.

The Lost Roller

CHAPTER ONE

I was angry, screaming and fighting with all my strength. "You will put these pyjamas on," my father growled. "No, no!" I was screaming. I felt the big strong hands forcing the sleeves onto my tiny arms as I struggled and fought. Then another sharp pain as the big hand slapped hard again on my bare backside. The more it hurt the more I fought. My Aunt Daisy took control and carried me out of the room, just in time, as my father was removing his leather belt. That is my first vivid memory from fifty-seven years ago. I was four years old.

Aunt Daisy wasn't really my aunt. She was my mother's aunt and a sitting tenant in a very small basement flat at 36 Danube Street in Stockbridge, Edinburgh. My grandmother and grandfather died suddenly when my mum was very young and the family had to be split up. My mother's sister was sent to live with relations in the north of England, and my mother was brought up by Aunt Daisy.

My father was an army man. He had been a colour sergeant in the Royal Marines during the Second World War and had been responsible for transportation. Always smartly dressed in his tweed sports jacket and split pea hat, he never went out without his collar and tie and highly-polished shoes. He smoked John Players Special non-tipped cigarettes, sixty a day. He was a tall, slim, handsome man who had lost most of his hair early in life, but had a thin pencil moustache, sharply trimmed in a straight line. A very impressive, authoritative figure as he walked down the street with one hand in his right-hand pocket, as he always did, but he only had to look at you with those chilling eyes to put the fear of the devil in you.

Danube Street, in the early 1950s was not the sought-after, highly-priced property area that it is today. In fact, very few people could afford to buy properties and many in Stockbridge were run down and neglected by the landlords. In contrast, many of the Georgian properties were grand, imposing buildings with tall stone pillars marking the entrances to two floors of rooms with high ceilings and ornate cornicing, and basements below that would have accommodated the servants in times of greater wealth. The cobbled streets were wide and lined with high kerbs and pavements.

We lived in what was known as an "area flat". You could look down from the pavement through the railings into the windows below. A steep stone staircase wound down into the dark, damp, outside area that was paved with large flagstones. Wooden doors led to cellars under the road that looked like dungeons.

It was always dark and damp in the flat. Very little light got in through the windows. I remember my mother telling us the story of Leerie The Lamplighter, whose job it was to walk around lighting the gas street lamps that barely brightened the dark nights. Then, one dreary misty night as the light was fading, I looked up from the basement window and saw him! A shadowy figure in a black coat holding a long pole that lit the gas mantle in the street lamp. He looked down and saw me at the window and walked towards the railings. He had no face, just a black outline, and I screamed in terror until my mother grabbed me in her arms and looked out the window saying, "There's nothing there, it's alright."

I remember the area flat as an eerie place. The rooms were dark. The lighting had been converted from gas to electric but the gas mantles were still there, white fluffy balls sticking out of the wall. Everything seemed to centre round the range in the living room/kitchen cum bedroom. Aunt Daisy slept in the alcove behind a heavy woven curtain. My mother and father slept in the small front bedroom with the baby, Rosemary, while my older brother, Brian, and my younger brother, Norman and I slept in the same bed in the other room, two with their heads to the top and one with their head to the bottom. My sister Margaret, slept on the floor in the living room beside my aunt. We were kept warm with coats over the bed and a stone hot-water bottle pushed into a large sock, which we were always fighting over.

My father would be up early every morning firing up the black cast iron range with paper sticks and coal. All the cooking was done on the range. In fact all activities took place in front of it where it was warm. There was always a kettle boiling away, and a teapot simmering on the hot plate. My mother would heat water in a large metal pot and pour it into a tin bath and bathe us one after the other in the same water.

I will never forget the smell in that flat, from the soot out of the chimney and the dampness in the walls. Once, my mother and father's bed fell through the floor in the middle of the night when they were sleeping. Dry rot and woodworm had eaten away the floor joists and the whole family was wakened by the noise and commotion and gathered around the bedroom doorway looking at the half-submerged bed and the hole in the floor. I thought we were all going to be swallowed up.

Aunt Daisy was a wonderful person. She was short and stout and always wore her floral-patterned apron which had one large pocket in the front where she kept her clothes pegs. Her hair was always in curlers under a hairnet and when we were cheeky she would shout sharply, "Wheesht! Hold your tongue!" and I would walk behind her holding my tongue between my thumb and forefinger and making cheeky faces to make the others laugh. She expressed an air of sternness and authority, but really she was soft and reassuring.

In the basement flat next door lived Mrs Kirkhope. She too was never seen without her floral apron with the big pocket, where she kept her pegs, curlers and hairnet—it was the fashion of the day. I loved going down to see her. She had a budgie that talked non-stop in a cage that she hung outside, under the stairs, and a strange husband who sat in a chair beside it never saying a word. She would make us jam sandwiches and juice, and tell great stories of her childhood.

We were allowed to play in the street in those days because you rarely saw a car. When one did come along, everyone looked out their window at the spectacle. You were more likely to be trampled by the store horse delivering milk.

Straight across the road from Mrs Kirkhope's flat was 17 Danube Street (Dora's famous brothel). I was too young to know what was going on, but I remember sitting on the steps opposite and watching the sailors arrive in taxis from Leith docks. They would throw pennies across the street to me. I watched them being greeted at the door by glamorously-dressed women who always smiled and waved across. They would enter the hallway and go up the winding staircase with its ornate banister to the first floor. Through the open front door I could see the walls were rich and plush with fancy red and black wallpaper, and in the corner at the bottom of the stairs was a white stand with a large pot on top with two long, green leaves partly covering a painting hung on the wall in a golden frame.

There was always something going on in the street. A wedding in the house upstairs attracted all the children in the area because all weddings had a "poor oot", when the father of the bride would open the car window and throw handfuls of pennies and ha'pennies out into the street and all the children from poorer families would scramble about on the ground picking up as much as they could find. I suppose we must have been poor.

Then one day everyone was so happy… the Queen was coming! The stables for the Horse Guards were in the mews at the top of St. Bernard's Crescent nearby, and the Queen was coming to inspect the horses. My father was at home for a change, he was never usually around during the day. We were all dressed in our Sunday best and my mother looked beautiful. She always looked beautiful. Aunt Daisy even had her curlers out, and her apron off, and she was wearing her best coat which was normally kept in the cupboard with the mothballs. We all walked round into St. Bernard's Crescent and stood with all the other people dressed in their best clothes, lining the street, standing for ages and ages. Then I heard the "clip clop, clip clop" of the horses' hooves on the cobbled road coming up the hill. I was jammed between the legs of the grown-ups, hanging onto my mother's coat and I caught a glimpse of a horse's leg and a wheel, but nothing else! The Queen must have been there because everyone was waving and cheering.

My mother made a meat loaf that day to celebrate. It was a special dinner whenever my mother made a meat loaf. Her recipe included ground beef, or mutton, mixed with breadcrumbs, oatmeal, beef dripping and, of course, her secret ingredient that she never divulged to anyone. It was all fun and laughter until some strange men came to the door bearing small toys for the children, and my father went off with them. I could feel the atmosphere in the house change.

Things were always different when my father was around. We were kept out of the way. Of course, the baby Rosemary got all the attention, but the other four of us were not to be seen and not to be heard. When he wasn't there we had the freedom to do what we wanted.

One thing I remember as clearly as if it was yesterday: we were playing outside in the area, when my older brother Brian locked me in the cellar under the street. It was pitch black and water was dripping from the vaulted ceiling. All I could see was light through the cracks between the wooden slats of the door. I was terrified, screaming and panicking but no one came. I had imagined all sorts of evil monsters hiding in these dungeons under the street, ready to grab the first child that set foot in their trap. I was screaming for what seemed like an age before he let me out. When I ran into the light, I had a giant black spider on the back of my hand! I was frozen with fear until Brian knocked it off. I can still feel the terror when I think about it now. I have had a deep fear of darkness and spiders ever since, as well as a recurring nightmare of something touching my back as I'm trying to run away, taunting me as if to say it's futile to try and run.

My younger brother Norman was the accident-prone child in the family. He was aged two when he fell in the street while carrying his glass feeding bottle and almost cut his hand in half. He was just recovering from that when he put his hand down a street drain (what we used to call a siver) and contracted scarlet fever. If the flat was crowded before, it was a lot worse now—he had to be isolated in my mum and dad's bedroom, so the whole family slept on the living room floor. Our family doctor came to see him everyday. Dr Scott had brought us all into the world and saw us through every illness. He was a creepy man with a low, soft-spoken voice but I didn't like his pencil moustache or the way he looked at me. When Norman was no longer contagious we were allowed into the room to see him. I stood at the bottom of the bed and watched him holding his hands up in front of his face shouting, "Stop! Stop! Horses on the bed!" My mother said he was delirious and seeing things.

It hadn't always been like this.

When the Second World War had ended my father was demobbed from the army and took an interest in the clothing industry. He started working as a salesman in a men's tailoring shop and definitely had an eye for style. He met my mother at the Marine Ballroom in Portobello. It was the only ballroom in Edinburgh which had a roof that opened up, and during the evening it would slide back so couples could dance under the stars. After they married, my father went into partnership with a well-known tailoring business in the capital which had shops in Lothian Road, Leith Walk and Dalry Road. Everything must have been going very well because my parents bought a large house in Corbiehill (a respectable area near Blackhall, Edinburgh). My brother, Brian, was born there in 1948. He's two years older than me and vaguely remembers that house.

It's been very difficult to find out exactly what happened back then because no one ever talked about it, but apparently money started going missing from the business and eventually the shops were all gone. My parents lost everything and had nowhere else to go, which is why they moved into Danube Street with Aunt Daisy.

My mother confessed to me, later in life, that they hadn't planned to have five children. There was no contraception in those days so some of us had come along by accident. I have no idea which ones, and don't much care to find out because she gave us all love and affection through very hard times.

All my life I thought I was born in Danube Street, but in my research I discovered that I was actually born in a five-bedroom

Victorian villa at 20, St. Bernard's Row, Stockbridge. My mum cleaned the house for the owner but she was treated like one of the family, and when I was due the lady of the house suggested that my mum stayed there until the baby was born.

In the early 1950s there was a lot of building development going on in and around Edinburgh and my mother registered on the council housing list. After a long waiting time she was offered a house in what was to be a new housing estate at Clermiston, on the west side of Edinburgh. The house at 110 Drum Brae Drive was one of a few just completed and we prepared for the big move. I know we didn't have many possessions because most of it fitted into large suitcases and two tea chests. My father had taken a job as a travelling salesman, selling shirts and ties, and had bought an old car from one of his dodgy pals. We drove in the car to what seemed like the other side of the world and arrived on a building site. There were no roads or pavements but there was a lot of mud, and wooden crosses all over the place marking out where the houses would be built.

Our new house was amazing: three-bedroomed, semi-detached, living room and separate kitchen, a back porch, a coal cellar, hot and cold running water, and a real bath. This was something my mother had only dreamt of and here it was! It had large gardens to the front, back and side. (Well, when I say "gardens" I mean bare earth with potential.) This was a new start and I was happy to see my mother was happy.

I wasn't intentionally a difficult child. I just had a wild imagination and wanted to investigate and explore, which resulted in me spending a lot of the time on my own. I don't know why, but I felt separate from the others—we didn't get on as brothers and sisters, but I suppose that's not unusual in a large family—and I wasn't happy when the time came to go to my first school. On the first day my mother had to drag me, screaming, up the path to the school in front of all the other mothers. She must have been very upset at having to leave me in such a state that day, but I grew to love the place.

Fox Covert Primary School was in Fox Covert House, a large stone built country house surrounded by an orchard, trees, bushes and a walled garden with greenhouses. Instead of having defined play areas we had grass mounds to roll down and sledge on. There were trees to climb and swing from, bushes and shrubs to crawl through and hide in. The only restriction was not being allowed outside the school boundary into the woods, which only served to arouse my curiosity as to what lay beyond.

The community held a garden fete in the grounds every springtime. There were stalls set out on the front lawn, adorned with coloured ribbons and flags and selling homemade tablet, cakes and jam. There was country dancing and games for the children. It was something everyone in the neighbourhood looked forward to.

Fox Covert House was situated in a wooded area on the north side of Buttercup Dairy Farm.

I remember the whole family walking up to Corstorphine Hill and along the dirt track road, now known as Clerwood, to the imposing entrance leading to Buttercup Farm. You were drawn in between the lodge house and the cottages on either side, through an avenue of trees, down the long drive to the big white house, with its walled gardens and the buildings of the dairy. On a beautiful summer's day it was something to behold. We looked down over the sprawling fields of the working dairy farm (of which there is very little evidence today). To the south of it were the private grounds and trees surrounding the just-visible roof of the magnificent mansion, Clermiston House, which later became so familiar to me.

I often go to the same spot now and remember what it was like before the deluge of poorly-designed houses came along, and unashamed planners allowed the destruction of so much heritage and history.

At the age of six I was, sadly, moved to the newly built Clermiston Primary School in the Parkgrove area, beside the Queensferry Road: a purpose-built school with no character and no heart. It was not at all like Fox Covert which was in line for demolition to make way for progress.

The headmistress of the new school was a tyrant. She had a huge wart on the end of her nose with hair growing out of it, one eye was higher up her face than the other, and her teeth were like a handful of cigarette ends. She had bandy legs with veins sticking out and gave off a terrible smell. Well, that's how I like to remember her! The whole school lined up for inspection every morning. Every pupil was expected to bring a hanky with them, and, as I didn't have one, she took a long wooden ruler to the backs of my legs and humiliated me in front of the whole school because I screamed with the pain. I decided there and then that no matter what she did she would never control me. I was given the same punishment a number of times, and the more it hurt the more rebellious I became. I hated that school.

More and more families were moving into the area as the houses were completed and there were lots of children playing out in the streets. Everyone knew each other and there was no fear of going off on your own, or worry about who you were playing with—we just ran around wild.

Most of the children I knew had a "guider" made from pram wheels acquired from the children's home on Corstorphine Hill, and old bits of wood nailed and tied together. There were no brakes, you just hurtled down hills and guided the front wheels with your feet. Needless to say, there were many accidents. We played peevers, kick-the-can, statues, tig, and hide-go-seek in the gardens. There were no telephones, televisions or computers and we had a great time.

The rag and bone man would come round on his horse and cart. You could hear him from miles away, blowing his bugle to let everyone know he was on his way. My mother would collect up old woollens and worn out clothes which she would exchange for a small amount of money. In the summer, Onion Johnny would come up the street on his bicycle with strings of onions hung over the handlebars. He wore a black and white striped jumper and a black tammy on his head.

I was becoming a bit of a wanderer and would go off exploring, sometimes forgetting to come home. One night my father came out looking for me after a drinking session at the pub. He dragged me all the way home and hit me so hard with his leather belt I couldn't walk. I couldn't sit down for days and had to lie face down on the bed. What did I do that was that bad?

I watched my mother struggling to make ends meet. Sometimes she would have some money and spend it on essentials like clothes and food for us all, but often she would have nothing, and relied upon dividends from the stamps she collected at St. Cuthbert's Co-operative Society. Everyone called it "the Store". The Provident insurance man would come round to collect payments from her: it was a scheme which she paid pennies into and got back a small lump sum. The gasman would come and empty the meter and give her back a rebate in shillings. She always seemed to be worried and sad.

It was around this time that I started to sing. I liked the attention I got and it made my mother happy. She was always asking me to sing, but the only song I knew was *Little White Bull* by Tommy Steele. So I became the entertainer in the family.

Aunt Daisy had a sister, Jenny, who lived with Uncle Tommy in the Grassmarket, within the shadow of Edinburgh Castle. The Grassmarket lies in a valley between the West Port and the Cowgate of Edinburgh and was the site for public hangings in the 17th century. Its buildings were originally designed to accommodate the horse and cattle markets and it was said to be frequented by such famous figures as Robert Burns and William Wordsworth. During the 19th century the Grassmarket became known as Little Ireland as it was home to a large number of Irish people who migrated to Scotland after the potato famine. The St Patrick's Church founded a Catholic Young Men's Society, and Canon Edward Hannan suggested forming a football team to help integrate Irish Catholics into the wider population, and to encourage a life of temperance. So in 1875, Hibernian F.C. was founded.

The Grassmarket was also an area renowned for its homeless hostels and a gathering place for those whose lives had hit rock bottom through alcoholism. It was somewhere I was drawn to later in life as my own addiction took hold, but back in 1957, when I was only seven years of age, it was a different story. When we all went to visit Aunt Jenny and Uncle Tommy I saw my very first images of stereotypical alcoholics, sitting in doorways and lying drunk in the street. It was a frightening experience for a child—I didn't understand what was wrong, or why no one was helping them.

We didn't visit there very often but, every time we did, Uncle Tommy was drunk. I thought he was a fascinating character. He would sit back in his armchair in his dirty old white shirt with no collar and the sleeves rolled up to his elbows. His braces were attached to his trousers but hanging down, off his shoulders on both sides, and he would play the harmonica. I was mesmerised. I had never heard anything so wonderful! His leg would bounce up and down in time with the music and we all listened intently. He started to teach me how to play and the first song I learned was *I Love To Go A-Wandering, With A Knapsack On My Back*. I was so excited, I couldn't wait to see him again.

We only visited them on two other occasions and each time he would teach me a new song. On the last visit, we were just getting ready to leave when Uncle Tommy stood up and handed me a box. I held it up in both hands and he said, "Well, open it then."

There was a brand new harmonica inside and my face lit up from ear to ear. "You'll have to practice," he said. I promised I would and thanked him enthusiastically.

I never saw him again, but I did practice every day. It must have driven the family crazy.

One thing's for sure, they won't want to hear *I Love To Go A-Wandering* ever again.

We had a second Aunt Daisy, who was my father's sister. She lived with my grandmother at Rosebank Cottages, near Fountainbridge in Edinburgh and when my grandmother died Daisy inherited all her worldly goods, including the house. Sadly my grandmother died before I was born, but I was intrigued by the stories Daisy told me about her. She had been a spiritualist and was said to be in touch with the spirits from the afterlife. She held meetings in a hall at Gayfield Square and, apparently, was quite a well-known figure in that circle. Daisy would say to me often, "I think you have the gift you know." I didn't know what she was talking about.

I had a slight problem with authority, and authority figures, so when two of my friends joined The Life Boys I wasn't keen at first, but when they came back and told me what a laugh it was, and about the great games they played, I warmed to the idea and went with them the following week to join up.

The Life Boys was the Royal Navy's equivalent of the Boys' Brigade and was on every Wednesday evening at Drum Brae Primary School. I suppose it was designed to encourage young men to join the Navy eventually. There was a lot of regimented stuff going on and I couldn't really take the marching and saluting seriously. When I think back on it now, I must have been a nightmare because I was knocking boys' caps off and tripping them up when they were marching. They all had their smart navy blue uniforms with banded cap and sash. Everyone that is, except me, who stood out like an impostor. I was given a form to take home with all the details of costs and where to buy the uniform, but my mum said she couldn't afford it. Aunt Daisy, who was at our house most of the time, had heard us talking about it and called me over. "If you stick it out for another two weeks I will buy the uniform for you." So I did. I stuck it out for two weeks and got the uniform, which consisted of socks, ribbon that hung down from the socks, belt, top with epaulettes and padded shoulders, neckerchief, cap and sash.

The first night I wore the uniform to the Life Boys I was a bit hyper and got pulled up a few times for not following orders and for laughing too much. The week after that I was in trouble for putting wild rosehip seeds down the backs of boys' jumpers. (We called them "itchy powders") The week after that, I was taken aside and told not to come back—my membership was terminated. I think the final straw had been the badges... they had a row of boxes on a table and you had to take a different coloured badge to show you had completed a specific task. Each box had a sticker on the front telling you what task the badge in the box represented. I took the stickers off the front and mixed them all up.

I didn't have the nerve to tell my mother, and certainly not my Aunt Daisy who'd paid for my uniform, that I was thrown out. So every Wednesday night I got my uniform on and ran out the door saying, " I'm off to the Life Boys," and had to find something to do for two hours before I could go back home. I did that for four weeks before I had to confess.

I stayed out of the way for a while. I would go down into the wheat fields near Cammo Tower and lie flat on the ground amongst the wheat and listen to the skylarks singing, hovering high up in the sky and lose myself for a few hours.

Clermiston House

CHAPTER TWO

It was the school holidays in the summer of 1959 when I first discovered Clermiston House and I will never forget it. I was off on one of my expeditions to explore the undiscovered world beyond the trees. To get there I had to negotiate my way through the building site that now engulfed Buttercup Farm. When I reached the uncharted land I climbed over the fence and fought my way through the brambles and jaggy nettles, fighting with snakes and Indians on the way and arrived wounded, but alive, at the field beyond. I took in the view that confronted me and saw at the far end of the field, farm buildings that looked deserted. There was no one in sight so I walked slowly further into the field.

I couldn't believe what I was seeing... I was standing in front of a high wall with stone balusters along the top. There was a double stone staircase rising up from the field to a higher level, where a statue of a man on horseback towered over the entrance guarding the way to the mysteriously grand mansion house beyond. I felt like I had walked into another world which wasn't like anything I had seen before, telling a story of another time, and of wealth and wellbeing. I didn't dare go any closer but I knew I would be back.

The following day I entered the private grounds to the north side of the mansion house and slowly made my way through the bushes, staying undercover for fear of the unknown. I came across pear trees with branches straining under the weight of the abundant fruit. I didn't have much experience of pears but this was the most delicious thing I had ever tasted! I tucked my jumper into my trousers, and filled up my dukes with pears as quickly as possible.

I could see the side of the house in the distance between the trees, and in my attempt to climb between two holly bushes, without being scarred for life by its sharp prickly thorns, I kicked my foot against a large flat stone which looked to be deliberately placed to cover something. I pulled at it with all my strength and it slipped away exposing a hole in the ground. With the help of the daylight I could see down into a tunnel running towards the house. My wild imagination kicked in, and I could see pirates and buried treasure with chests full of gold. "I'll need to go back and tell someone about this," I said to myself, thinking I had discovered something of real importance.

I ran back all the way to where I lived, hampered by the weight of the pears bouncing up and down in my stretched jumper. It was late afternoon and I knew I would have to be back soon for my tea or I would be in trouble, but there was enough time to go round to Duncan's house. He was a school friend I knew I could trust with a secret.

"Duncan," I said excitedly as he answered the door, "taste that!" and handed him a large pear. "Where did you get them?" he enquired looking down at my bulge. "I found this amazing place away over the other side of the trees," and pointed in the direction of the house. "I found this tunnel under the bushes. Do you want to come with me tonight? I'll show you where it is, bring your torch." "I'll come round for you after tea," Duncan said excitedly.

That night, before it was dark, we gathered up two other pals, Ian and Allan, and headed off with torches in hand. I led the way through the woods to where I had found the flat stone and showed them the tunnel. "I'm not going down there," Ian said. "You can go. I'll keep watch up here." "I'll go" said Duncan." "What about you?" I said, turning to Allan. "Yeah, alright but I'm not going very far." I could sense the fear in his voice. I was beginning to think maybe this wasn't such a good idea.

The daylight was starting to fade as we climbed down into the tunnel. The tunnel was built in stone with a vaulted ceiling, very low and narrow. We had to crouch down and walk in single file. Duncan up front, Allan in the middle and me at the rear. It was exciting to begin with but it started to feel more and more enclosed the further we got away from the opening.

I could see the torch beams shining ahead making long, scary shadowy shapes on the walls and I could feel the darkness creeping up behind me. "Hey! Listen. What's that?" I said loudly, creating an eerie echo. We stopped for a minute. There was a deep rumbling noise in the distance. "I don't like this," I said in a low, shaky voice, beginning to panic as we crept along further, "I think we should turn back." "So do I," Duncan murmured, and so we about-turned.

This time I was leading the way into the darkness and the torches behind me were beaming long moving shadows in front of me. I could only see so far in front then it was pitch black. We seemed to be walking a long way. I turned to the others and said, "I don't remember coming this far." "Neither do I, keep going!" someone yelled from behind as the two of them anxiously pushed me forward. My torch was getting dim as the batteries faded and the vaulted ceiling seemed to be getting lower when, all of a sudden, the tunnel ended: it was filled in with earth and stones. "The tunnel's collapsed! What are we going to do?" I shouted, panicking, shining my torch into the tunnel behind us expecting something horrible to appear out of the darkness. There was silence for a moment before everyone started to panic. "Shout for help!" Allan yelled, as if he thought someone would hear him. We were all getting in a state. I felt the fear rising up inside me and I wanted to start shouting myself but managed to stifle it. "What if we can't get out?" Allan cried, "We're stuck, nobody will find us, we'll never get out." Duncan was trying to stay calm and suggested we go back the other way. I agreed, "Come on, we'll have to try it."

There was barely enough room to turn around but we headed back in the other direction, faster this time, grabbing each other's jumpers and tripping over each other's feet. After just a few yards I caught a glimpse of light above my head and looked up. There it was: the entrance. Crouched down in the darkness, we had walked right past the opening. What a relief. We were trying to climb over each other to get out of the hole. "Where were you, you idiot?" we were all shouting at Ian. "You were supposed to be looking out for us with your torch!" "I was just having a look around," he said sheepishly. "What happened?" "Oh god, we nearly got trapped in the tunnel!" I told him what had happened and we laughed uncontrollably, but I was still shaking...

I don't think any of the others had a desire to ever go back there but, a few days later, I wandered into the gardens of the mansion house once more with an unfulfilled desire to find out more about this curious place. I was climbing a tree when two children appeared from nowhere. One of them was a boy a bit younger than me, the other a young girl who looked around six years old. "You're not allowed in here you know," he said, sounding like he thought it was a stupid rule. "I'm not doing anything, just wanted to see the house. Do you live here?" "Yes we do, my dad's the caretaker." "What's your name?" I asked. "Alan," he replied "and this is my sister." There were a few awkward moments before he said, "Do you want to come and see something?" "What is it?" "Come on, I'll show you."

He led me right across the front of the house, and up close to the statue I had seen from the field days before. It was gigantic. Carved out of stone, it was a man on horseback with a beard, and curly hair with a funny hat on. He was wearing heavy clothing and his arm was raised to the side. The horse was rearing up and another figure of a man was holding the horse's head with one hand and a sword in the other. He was also wearing a floppy hat and big boots. It was so full of life I couldn't help but walk round and study its detail. "No, that's not it," Alan stated, "it's over here." I followed him down a tree-lined path which forked off to the left and right.

"Do you want to see the swimming pool?" Not waiting for an answer he walked through an opening in a high wall. "Wow!" I was amazed. It was an open air swimming pool. The water had been drained out and it was obvious that it hadn't been used for a long time. (I discovered later on in life that the pool had been used to train R.A.F. pilots in survival during the Second World War). The bottom was covered with leaves and dirt, but you could see the shape going down from the shallow end to the deep end. It was sad, really, to see it in this condition as I could imagine what it would have been like when people were jump-

Statue of King James the V. at Clermiston House.

ing in and splashing around in the water. "Come on, it's this way," shouted Alan as he ran off, back down the path with his sister and me in pursuit.

Through neatly trimmed hedges we entered a sunken garden which led into a maze on the left-hand side and had a pond in the centre of the grass with a carved stone fountain rising up through the middle. "Here it is!" Alan shouted, running to the side of the pond. It was full of frogs and newts. They were leaping off giant lily leaves all around. For an eight-year-old this was heaven.

Then he showed me the orchard and the squash courts and the curling rink. I looked up the long driveway coming down the hill, lined with rhododendron bushes and I imagined horse-drawn carriages and hound dogs. On the lawn near the statue was a rotating wooden summerhouse that we pushed round and round. All the way home that day I had the feeling that I was privileged to be experiencing this amazing place which stood suspended in time.

I went back many times over the next few months and, every time I walked through the gardens, Alan would appear with his sister. It was quite strange. The old farm buildings at the far end of the front field were a real attraction to me and we would have great fun playing in the hayloft. Everything was in its place: the hay bales were piled up ready for use; sheds penned off into sections with empty troughs for feeding the animals; wooden doors with broken hinges hung precariously, requiring attention; an old tractor and machinery lay awaiting repair while pigeons and swallows moved in and made it their home. The only things missing were the animals and people. It felt like it had just stopped one day, all of a sudden. I found it quite disturbing and sad.

I did have some very happy times there. I will never forget running around the gardens and climbing on the statue, sword fencing with the man holding the horse. I was even invited into the basement of the mansion house to meet Alan's mum and dad, and had dinner with them sitting round a huge, rough, wooden table. This would have been the servants' quarters at one time, long ago, but now there was no one left to serve.

The house had last been occupied by the Inverarity family, who moved to Ireland after the house was sold. We weren't supposed to go upstairs to the main house, but when Alan's parents were out of the house one day he led me up the dark staircase from the basement into the hallway of Clermiston House. I stopped in the middle of the floor in front of an imposing ornate fireplace where I could picture the gentry standing around on a cold winter's night, indulging themselves in the warm glow of a roaring fire. The hall was overlooked by a wide staircase. I imagined I was Robin Hood leaping up the stairs sword in hand then sliding back down the banister taking out three of the sheriff's best men on the way. While I was daydreaming Alan ran up the grand staircase to the first floor shouting, "Come on, we can play hide and seek." By the time I got up the stairs he was gone and I could just hear his footsteps on the bare wooden floorboards.

I looked to the left and saw two big rooms with a large open doorway between the two, then through to a window on the far end wall. On the other side of the landing there were similar large, empty rooms with no furniture or curtains. There was another smaller door to the left and I opened it and looked in. It was a bathroom with a huge bath with gold taps and marble walls all the way up to the ceiling. I closed the door and stood in the hallway. For a few seconds there was an absolute eerie silence and I felt isolated. Then I heard a noise from the floor above and ran up the staircase to the next landing. It was dark and musty. The rooms on the right-hand side had nothing in them, just great big chandeliers hanging from the ceiling. I looked left, through the first room where a big double doorway led through to the far away room, and I thought I saw something moving.

Suddenly a woman appeared in a long, black dress with a white lace outline. Her hair was tied up and covered with a small white cloth. She walked slowly across the open doorway between the two rooms, looking down at a book. I froze. She stopped in the middle of the doorway and she turned her head slowly towards me and looked for a second, then turned back to her book and walked across the doorway and out of sight. I took off and ran down the stairs two at a time! When I got back to the basement, Alan was sitting there at the table laughing. I didn't say anything about what I saw. I just said, "I'm going to be late, I'll have to get home!" and left.

I never told anyone what I saw in that house. I had this feeling it was the end of an era, that something was coming that would change this place forever, and I was right.

The next time I saw Alan he told me they were going away and I never saw him again. The house lay empty for a time, then one day I was in the field in front of the house and the statue was gone. Not long after this they started to knock down Clermiston House, then the farm buildings, and before long it was all gone. I've never understood why anyone could have destroyed such beauty, grace and history and not recognise its value.

Forgive them, for they know not what they do.

Every summer holidays my father rented a caravan in Gilsland Caravan Park, North Berwick. We all loved it there, but the open-air, saltwater swimming pool by the harbour was too cold to swim in, and seemed a bit pointless surrounded by the sea. The paddling pool was in the sea, with a wall around it that trapped the water as the tide went out, but every parent was too frightened to let their children play in it because the tide came in so quickly and submerged the pool area. I would say, "Mum can I go in the paddling pool?" "No you can't, the tide's coming in." "Where? I can't even see the sea." "Oh go and dig a hole in the sand or something."

It was a long walk from the caravan park to the beach and most days the whole family would trek down there, loaded with folding chairs, bags filled with food, towels and swimsuits, a windbreaker and a primus stove for cooking on. Then, when the day was over, we had to hump it all back up the hill, tired and in bad moods. Occasionally we children were allowed to go down to the beach without Mum and Dad, provided we all went together.

The sea front was beautiful, but when the tide was out it exposed the rocks which went out a long way. These rocks were extremely dangerous, with slippery seaweed on the surface and deep crevices that ran in lines out towards the sea. But that's exactly where I wanted to go. When the tide came in it brought with it large shoals of sprats, thousands of them trapped between the rocks, and with them came larger fish that we caught on hand-held lines, pulling them out on hooks two and three at a time. It was very exciting, but had to be timed precisely because the tide came in so fast.

One day I was walking across the rocks and slipped into a deep pool. The tide was coming in, I couldn't swim, and I was pulled down under the water. Each time a wave came in I was thrown against the rocks. I really thought it was the end when a huge wave took me right under and I couldn't hold my breath any longer. I was flapping around and came to the surface just in time to see my brother Brian dangling his legs over the side so I could grab on to his foot and he pulled me out. I lay there coughing and spluttering, and glad to be alive. That was very close. I made him promise not to tell Dad.

The next time we went to the beach on our own I wandered off along the coast, to a place way out of sight from the others where it was completely deserted. I was standing on rocks partially submerged in the sea when I saw these strange black shapes rising up out of the water, just yards away from where I was standing. These curved black shapes were rising out of the water, then disappearing, then rising again. Whatever they were, they were big and weird. I wanted to run but was frozen to the spot when, all of a sudden, I heard this strange noise—Whoosh! Whoosh! Whoosh!– coming from behind me and getting louder and louder. Suddenly, three giant birds flew right over my head at low level! It was like a living nightmare, I just saw these huge wings and went into a complete panic attack. I couldn't make any sense of what was happening, my whole body was shaking and my heart was pounding, the fear was so intense. I was having completely irrational thoughts. I ran to the cliffs, climbed in between two rocks and curled up. I couldn't move, for I don't know how long, and I lost all sense of time…

Eventually it passed, and when I looked around everything was back to normal so I ran back along the beach and met the others out looking for me. I tried to tell them what had happened but they looked at me as if I had gone mad. I told my parents when I got back to the caravan and my father came up with a rational explanation: he said the large black shapes I saw in the water were probably porpoises, the small dolphins that were common in the Firth of Forth in the 1950s, and what flew over my head were most likely swans flying low over the water. It all made sense, but I had experienced my first panic attack.

Back in Edinburgh, another summer holiday experience I remember vividly was when we put a raft together. That was the four stooges, Duncan, Allan, Ian and I. We got the idea from finding a couple of barrels washed up at the side of the River Almond, possibly at its deepest point as it roars its way down and over the waterfall en route to Cramond and out to sea.

"It's easy," says Duncan, "just a few branches tied to the barrels and a board over the top. Easy!" So we tied some branches to the barrels and a couple of old planks of wood on top. Just before we set off, in the excitement of it all, I had forgotten I had my new shoes on. The new shoes that my mother had told me NOT to wear if I was going out, the new shoes that were only for special occasions. So I took them off and put them down my jumper, which I tucked into my trousers, before the four of us clambered onto the makeshift raft and set off from the banks of the River Almond.

At first it seemed to float alright, if a bit lopsided, but I started to worry when we got further into the current and the raft started spinning round and round, but we had no means of control. Another worry was that we were bobbing up and down so much the barrels were completely submerged, and most of the time the water was over our feet. Watching Ian on all fours, rigidly hanging on to the rope, did nothing to raise my confidence but, most worrying of all, was the fact we were now travelling at some speed, getting faster and faster while heading for a sharp bend where a huge tree hung precariously over the river, with its branches dangling in the water.

For paddles we only had two bits of broken wood, and all I could hear was shouting, " You're not paddling!" " I **am** paddling!" "Well, paddle faster, we're going the wrong way!" but we couldn't stop it. The river went one way and the momentum of the raft took us another, right into the tree. Duncan and Allan were at the front and managed to scramble onto the branches. Ian leapt off and made it to the bank, but I was standing at the back of the raft and a large branch, stretching out just above water level, swept me right off the raft and I was left dangling in the water up to my neck, with both arms hanging onto the branch.

The current was fast and pulling me downstream. I was losing my grip, hanging on by my fingernails and swallowing water, when two legs appeared. Duncan realised I was in trouble and crawled along the branch to grab hold of my arm. I climbed out, exhausted, and lay on the bank coughing and spluttering, trying to catch a breath. I just lay there for a while. Everyone was quiet and in a bit of shock. Someone said, "That was close." I was sorting out my soaking wet clothes when I realised I only had one shoe. "Oh no, I've lost a shoe—I'll get killed!" The other one was gone, nowhere to be seen. So I arrived home in bare feet, carrying one shoe, hoping I would only be half-killed since I still had one, but no… I got the works, the full leather belt across my bare backside.

I couldn't count how many times I was brought back to the house by the police for being places I shouldn't have been, and for doing things I shouldn't have been doing.

I remember stealing apples from the garden of the Big White House on Buttercup Farm when I saw a large man come running round the side of the house, shouting. I ran and climbed back up the fence and jumped off, but a spike of the fence went up the back of my jumper and I was left hanging in the air with my feet off the ground. Of course, I got caught and held till the police came. But what always struck me was I got belted by my father for getting caught, not for what I had done.

I never knew this man. I knew he was my father, but I knew nothing about him. He never spoke to me, he just gave commands and doled out the discipline.

CHAPTER THREE

During one summer holiday in North Berwick we went to a café in the High Street for ice cream. While we were waiting in the queue I looked to the back of the café and saw a very strange-looking object against the wall, all lit up with bright colours. It was the first time I'd ever seen a jukebox. This was in 1960 and I was ten years old.

I watched while someone put money in and pressed a button. The song they played was *Born Too Late* by The Pony Tails, and it was just one of these moments that change your life. I was hooked! That song, and that sound, had such an effect on me there was no going back. Music would take over my life.

Back in Edinburgh I had another similar experience the day a new boy appeared on the scene and brought his mother's wind up gramophone record player into the garden. He put on a 78rpm, hard vinyl record of The Everly Brothers singing *All I Have To Do Is Dream*. It didn't get much better than that.

The early 1960s was a voyage of discovery. I feel privileged to have been around to experience the phenomenon that was Elvis Presley and to witness the birth of The Beatles and The Rolling Stones. But I'm away ahead of myself. I'm not even at secondary school yet. Where was I? Oh yeah...

The secondary school system was such that, for pupils like me, whose head was full of nonsense and with very little interest in academic qualifications, the choice was limited to schools with a practical outlook that directed you towards a trade. In my case this suited me because all my friends were going to Tynecastle Secondary School and we all enrolled there in September 1962.

It was a strange old place with uniform buildings laid out with formal classrooms for serious subjects, like maths, English, geography and history, on one side of the playground, and workshops for woodwork, metalwork, technical drawing and sciences on the other. All the teachers on the serious side wore black robes and looked angry, while on the practical side dressed more casually and looked more relaxed.

The first day was spent being shown round our classrooms and getting familiar with the place. The second day we were told to wait outside the school hall so that we could be taken to the nine thirty assembly of the entire school. The new intake of pupils were all seated at the front and I landed smack bang in the middle of the second row. The rest of the school were packed in and sat down behind us. A tall, balding man stood on the stage in front of a lectern with his black robes hanging off his shoulder on one side, looking contemptuously down his nose at the disappointing bunch that sat before him. The first thing I noticed was his pencil moustache, and I immediately took a dislike to the man. He said, "Good morning," and everyone repeated it. He then introduced himself as the deputy headmaster (who we later referred to as The Don) and he went on and on about the school. I had no idea what he was talking about because I wasn't listening, but he got my attention when he introduced the headmaster, who approached from the right-hand aisle and came onto the stage carrying a handful of papers.

Apart from his grey hair he had no really distinguishing features. When he spoke it was with a relaxed tone, and his welcoming speech made us all feel at ease. We were told to learn the school song: "*Tynecastle, Tynecastle, we vow to be true, always to honour the silver and blue.*"

I was quite excited and eager to please, so when he directed a question towards the new pupils I was keen to answer. His question was, "Have any of the new pupils been reading any books recently?" I immediately, without thinking, put my hand up, "Yes!" What is your name?" he asked, looking directly at me. "Gordon Clark," I squeaked out, realising this wasn't such a good idea. "Well! Stand up, Gordon. You will refer to me as Sir from now on. Tell us what you've been reading." "*Shadow the Sheep Dog* by Enid Blyton, Sir." There was a short, uncomfortable silence before he growled, "That's a children's book. Sit down." I heard the whole school laugh as he humiliated me.

First year pupils spent their first two terms at Pentlands, which was the annexe to the main Tynecastle School. I liked it a lot, we had some great laughs there. I was even recognised for my singing ability and asked to sing with the choir. One of my biggest regrets is that when I was asked to sing a solo at the Usher Hall, in front of all the Edinburgh schools, I turned it down because my pals were taking the piss out of me.

I was always in trouble with my big mouth. A fight broke out in the playground and all the boys formed a circle around it. Out came Mr Pierson from the metal workshop, marching across the ground like a sergeant major and proudly presenting his pencil moustache, neatly trimmed in a straight line. He pushed his way through and pulled the fighting boys apart saying in a stern voice, "Have a break lads." I cupped my hand round my mouth and shouted "Have a Kit Kat!" It was out before I could stop it. That remark resulted in six double-handers from the most feared belt in the school. I had bruises up my wrists for days. Mr Pierson kept his thick, double-pronged, hard leather belt over his right shoulder, under his jacket. It was rumoured that he soaked the belt in vinegar to harden the leather. I could believe that.

The real work started in second year when we moved permanently to the main school. It was quite obvious to me that most of the boys, and a large proportion of the girls, were not interested in learning. I personally found it difficult to take many of these teachers seriously, although there were one or two practical teachers I had respect for.

I just couldn't stay out of trouble. In an effort to brighten up the corridors, flowering plants had been placed on all the window ledges—they lasted for one day and were all chopped off at the base. I was one of the suspects just because I was in the vicinity at the time.

In order to encourage more sports activity some waste ground behind the workshops, between the wall of Hearts football ground and the school building, had been dug out and filled with sand to make a long jump. It wasn't long before the sand was thrown over the wall into the football ground. One of my school reports read: "He sets himself very low standards and continually fails to live up to them."

Every pupil who went to Tynecastle School will go through their lives with the smell in their nostrils. Depending which way the wind was blowing, you could have the smell of boiling hops from the brewery, or the smell of boiling horse bones from the glue factory. Sometimes both.

I got into a few scrapes and fights but it wasn't really my scene, I just wanted to have a laugh and get on with everybody. But there was one boy who everyone steered clear of—he was taller than everyone else and had a reputation. I watched him pick on boys much smaller than himself, but he still had to have his pals around him to back him up. He decided to pick on me one day. I remember not feeling great that morning, waiting outside the woodwork class, when this bully pushed me, then he pushed me again and I lost the plot—I swung a punch that caught him right on the side of the face. He put his head down and was swinging wildly so all I had to do was dodge his punches, and land a few sore ones. He gave in, saying, "I've had enough," and backed off. I couldn't believe it, it was a fluke! After that my status at the school rose to a new level.

Somewhere down the line I had picked up the nickname "Nobby" Clark. It came about when I knocked on a friend's door one day. His father answered and said, "Ah, here's Nobby Clark." He had been in the army where, apparently, all men with the last name Clark were called Nobby. It caught on at school like a house on fire, now everybody called me Nobby. Many people have put their own interpretation on it over the years, believe me, but the true source is that the clerks who worked in the banking sector in the City of London wore a distinguishing hat with a round top called a Nobby hat... it's as boring as that.

It was around then that I met Derek Longmuir. Our classes shared certain subjects and we first met in technical drawing where I sat a couple of rows behind him and watched him drumming on the desk with two pencils. After the class finished I went over and introduced myself and asked if he played the drums. "Yeah," he said, "I play in a group with my brother, Alan, and my cousin, Neil." I told him I was a singer and played harmonica. "I sing in the choir and I've got a group with some pals," I exaggerated. The nearest we'd got to a group was standing on top of water storage tanks on a building site, pretending we were The Shadows. Derek and I got talking about songs we liked and he asked me if I wanted to come along to one of their practices. "Yeah, why not?" I said, trying to sound cool.

Alan and Derek Longmuir lived on Caledonian Road, in the Dalry area of Edinburgh. All I knew about them was their dad was an undertaker, they had two sisters, and they practiced in the front room of their mum's house. I went along to hear their group and watch them practice. I had no expectations but I was really surprised—they seemed quite organised with proper guitars, amps and a microphone. I wasn't sure about Derek's drums, though, when I saw the photographs of Ringo Starr on the skins.

Alan was playing bass guitar and doing all the singing, Derek was on drums and Neil Porteous, their cousin, was on electric guitar. I thought they were really good. They played *Too Much Monkey Business* and *Jump Back, Baby, Jump Back*, then they asked me if I wanted to try out a song. I was terrified. I had never sung with a microphone and speakers before, but I gave *Down at The Club* my best shot and joined the band.

It was spring, 1965 and this was something good happening. When I headed home that night my head was buzzing with excitement. I was walking slowly up my street when I heard *Just One Look* by The Hollies playing loud through an open bedroom window on someone's Dansette record player. Three houses further on and another open window was blasting out *Wonderful Land* by The Shadows, and when I got home my older brother, Brian, was playing *Ain't that Peculiar* by Marvin Gaye. Now **that** was a shower of colour, like walking through a rainbow.

Derek and I became good friends very quickly and were hanging out together at school. Alan had been at Tynecastle Secondary School too, but he'd left to start a plumbing apprenticeship. He'd just turned seventeen and was a year and a half older than Derek and I.

I spent quite a few evenings over at their house and when we weren't practising we'd be listening to music, strumming guitars and singing songs, sitting around talking about what we wanted to do with the group. There was an air of excitement and anticipation about it, like we were too early for a football match, eagerly waiting for the start.

The group was called The Saxons. After just a few weeks of practising as many nights as Derek and Alan's parents would allow, we had a list of twelve songs we could play. Or we thought we could, until we were asked to play at the youth club in Cairns Church Hall on Gorgie Road. A lot of girls from our school went to the youth club. Alan had a job so he could afford to buy some trendy threads. He had good taste in clothes and already had the makings of a mod. I bought a grey, striped jacket and a black cardigan from a jumble sale, while Derek had his school shirt on under a crew neck jumper, and Neil was even less trendy in his short-sleeved shirt and red tie.

We got up there and did our thing. I don't think it went too badly as we got through some of the songs without stopping. But the buzz was incredible! You know what they say about taking drugs: make the first time last, you will never be there again. Well, that's how it was. We were just trying to crash out some music, albeit interwoven with inexperience, nervous mistakes and embarrassing blunders—it was great! Adrenalin was the drug, no doubt about it.

To look back on Edinburgh in the 1960s, and compare it to nowadays, it's almost unrecognisable and not all the changes are good. I don't see the facilities for kids and teenagers that we had. When I was fifteen, you didn't need an entertainments licence: just book a hall, and book a group. There was live music in every available space.

The first group I saw were The Saints, in Davidson's Mains Church Hall. Their stage gear consisted of black shirts and red ties with "The Saints" embroidered down the front. I was hearing songs for the very first time like *Louie Louie* and *Memphis Tennessee*. While the other boys were chasing the girls, I couldn't take my eyes off the stage.

Alan had been going round the dance halls for a while, but Derek and I were just getting started. Neil wasn't really into that sort of thing. But we had the makings of a plan: we would split up and go to different clubs and dances and see if anyone would give us a spot. The first step up the ladder was the Gonk Club at Tollcross. I especially remember that night because I was late getting ready at my house. I had a pair of white trousers which I had dyed salmon pink using a tin of Dylon. When I tried them on they were all crushed so I thought, to save time, I'll just iron them while I'm wearing them... I burned the skin all the way down my thigh.

The Saxons were to go on stage first, before Tiny and The Titans, who had a young singer that looked about nine. (His name was Colin Chisholm, and he later went on to sing with Bilbo Baggins and Chisholm & Spence.) I heard he was very good so I was nervous. We went on stage when the club was about half full, with everyone standing around waiting for the music to start. My heart was pounding so fast I thought it might explode. We got into the first song and got a bit mixed up, so had to stop and go back to the beginning. I didn't know where to look—I got in behind the drums with my back to the audience until we started up again. We stumbled on and just managed to get through about six songs. It was rough to start, and not very smooth to finish, but it was an experience nonetheless.

The group was starting to take up more time, which was great for me, Alan and Derek. But Neil had other plans and missed a few practice nights. Eventually he wanted to leave and do other things so we started the search for a new guitarist. We ran an advert in the local paper and got three responses.

The first guy who turned up was very posh, spoke with a bool in his mouth. I could see Alan standing with his head down, trying not to giggle. We were working-class guys who spoke the best Edinburgh slang. "What would you like me to play?" he asked, very confidently. "Oh, just anything you know," we said, as he launched into some classical piece. I didn't think people could move their fingers so fast. When he finished we said, "That's great—we'll be in touch." We just looked at each other and Alan said, "He's too good for us."

The second guy was a good player, but didn't look right. It's funny how we were aware of image even in these early stages.

The third guy was David Pettigrew. He wasn't bad on the guitar but, more importantly, we thought he looked the part and fitted in. He became Dave the Rave, the new guitarist in The Saxons.

By now we were getting more bookings and the next step up came at the Greenhill Club at Morningside. It was just a bare hall with a long, thin stage running from one side of the hall to the other, just deep enough to get the drums on in the middle so I had to stand on one side with Dave the Rave, while Alan stood on the other side on his own. Derek counted in the first song. Dave the Rave and I went straight into the intro for "Down at The Club" and Alan started playing a completely different song while Derek was lost somewhere in the middle. I looked over at Alan and shouted across the drums, "You're playing the wrong song!" but he couldn't hear me and with a big grin on his face, mouthed back, "Yeah! It's great."

We did get better, but it took a while.

Dave the Rave had brought along Charlie Smith to one of our practices. The two of them had been at school together and Dave was very impressed by Charlie's big ideas. He was a nice guy, very funny. He became our manager and roadie rolled into one, and he also got us some bookings along the way.

CHAPTER FOUR

The big one to crack was The Top Storey Club—everybody wanted to play at The Top Storey and it wasn't easy for a group to get in there. Situated at the top of Leith Walk, up a winding staircase to the fourth floor above a snooker hall, there was no other place that had that atmosphere. It was nothing more than a dark hall with a low ceiling, a large stage, and a soft drinks bar in the back corner, but there was something special about it. Out of all the clubs and dance halls I went to, and played at, this was the best.

The club was run by Jimmy Craig—a short, smiley man who stooped slightly and had sticking-out ears. Alan approached Jimmy and asked if we could play there some night. Apparently he wasn't showing much interest. All he said was, "Are you any good?" but a voice came from behind, saying, "I've heard them. They're very good. You should book them." It was Tam Paton. He didn't have a clue who we were, but it got us the booking and we played there many times over the next couple of years along with The Hipple People, The Embers, The Boston Dexters, The Moonrakers, The Beachcombers and many more.

That first night that Alan met Tam Paton he asked him if he would come along and hear us practise one night and, true to his word, he turned up. He listened to a few songs and advised us to get a keyboard player, because every group had a keyboard player.

Tam Paton was quite a well-known figure around the clubs and dance halls. He had played keyboards and led The Edinburgh Crusaders before putting together The Tommy Paton Show Band which played at the Edinburgh Palais De Dance. I remember going there with Alan to see Tam's band. It had a revolving stage and we could hear the band playing behind the scenes before gradually appearing as the stage turned. I was thinking there must be a huge amount of machinery to make that work, until Alan pointed to a space at the side of the stage where you could see down underneath—there was a man sitting on what looked like part of a bicycle attached to a long chain, and he was pedalling frantically, turning the stage.

Tam also managed a group called The Hipple People, one of Edinburgh's most popular bands. At a time when all groups were playing cover songs, and were judged by how close they could get to the original record, here was a group who put their own interpretation into it, and it was brilliant. I heard great songs like *Keep Your Hands Off My Baby*, *He's A Rebel* and *One Fine Day*. This was all a learning curve for me.

Tam Paton was an impressive figure in his late twenties. He knew how to dress to impress, and wore a smart-but-casual suit, with a white shirt hanging outside his trousers and unbuttoned down the front, his hairy chest displaying a large gold chain and medallion. He had longish, fair hair that swept over his forehead, and he wore black pointed boots with high heels. He always had a cigarette in his right hand, the long thin ones, and blew the smoke out of the side of his mouth in a nonchalant manner.

He had spent some time in the army, being one of the last to do National Service. Maybe that had something to do with his covering up the fact he was gay, something I was completely unaware of until much later on.

His wheels were impressive too: a white Ford Zephyr with the windows tinted black, white wall tyres and a long aerial on the roof. This was the man we wanted to manage us.

Tam came along to a few of our practice nights and we got to know him better. I don't remember us ever actually discussing it with Tam, I think we all just knew it was the right thing and that was it—we had our manager.

He was a big man, bulky round the shoulders and very strong. He spoke with a high-pitched voice but with loads of confidence. His father had established, and built up, Thomas Paton and Sons Potato Merchants, and Tam drove one of their three lorries during the day, delivering large bags of potatoes to restaurants and chip shops all over Edinburgh. His brother, David, ran the business in Port Seton where they had a warehouse and garage, to store the potatoes and keep the vehicles. At the back of the garage was an empty office area. It was small, had no windows or ventilation, but we eventually made it into a practice room.

Tam lived with his mother and father in Prestonpans, and had a bedroom upstairs to the front. The first time we visited Tam's house, his mother made us the best egg and chips I have ever tasted. I know that sounds crazy, but she had a very precise way of making chips that made them taste different. Then Tam showed us his bedroom, "How can I make this into an office and still have it as a bedroom?" he asked in his high-pitched voice. Well, there were two apprentice joiners in Derek and I, so we built him a desk and we all painted the room, got the phone connected and the pictures up on the walls.

Tam Paton's taste in decoration was a bit suspect—he liked to have fake rifles and hand pistols on the walls, and had crossed swords over the fireplace. It was a council house, for God's sake, not Edinburgh Castle! But that room became the hub of all the incredible activity that was to come.

Things were getting quite serious at this point. It was 1966 and I was sixteen. I had not long left school and started a joiner apprenticeship with Wimpey Construction on their large building sites. In these days tradesmen had a lifelong job with construction companies. They were directly employed and had their pensions tied into length of service. My clocking in number was J45—I've never forgotten that. I collected my wages, like all the other men, every Thursday at the pay hut, in cash, in a brown sealed envelope. My wages for my first year were one pound, six shillings and sixpence a week. I'd give a pound to my mother and keep the rest.

It was like one huge extended family. There were hundreds of men on site and yet everyone knew each other, I loved it. I was picked up not far from my house at Drum Brae every morning in a covered lorry and climbed in the back with all the other men, sometimes twenty or thirty men. We'd sit squeezed up on wooden benches, all the way to the building site, some fifteen miles away, and back again at night-time. It became known as the meat wagon.

I was so tired out doing stuff with the group at night and getting up at six thirty every morning, I slept all the way there and back again and was a target for a good mickey-take, especially with the name Nobby Clark, I got ribbed a lot but I took it in good spirit. I will always remember my mother saying to me, "Just finish your time, son, do your apprenticeship then you can do what you like." I didn't know the value of that at the time, but I do now.

The year was 1966: the height of Beatlemania The Beatles were at number 1 in the charts with *Paperback Writer*, The Walker Brothers just had a big hit with *The Sun Ain't Gonna Shine Anymore*, and The Beach Boys had just released *God Only Knows*. It was heaven on earth.

I was looking forward to my first "trades holiday". We would be getting three weeks wages in one go, and off work for two weeks. The final Friday came and we got paid in the morning so we could finish up at lunchtime. The site we were working on was in Penicuik, just south of Edinburgh, and all the men I worked with were going to the Cuiken Inn for a drink before they went home. "Come on—you're a man now—come and have a drink," they insisted. I wasn't even seventeen yet, so I was well underage. I'd never drank alcohol before, other than a sip of my mother's Advocaat, and I didn't like the taste of that much. So they sneaked me in and sat me down in the corner and put a pint of lager in front of me.

I knew I was playing with the group that night at Westfield Halls and would be picked up by Tam and the boys at six thirty, but as soon as I got the effect from the alcohol, I immediately wanted more and by the time we left the pub I couldn't walk or talk.

The men lifted me into the back of the lorry and dropped me off at my mother's house. I was legless, and sick all over the front step. She was mortified. My mother had put up with years of my father's drinking and the last thing she needed was to see me in this state. She tried to sober me up with coffee and food before they came to pick me up, but it didn't work—Tam Paton and the boys arrived but I was not in a fit state. Tam kept saying, "He can't sing like that," and I kept saying, "I'm alright, I'm alright." So they got me to the gig and I was still drunk when I went on stage. Thankfully I can't remember much about it, but apparently I was staggering about so much that Charlie Smith, now demoted to just our roadie, was crouched down beside the drums, with a brush handle against my back, trying to hold me up against the microphone. I made a fool of myself, and the band, that night, and I vowed it would never happen again.

We were practising two nights a week, and sometimes at the weekend, in Alan and Derek Longmuir's front room. We were playing here and there but musically it wasn't coming together. There were a couple of nights we played really badly and everybody was a bit down so we decided to change the name from The Saxons to The Deadbeats. I'm embarrassed to admit that it was my suggestion. I can't imagine why—I must have thought it was funny at the time. But, there was something good happening... girls were beginning to follow us round the clubs. Then, at a practice one night, Alan brought along Greig Ellison. They were serving their plumbing apprenticeships with the same company, and were working together at the City Hospital. Greig brought along his guitar and played some songs with us. He was a good player, and looked good, so we asked him to join the band. Dave the Rave moved onto keyboards while Greig took over on guitar.

We were experimenting with different ideas, and for a short time we were a six piece with Greig's brother, Mike, singing up front with me, but it didn't last long and Mike left.

I know this is confusing but we went through so many changes, some planned and some forced upon us trying to find the right formula.

It was time for us to step it up a gear and to find the right name for the group. I don't think anyone believed we could make it called The Deadbeats. We needed to find the right name, something big, something American-sounding because everyone was into Tamla Motown and Stax music at the time. We were in Tam's office in Prestonpans, discussing what to do about the name. He had a map of Scotland on the wall above his desk where we stuck coloured pins in to mark all the places we had played. On the other wall was a map of America. Alan and I decided to randomly stick pins in the map of America to see if we could come up with an idea for a name. The first few times there was nothing of interest, I seem to remember Wisconsin was one of them, and then someone stuck a pin right beside Bay City, Michigan and right away we thought we had something! We tried tagging names on the end like Bay City Stompers, Strollers, but they didn't sound right. It was a couple of days later after throwing it around, and arguing about it, that the name "Bay City Rollers" emerged. I honestly don't remember who came up with what—let's just say it was a team effort—and I thought it was brilliant. The new name gave us much more confidence. We were now officially called The Bay City Rollers.

We were unaware that the name Bay City Rollers was already well-known on the east side of America. Bay City was a famous surfing area and the waves were known as the Rollers.

(That's just the official story we released to the press—later I will divulge the truth.)

Working so hard was taking its toll on us all, so we decided it was time we had a holiday. None of us had ever been out of Scotland before and Tam suggested we drive down to Spain in his car. I remember we were all so excited the day we were leaving. The street outside Alan and Derek's house was full of girls all waiting to see us off, and the five members of the group, plus Tam driving, all crammed into his Ford Zephyr and headed for Spain. We drove all the way down to Dover and got on the ferry across to France.

It was July 1968, extremely hot, and Tam was having trouble keeping us rounded up. Alan and Greig were the oldest in the group and wanted to go for a drink on the ferry, so they sneaked off while Tam was trying to sort out the cabins. Most of us went for a rest that afternoon, but Greig had gone up on the deck of the boat to sunbathe, and had fallen asleep. Greig was a redhead with very fair skin, and when we eventually found him, two hours later, he was lying face down on the deck, his back bright red and covered in blisters. We got him down to the cabin in agony and took off the vest he was wearing. The white bits, where his vest straps had been, made his back look like a flag and Tam burst out laughing, which started the rest of us off. Greig was really in pain. "I know the best thing for that," Tam said, grabbing his bottle of Old Spice aftershave and pouring it all over Greig's back. The poor guy was in agony. We were shouting "Stop it Tam, it's too painful!" while giggling at the same time. "He needs to get some cream on it," he said, and went into his bag to get his big, cheap bottle of sun cream. Greig was lying face down on the bed moaning, and Tam stood over him squeezing the sun cream bottle, but nothing came out. He tried again, but was squeezing so hard the top burst off and the cream splattered all over his body, his hair and all over the bed. We all just fell apart, rolling about the floor in stitches while poor Greig lay there moaning in agony. That was the first sign of Tam's sadistic tendencies.

Tam had worked out the route we would take, down through France and over the Pyrenees mountains, into northern Spain and down to the coast. It meant sleeping in the car overnight. We drove, or should I say Tam drove, because he was the only one with a licence, through Perpignan and as far south as we could before it got dark, and stopped at the side of a country road in the middle of nowhere. There were three in the back seat and three in the front seat, all lying on top of each other, trying to get comfortable. It was so warm we had all the windows open, but it was too uncomfortable so Alan, Greig and I got out and lay on the grass verge beside the car. We were surrounded by woods and there were no lights other than the stars in the sky.

I was just getting comfortable, when Tam, through the open car window, said he had read a true story about a couple who went touring through France, but their car broke down so the man went off looking for help, while the woman waited in the car. She fell asleep and was awakened by loud banging—a maniac had climbed on top of the car and was banging her husband's severed head off the roof. You never saw anybody move so fast! We were shoving each other out of the way to get back in the car and firmly closed the windows and locked the doors. The only person who slept that night was Tam.

The journey over the Pyrenees was spectacular. There were no motorways back then, and the only way across was over mountain passes. We drove down through northern Spain, all the way to the coast, and stopped at the Mediterranean Sea. It was a beautiful, hot, sunny day and we ran from the car, across a field, onto the beach and dived into the sea. When I looked back at the coastline, there were a few farm buildings and one or two old, Spanish style houses, then fields as far as you could see. There were some people in the distance on horses riding along a dusty track. It was remote and breathtakingly beautiful. This was Lloret De Mar, which nowadays is a busy, built-up holiday resort with skyscraper hotels, bars and night clubs.

We needed to find somewhere to stay, so we got back in the car and drove up the coast to the nearest town. The first small coastal town we came to was Calafel, where we booked into some holiday apartments and went through the ritual of Tam deciding who would be sharing rooms. Once we got settled we were all straining at the bit to go out and explore, so when Tam said, "I'll just let you lot go out together. I'm going to have a sleep," we were excited and couldn't wait to get away. It was early evening, the sun was still shining, and the five of us wandered the streets looking for a bar to go into.

We found a place that had music playing and a small dance floor. A bottle of Champagne was the equivalent of one pound in pesetas (the Spanish currency at the time) and being so young and naïve, we agreed to buy a bottle each. A couple of hours later, after girls had started to arrive, I remember everyone dispersing around the bar. Some were dancing, some were chatting up girls, I was trying to have a conversation with a French girl who didn't speak any English, and I didn't speak any French, and that's the last I remember… until I was found down at the beach, sitting on a wall under the starlight, staring into her eyes, with Tam standing over me, steam coming out his ears and raging. Four of the other boys were standing behind him, drunk out of their faces. "Where's Dave?" Tam was shouting.

Dave the Rave had disappeared. I was told to join the ranks and we all set off to look for him. Tam marched in front with the rest of us staggering along behind. Somehow on the way we lost Derek, and we ended up back at the apartments. Tam was going crazy, pacing up and down, shouting and swearing, and then Derek walked in with Dave the Rave. "I've lost my false teeth," Dave said, and opened his mouth to show his gums right across the front. "Where the fuck did you lose them?" Tam shouted. "I don't know... I was sick in the town somewhere." So we all went back out to find Dave's teeth. But we got split up again and Alan, Greig and I ended up back in the same bar, while the others searched the streets. They found Dave's teeth on the ground where he had been sick. He picked them up and put them back in his mouth.

When we got back to Edinburgh, we were feeling great, looking tanned, and dying to get back on stage. I had been going to a coffee bar in St John's Church at the west end of Princes Street. It was down in the vaults at the back of the church, and the only access was through the graveyard, so they called it The Coffin. Its original purpose was just to give teenagers a place where they could meet up, but it had become the "in" place to go and—wow!—what a place... it was filled with artists, and musicians, and colourful young people with a purpose, who all generated a lot of energy. It was the beginning of the hippy period and I was in there on a Saturday afternoon, surrounded by great people, waiting for one of the first copies of *Sergeant Pepper's Lonely Hearts Club Band* to be brought straight round from Bruce's Record Shop to The Coffin. I remember when Moses walked in with the album and I saw the cover—that in itself told me it was something special. It was played on a gramophone record player, the type with the lift-up lid and built-in stereo speakers. The whole place just stalled, and everyone was staring at the record player. I didn't take drugs at the time, but I remember all these colours coming out of the speakers.

For me it was a moment frozen in time and marks my meeting with Keith Norman at The Coffin. Sometimes in your life you cross paths with someone that you immediately make a connection with and we became very good friends, especially when I found out he played keyboards for a group called The Images. I wanted him in our group, so I asked the rest of them to come along and see him play one night. There was no hesitation, Keith was right for the group. He was a great-looking guy with very dark, almost black, shiny straight hair down to his shoulders and a cheeky smile. He was a very deep guy. Something was lost about him—he was sad but with a sense of humour. The girls loved Keith and I liked him a lot as a friend.

Tam Paton suggested we try something different and have two keyboard players, one on either side of the stage. So we bought two Vox Continental organs. All the best bands from Glasgow, The Pathfinders, The Poets and others, had Vox Continentals and they were wiping the floor with most of the Edinburgh bands.

We were getting somewhere. The Bay City Rollers were now: Nobby Clark on vocals; Alan Longmuir on bass; Derek Longmuir on drums; Greig Ellison on guitar; and Dave Pettigrew (Dave The Rave) and Keith Norman on keyboards.

We would sit in Tam's office/bedroom in Prestonpans discussing what it would take to make it big, and how dedicated we would have to be. Tam strongly believed that having girlfriends would be a distraction and we agreed, to the best of our ability. One of his ploys was to tell us stories that would put us off girlfriends. He told us that a young couple had been having sex in Princes Street Gardens and had got stuck together. He told us women had a bone that could come down and stop you from pulling out. He told us they'd had to carry both of them on a stretcher through the gardens, in front of all the people sunbathing.

Tam also detested alcohol, having watched his alcoholic father mistreat his mother, and it all became very important that we stuck to the rules of no steady girlfriends and no drinking.

There was a very strong bond built up between Alan, Derek, myself, and Tam. I don't think we were convinced that Dave the Rave was committed to the group, Keith was new, and as a new

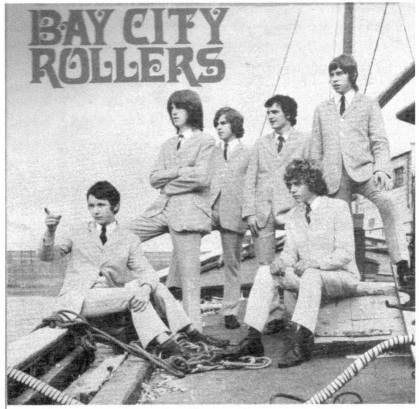

Standing (left to right): Greg Ellison (Lead); Allan Longmuir (Bass); Dave Pettigrew (Organ); Derek Longmuir (Drums).
Seated: Left—Keith Norman (Organ); Right—Nobby Clark (Vocalist).

member would still have to prove he was keen and interested, but there was an amazing chemistry between us, and an energy that was almost tangible.

We were improving musically too. Keith had been taught classical piano so it raised the game slightly, and by now we were playing regularly around Edinburgh and beginning to spread our wings a little. To our joy and amazement we were building up a huge following of girls, and a few guys.

Tam Smith had been working with us as a roadie for some time. I don't even remember how it came about—maybe we poached him from another group—but he was with us a long time. He became one of the boys and looked after us in the dressing room and he was always on the button. It was becoming difficult to get in and out of dance halls because so many girls were waiting at the back door. Tam Smith would hustle us through, but Tam Paton would get a bit frantic, because there was a fair bit of kissing and touching going on.

Everything was coming together and it was time for the next stage of the plan. The map of Scotland which hung above Tam Paton's desk in Prestonpans had a few coloured pins stuck in it to mark the places we had played, but it was now our ambitious plan to have a pin in every city and town on that map and, you know, by the end, we almost achieved it.

The Bay City Rollers (circa 1968)

CHAPTER FIVE

The newspapers and magazines were starting to take an interest so we were doing more and more interviews and gaining experience. In September 1968 we were asked to take part in a charity walk with Jimmy Savile (Radio One DJ, and TV presenter) which would later end in a football match with teams made up of Jimmy Savile and Friends Vs The Bay City Rollers and Friends. We had the advantage of having Linnie Paterson (lead singer with The Writing On The Wall) on our team, who was a great player. We won the game, which made the front page of The Evening News and raised a lot of money to build a swimming pool for over three hundred severely handicapped children at St. Joseph's Hospital, Rosewell.

I remember meeting Jimmy Savile for the first time in the dressing room (although our paths crossed many times in the following years). I tried to make conversation, but every time I asked a question he blanked it, or diverted it with a stupid, humorous comment. He was so full of himself. I remember saying to Alan, "What a dick he is, he gives me the creeps!"

Tam Paton was out there with a purpose and a focus. He had this brilliant idea of spray-painting the name, Bay City Rollers, across all the bridges over the M8 motorway and in big letters on the wall at the east end of Princes Street. Although we got charged with defacing property, and had to scrub it off the wall, we had the photographers there from the newspapers and got some great publicity.

Our diary was filling up with some of the best dance halls in the country, including the J.M. Ballroom in Dundee, The Trocadero in Hamilton, The Locarno in Glasgow, The Kinema Ballroom in Dunfermline and The Beach Ballroom in Aberdeen. Then there were the other not-so-good places, like Shotts Town

Hall, where halfway through the set we had to get off the stage because the whole crowd were fighting and smashing chairs up for weapons. There were bodies and blood everywhere. They had to let two Alsatian dogs into the hall to break it up. When we got outside there was an angry mob waiting for us who'd slashed the tyres on the car and smashed all the windows in the van. We had no choice, we had to run to the car dodging missiles and get out of there quickly. We drove about two miles on the rims of the wheels.

Then there was Prestonpans Town Hall. I remember it well because the place was mobbed with fans. I was wearing a pair of green satin trousers I had made using my mother's old sewing machine. I had started making clothes for the group and these were one of my early attempts. The night was going great. We were a few songs into the set, and the girls at the front were grabbing my hands and trying to pull me off stage, when the satin trousers ripped right up the back seam. I never wore underwear on stage so I was trying to stay facing forward while the rest of the group were cracking up behind me. Then during the next song, while I had my shirt wrapped round my trousers, the power went off on stage and the sound ground to a halt. We stood there looking at each other like a bunch of fools, before awkwardly backing off the stage into the dressing room, only to find that the caretaker had pulled out the plug so he could boil the kettle for his tea.

Everywhere we played we handed out hundreds of photographs of the band and were building up a huge following. Tam Paton was always thinking up new ways to boost our fan club. He bought all the teenage magazines that had lists of girls all over the country looking for pen pals. He copied all these addresses into a book and sent them all photographs of the group and details of our fan club—the mail started rolling in.

By 1968 things were really happening. I had girls gathering outside my house on a regular basis while Alan and Derek's house was constantly besieged with hordes of fans because they knew that was our meeting place. They followed us everywhere.

There was a dance hall just outside of Edinburgh called Rosewell Institute where we had played a number of times. Tam had got involved there as a promoter and he booked the Bee Gees, who had a number 1 hit with *Massachusetts,* and we were to be the support act.

It was sold out. You couldn't have got another person into that hall. I stood at the side of the stage and watched Barry Gibb performing in this fabulous gold, silk shirt with puffed sleeves and frills all down the front. Later, when they came off stage, one of our fans ran into their dressing room and took the shirt. After the Bee Gees had driven away we were getting into the car when she handed the shirt to me. I wore that shirt on stage a couple of times before playing at Motherwell Town Hall where things got a bit out of control and I was pulled off stage by the fans—they ripped the shirt to shreds... Can you imagine what that shirt would be worth today? Sorry Barry.

A few weeks later we were back at Rosewell Institute, supporting Robert Plant and his Band of Joy (before they became Led Zeppelin). I watched them arrive in their scruffy clothes, but they got changed into even scruffier clothes to perform on stage. That's the point when I really got in touch with how important image was.

We were booked to play a gig at the Flotilla Club at Rosyth dockyards in Fife, it was a Navy dinner-dance. Top of the bill was Johnny Johnson and the Bandwagon who had a number of hits, including *Blame It On The Pony Express*, all written by Tony Macaulay who later wrote a song for The Bay City Rollers. Unfortunately for Johnny Johnson, they had another gig after this one and had to go on first. All the navy personnel and guests (around six hundred of them) were still having dinner in the mess hall, so the band came on stage to just three people, and two of them were doormen. I stood in the wings and watched Johnny Johnson dressed in his sparkling white suit and black Afro wig, dancing up and down that stage for an hour and a quarter, giving an amazing performance. Afterwards, I spoke to him in the dressing room and said, "That was fantastic! I'm amazed you bothered, considering there was hardly anybody in the hall." He replied sharply, "It doesn't matter whether it's one or a thousand, you should always give your best performance—

you never know who that one person might be." I never forgot that.

Another gig I'll never forget was at Butlin's Holiday Camp in Ayrshire. We were on the bill with Hamish Imlach, the Scottish folk singer, and The Humblebums, who were Gerry Rafferty, Billy Connolly and Joe Egan. We were given chalets to stay in overnight. Our chalet was next door to the Humblebums, and we dropped our stuff off in it and walked down to the hall for a sound rehearsal. We must have left the chalet door unlocked, because when we got back all the beds had been upturned, all the bedclothes were thrown outside on the grass and our cases were emptied out on the floor. Billy Connolly and Joe Egan had slipped in when we were out and trashed the place. We had a good laugh with them after the gig.

Tam Paton was still driving a lorry for the family business, delivering potatoes to chip shops and restaurants around Edinburgh. To keep us occupied when we weren't playing we would take turns working on the lorry. The group was earning a lot of money from our live performances and Derek Longmuir was put in charge of the finances, but none of us took any money—it was all invested back into making the group more successful.

Tam had spotted David Paton (no relation to him) playing lead guitar with an Edinburgh group called The Beachcombers. They had been to London and released a single called *The Animal In Me* but it hadn't done so well, and David came back from London disillusioned with the music business and ready to give it up, get his hair cut and do something else. So Tam offered him a job on the potato lorry. This was his devious way of enticing him into The Rollers. David Paton was perfect for The Bay City Rollers. He was a great-looking guy, slim, with long, straight fair hair and he was very popular with the girls. After some gentle persuasion he joined the group in 1969.

Once Davie was settled into the group and had played a few gigs with us it was time for another holiday trip to Spain, but this time we would go in the new transit van we had just bought. Tam had discovered a new way of getting a tan. It was out of a bottle called Q.T. (quick tan) and he was ladling it on saying,

"You need to get some of this on you—it's brilliant." So we did, slapping it on. Two hours later when it developed, we were all covered in big brown patches all over our faces and bodies, and we couldn't get it off! We had to go on holiday looking like that.

We drove down to Dover and took the ferry across to France, but this time we took a different route down through Le Mans, where they hold the motor racing. On the way the van started overheating and we had to stop every few miles to fill up with water until, eventually, it ran out completely.

Luckily the police were passing and stopped to see what was wrong. They were talking away in French, which none of us understood a word of, when Keith jumped out of the van and started having a fluent conversation with them. We were gobsmacked. Keith was from a well-off family and had been taught at private school, not like the rest of us. The police got us on our way and we made it to a garage in Le Mans. The mechanic had a look at it and said, "You need a new radiator. I'll have to order the parts and it'll take a week."

There was nothing to do. The motor racing season hadn't started yet and the town was pretty much deserted. We slept in the van at night outside the garage and were bored to tears during the day. When the van finally got fixed, we decided it wasn't worth driving to Spain and headed for Paris instead.

Paris was like another world to us boys who had hardly been out of Scotland. We were up the Eiffel Tower and down The Champs Elysees. The fashions were out of this world—all the guys in the streets were wearing see-through lace shirts and trousers. We had to have them!

We arrived back in Edinburgh and were on stage the following night with the new gear on. I had black, see-through lace shirt and trousers; the other guys had the same but in different colours. The girls went wild and tried to rip them off us when we came off stage.

But we had a problem. It was rumoured that Keith was seeing a girl on the side. One night Tam picked us all up and we went and sat in the car outside Keith's house in Kaimes Road until about ten thirty when we saw him get off a bus and walk up the road to his house. He was obviously shocked to see us all sitting there and Tam got out and confronted him. He confessed to having a girlfriend and left the band shortly after. I felt terrible… he was a close friend, and we had just bought him a brand new Hammond organ and Leslie cabinet.

I knew that some of the guys in the band were having flings with girls on the side, and I was no exception. We had girls throwing themselves at us on a daily basis. But if members of the group were getting involved in relationships it meant they had to leave the group, so something had to be done about it. I decided to lead by example, and for the next five years I remained celibate.

One day we were working on the potato lorry with Tam when this great-looking guy came walking along the road. Tam immediately approached him and asked, "Can you play the guitar?" and the guy said "No." "Well, would you like to be in a group anyway?" asked Tam. This was Eric Manclark, who joined The Bay City Rollers but never actually ever had his guitar plugged in. Billy Lyall was the next to join, but he was the complete opposite, a trained classical pianist and flute player.

So now we had the new line up: Nobby Clark, Alan Longmuir, Derek Longmuir, Davie Paton, Billy Lyall and Eric Manclark. The image was right and, with the exception of Eric Manclark, the band was on a musical high. Davie Paton became the musical director of the group and took on the thankless task of teaching Eric to play the guitar.

To try and encourage Davie to stay with us we bought him a Gold Top Les Paul guitar, along with a Fender Jazz bass for Alan, which we got on hire-purchase (payment agreement) from Pete Seaton's music shop. Two weeks later, the van was broken into and both guitars were stolen and never seen again. We had no insurance and had to keep making monthly payments until they were paid off two years later.

Billy Lyall (or Hot Lips, as we called him, due to the fact he heated his flute up at the fire before he played) was very effeminate, very good-looking, extremely funny and a wonderful piano player. He did dabble in relationships with girls on the quiet, but we all knew which side his bread was buttered. He said in a newspaper article,

"I didn't know what group it was when I answered an advert for an organist. Just my luck it was the Rollers. I didn't realise how popular they were until I played the first gig at The Trocadero in Hamilton. I was shaking like a leaf when I saw the place was bursting at the seams with girl fans."

I was still making clothes for the band and Billy came along one day with a pair of curtains from his mother's house and asked if I could make trousers out of them. They were gold velvet with a floral pattern, and he wore them on stage nearly every night. Billy got everybody's back up because every night, after a gig, he would quickly get changed and run out to the car first, so he could get the front seat while the rest of us had to cram in the back.

We had a long-standing booking to play Tranent Town Hall (a small town just south-east of Edinburgh). We had to honour the booking, even though we hated playing there. It had a reputation for fights, and the guys there hated the Rollers because of the adoration we got from the girl fans, who travelled from all over the country to see us.

We set up all the amps and equipment in the afternoon so we could do a sound check. It was a typical town hall with a high stage and a door to the rear of the stage leading to the dressing room. After the sound check we left the hall to go for something to eat and get ready for the gig. When we arrived back, the place was mobbed. All the girl fans were packed tight in front of the stage, and at the rear of the hall were all the guys, standing around in packs. As soon as we walked on we received the, now-established, reception from the girl fans trying to pull us off stage by climbing up and grabbing our legs. I would tease them by putting my hand down, but I noticed that some guys had pushed their way through the crowd and were trying to grab my hand. The next thing I knew, a bottle was thrown from the back of the hall and smashed on the wall above the dressing room door. Then it all kicked off. Guys were climbing onto the stage and the roadies were pushing them back, they were grabbing the microphone stands and throwing them off stage. I looked over at Billy Lyall who was standing back from his Hammond organ—he took off and ran to the dressing room, closed the door and locked it from the inside. The rest of us followed and were banging on the door shouting, "Let us in!" but he thought it was the mob and wouldn't open the door. I looked round and saw them throw the Hammond organ off the stage. Then the drum kit went flying while the roadies were fighting them off with mike stands. The bouncers were tied up at the back of the hall trying to break up a battle royal between rival gangs. The place was mayhem until the police arrived and broke it up. We never played in that area again.

The group was moving on to better things, and under Davie Paton's influence we were developing musically and vocally. We now had four voices and I introduced more close harmony songs into the live set. The group, and Tam, went everywhere together and quite often we would go to our favourite restaurant, The House of Choi, for a Chinese meal. But we knew it wouldn't be long before a line of faces would appear at the restaurant window watching every mouthful. The fans were very astute at finding out where we were. We were like monkeys in a cage.

It was the same when we went to the pictures. We could rarely watch a film without being disturbed, so Tam hired the Regal Cinema in Bonnyrigg (just outside Edinburgh) for a private showing of *The Guns of Navarone*. But Tam mixed up the dates, and the cinema was left with a full staff and no audience. Tam was never on time for anything, he always kept people waiting. We called him "the late Tam Paton".

Horse riding was our favourite pastime, and at every opportunity we would go trekking up in the Pentland hills, but there were always girls waiting when we got back. We had to have some place for a hideaway, so we converted the practice room at the back of the potato garage in Port Seton into a studio. This was the one place where nobody disturbed us. Strictly "Rollers only" was the rule. The advantage of having our own studio was that we could practise whenever we wanted. Tam said once, "I don't know how they do it. I've seen them play a late night in a ballroom then drive straight back to the studio and play till five in the morning."

One night when we were practising, Tam walked in with a big lump of cannabis in his hand. We had no experience of drugs. Of course we had heard of people taking speed and dope, but there was no big drug scene in Edinburgh at that time. We gathered round to have a look. "What do you do with it?" Alan asked. "You heat it up and mix bits of it with tobacco and smoke it," Tam replied. Well none of us even smoked at the time, except Tam, so he rolled one up and gave it to us. I just remember being so dizzy and feeling sick—it was horrible. I never understood why Tam introduced us to it. There was a dark side to him that I found quite disturbing sometimes.

Just when things were looking up, I was given the bad news that my father was diagnosed with throat cancer. He had been a heavy smoker most of his life, but gave up immediately he was told of his illness. His last packet of cigarettes was put in the cupboard beside his chair and stayed there, but it was too late. I wasn't around much because we were so busy, but each time I came home he was worse. Eventually the surgeon had to carry out a tracheotomy and insert a tube through his neck into his windpipe so that he could breathe. I have to say he was an extremely brave man. I never heard him complain or moan about anything. He wore a cravat around his neck to hide the tube, and put his finger over the hole when he wanted to speak, and just got on with it.

I got back late one night. It was around two o'clock in the morning when we pulled up outside my house at Drum Brae Drive. I could see through the curtains that the lights were on in the living room, and I immediately thought something must be wrong. When I got inside my father was sitting in his chair—he had been waiting for me to come home. He asked me to sit down and tried to talk to me about the past… and why he had treated me the way he did. He went on to say he had followed my career with the group and could see all the hard work I had put into it. I just sat there silent, but in my head I was saying, "Don't you dare lay this on me now, to salve your conscience." Just then my mother burst into the room—she had been standing behind the door listening. She pointed at him and said, "Don't you fill his head with that nonsense," and told me to get to bed.

I suppose in his way he was trying to apologise, and say he was proud of me, but he never actually said the words. As his illness progressed he spent more and more time in the hospital. It was discovered that not only had his cancer spread, but he had also contracted tuberculosis. It wasn't long before my mother was told it was just a matter of time. She took the brave decision to bring him home and look after him. I felt so sorry for her. She had support from my sisters and brothers, but I was the only one still living at home and unfortunately I couldn't be there enough to help her. I remember him lying on the bed and Mum asking me if I would give him a shave. I tried to, but I couldn't—I could see it was hurting him. At that moment I saw my dad as a helpless human being, and not someone to be feared. I went into my bedroom and cried my heart out. I'd told myself for so long that I hated him, when really I loved him and just wanted him to show that he loved me.

He died on the 25th January 1970.

CHAPTER SIX

Interviews and photograph sessions (smudges, as we used to call them) were coming thick and fast, and were always mayhem with us laughing and fooling around. We were just a bunch of young guys having the time of our lives. I loved the excitement and the buzz that surrounded the group, but most of all I loved playing live on stage.

We had a fantastic live set. Some original songs, and some cover songs, carefully chosen and built-up over a long period. *Bye Bye Baby* was a song I introduced quite early on and it was one of the most popular songs with our fans. I took it from the original by The Four Seasons (written by their keyboard player, Bob Gaudio) and we did other songs of theirs over the years: *Beggin'* was a fairly unknown song when we did it, now everyone knows it, and very early on we did a version of *Rag Doll* (both of these were Gaudio songs). When we played in Scotland I couldn't get off the stage without singing *Please Stay*, a very early Burt Bacharach composition originally sung by The Cryin' Shames. I must have sung it hundreds of times, and it became a Bay City Rollers anthem.

I had a strange feeling of disloyalty to fans in Scotland when our attention was drawn towards London and the south. They had supported us through thick and thin, and followed us everywhere. We had made a success of it and were about to step into the unknown. We got hundreds of fan letters begging us not to go to London because we would forget them and not come back.

Gary Nichols, a reporter for a Scottish teen magazine, wrote this article:

Will the Rollers be following the usual trail to the big smoke? Not while there are still places to play in Scotland—and the main one is Glasgow.

"We've played all around and about—Gourock, Wishaw, Motherwell, Bellshill—but we've only played Glasgow once, at The Electric Gardens" says Nobby.

"The scene's only just starting for the Rollers in the west," agrees Tam. " It's like it was in Edinburgh two years ago for us." And the west also holds two of the Rollers favourite venues— Hamilton Trocadero and East Kilbride where they caused a near riot recently. "My hair was standing on end for them----."

Those stories of screaming and mass hysteria are no fairy tales. Even on a cold March evening our team found a group of girls waiting outside a club to get a glimpse of the group leaving.

There's not much chance of more than a glimpse. The Rollers are valuable property, and as soon as they're out of a club, they're guarded by the manager and five big roadies until they're safely into the big black windowed transit van.

It's a fair bet that no other Scottish group has collected such a following before a chart record. An amazing number of girls follow them from gig to gig.

Despite what many progressive groups may say, there's more to the Bay City Rollers than five pretty faces. They've been an easy target for the critics for too long now—it's about time they received the musical recognition they deserve.

So there it was in black and white, we were being noticed and right at the top of our game when the bombshell hit: Davie Paton announced he was leaving the group. That was a big shock to us all and we were really down about it.

Davie said later, "I just couldn't stand the lifestyle. After not having a girlfriend for a year I was getting quite depressed; I once arranged a date and took a girl out in the group's van. When I looked in the rear mirror I discovered we were being tailed by Tam. We were chased for about two miles before I stopped and got out."

What next? Every time we thought we had it right, someone would leave. If it hadn't been for the bond between Alan, Derek and me, I think the band would have split before now, but we were determined. There's no doubt we were at a low point. We had to pick ourselves up and sort it out.

Here we were again auditioning guitar players, and along came Neil Henderson from Glasgow in answer to an advert we had put in the papers. He had played with some Glasgow bands and wasn't a bad guitarist but was going to find it difficult to follow Davie.

Now the line-up was Nobby Clark, Alan Longmuir, Derek Longmuir, Billy Lyall, Eric Manclark and Neil Henderson. Both Billy Lyall and I had been writing songs for some time and we added some of them into the live set. Tam Paton had a very strange attitude, as he didn't like any of us being songwriters. Maybe he felt it singled us out from the rest of the group or maybe he had other motives.

We'd had a fair bit of interest from London talent scouts and the word was getting out about our popularity. An article written in the Sunday Mail on 21st June 1970 said:

"A popular Scottish group hitting the headlines is The Bay City Rollers. The Edinburgh group may soon record their first single and album on a new label. Said manager Tam Paton "The boys have had so many recording offers recently that choosing the right one has been very difficult. It's almost certain however that the Rollers will have a single out before the end of the year."

A follow up article shortly after said:

The Bay City Rollers, accompanied by their two roadies and a photographer, drove down to London last week to record their first single, with £12 between the nine of them.

Manager Tam Paton, who followed by plane after clearing up some business in Edinburgh, explained that pressure of work and a bad weekend financially had prevented him from supplying the group with ready cash before they left.

So the Rollers had to go down knowing they'd be sleeping in the van for four nights. The boys spent four days in the studio laying down possible tracks for the single. Billy Lyall's "Take One Or The Other" was at one time certain to be their first "A" side but it was decided to wait and hear all of the tapes before making a final decision.

Among the men seen in London in connection with the big Rollers publicity build up was David Apps, the promoter who has handled Tom Jones, Englebert Humperdinck, Humble Pie and David Bowie, among others.

Currently in Apps' possession is the 20 minute promotion film of the Rollers shot recently at Dundee's J.M.ballroom. Three cameramen were sent up from London to shoot the film, which successfully captured the mass hysteria which a Rollers gig has been known to provoke, and the powers that be in London are suitably impressed with the result.

So we signed to David Apps's record label called Realisation 7, and very quickly we had the realisation it was a big mistake. His intention was to sell the contract on to someone else in order to make some money, and that is exactly what happened. David Apps approached Dick Leahy from Bell Records and showed him the film. Dick came up to Scotland and experienced the hysteria surrounding the group and wanted us on the Bell Records label. He negotiated a deal with David Apps and bought out our contract.

The months that followed were very confusing. We had an idea of the musical direction the band should go down, and it was more rock and roll than light pop, but Dick Leahy and Tam Paton had other ideas. Different young producers were brought in to try out songs with the group but none of them worked.

In the process of all this, I noticed that Billy Lyall was becoming more and more disheartened. His song *Take One Or The Other* had been pushed into the background, and when I spoke to him he told me he was thinking of leaving the group. I told the other guys and we tried to persuade him to stay, but he left soon after to take up a job as a sound engineer at Craighall Studios, Edinburgh.

So we brought in Archie Marr. We knew Archie from an Edinburgh band called The Tandem who had supported us several times at gigs, and he took Billy's place as the new keyboard player.

It was all happening so fast. The next thing we knew, we were presented with a new recording contract with Bell Records (a subsidiary of Arista Records in New York, under the presi-

BAY CITY ROLLERS   PERSONNEL MANAGEMENT   FAN CLUB   RECORDING COMPANY
Tam Paton   Wilma, 27 Prestongrange Road   Bell Records
Prestonpans 380   Prestonpans, East Lothian   RECORD RELEASE 18th JUNE
We Can Make Music

dency of Clive Davis). The contract on offer was under New York law and the deal on record sales would be 4%.

I looked at the contract and told the other band members and Tam, "They must think we're stupid. I'm not signing that." Tam went ballistic, "You're going to fuck it up for everybody if you don't sign that contract! I'll have nothing more to do with the band. After all the years of hard work you're going to end up with nothing!"

But Alan Longmuir agreed with me, and that made it worse. I suggested we take the contract to a lawyer. The response from Tam was, "What the fuck do you need a lawyer for? You can see what's in the contract. A fucking lawyer?" Looking round at the others, his eyes bulging, his voice getting higher and squeakier, and his arms flying everywhere, "He wants a fucking lawyer!" The rest of the guys were too frightened to say anything.

But I stood my ground, and Dick Leahy called a meeting in London on a Sunday afternoon at the Bell Records offices in Wardour Street. I walked into their office wearing the latest fashion in Edinburgh, a black T-shirt with numbers all over the front of it, and to undermine me Dick Leahy said, "You shouldn't wear that, it went out of fashion down here ages ago."

The meeting was tense. We went through the contract and removed some of the less important clauses and got to the percentages. I said, "I'm not happy with that." Dick Leahy made this statement, "I didn't think you would be. Look," he said, "we'll keep it at 4% the first year, then 5% the second and third year." I signed it under pressure and against my better judgement.

Once I had time to study the contract properly, I discovered that it stated 4% of 90%, which was even worse. Also written into the contract was an advance of £5000 on signing. That may not sound like much now, but in 1971 it was a lot of money to us. I kept on asking, "When will we get the money?" and was told, "Don't worry, it'll be sorted out." The money never came.

Jonathan King was a successful record producer. He ran Decca Records for a time before creating his own label, UK Records. He discovered and signed Genesis, worked with 10cc and produced a string of hits including *Una Paloma Blanca*, and *Sugar Sugar* under the name of Saccharin, but was probably best known for his first hit song *Everyone's Gone to the Moon*. Dick Leahy approached him and asked him to produce The Bay City Rollers.

It was arranged that the whole band would go to his house, just off Bayswater Road in Kensington. It was a large white house, set back off the road, and stood on three storeys. Jonathan King met us at the front door and led us up to his music room on the third floor. He was very chatty and, on first impressions, seemed like a really nice guy. He had a pile of records laid out for us to listen to. The first one was *Crimson and Clover*, by Tommy James and The Shondells. It reached number 1 in America in 1968. I immediately thought it was too slow for us.

The second song was *Keep on Dancing* by The Gentrys. It had been a massive hit in America in 1965, reaching number 4 in the Billboard Hot 100 chart. At least this one was up-tempo, but very retro sounding. Then he played *We Can Make Music* by Tommy Roe, which had been a worldwide release but not a big hit. I didn't like that one at all, but I didn't say anything... I thought, I'll just go with the flow.

Then Jonathan King picked up his acoustic guitar and played two songs written by himself, *Jenny* and *Alright*. It was embarrassing—he could hardly play the guitar, even though they were both written on three chords. It was not a good impression and I hated both songs. However, Dick Leahy gave him complete control over the recordings, and before long we were in Olympic Studios in Kingston recording *Keep on Dancing* as a potential A-side and *Alright* (written by Jonathan King) as the possible B-side. Those days you could earn as much in royalties from the B-side as you could from the A-side, especially if you wrote the song.

The studio had been booked for an evening session, because the hourly rate was cheaper, and the recording went on right through the night into the following morning. To give Jonathan King his due, he did give the group the opportunity to play on *Keep on Dancing,* but when Derek Longmuir attempted the fast drum intro, he couldn't play it at the right tempo. It was taking up too much studio time, so he brought in session musicians and none of the Rollers actually played on the record. It was just my lead vocal with my over-dubbed harmonies and some backing vocals from Alan Longmuir and Archie Marr.

I still wasn't convinced about the songs, until he brought in the organ and the strings and then the whole thing came alive. *Keep on Dancing* sounded like a hit song. We weren't allowed to be there when he mixed the tracks, and were asked to leave the studio. We wandered around Kingston for hours until the final mixes were done, then we went back to listen to them. The tracks were given to Dick Leahy and the decision was made that *Keep on Dancing* would be The Bay City Rollers first single, with Jonathan King's song *Alright* on the B-side. We went back on the road while awaiting a release date.

It was the first time I felt insecure in the band as I felt any control we had was melting away. I asked Tam when we were likely to get the advance of £5000 that we'd need to keep us on the road, but he confessed he'd found out Dick Leahy had paid it to Jonathan King. Tam did absolutely nothing about it. I was really angry and I had a feeling we were in trouble

A date was set for the release of *Keep on Dancing,* but then it kept being put back because of other releases on the Bell Records label, e.g. Dawn, The Partridge Family, Seals and Crofts, Edison Lighthouse, Johnny Johnson and The Bandwagon, etc. It was very frustrating…. and meanwhile, to top it all, Jonathan King was enjoying a hit of his own with, *JUMP UP AND DOWN, WAVE YOUR KNICKERS IN THE AIR*!

Eventually, *Keep on Dancing* was released on the 18th June 1971. To begin with we got one or two plays on the radio but the producers at the BBC's Radio One wouldn't put it on their playlist because of the track's strange ending. Jonathan King had thought it would be a novelty to fade out the song and then bring it back in again. But this worked against us because the producers were frightened it would catch out the DJs. It was beginning to look like it wouldn't get off the ground.

We had signed to a London agency called Starlight Artists, which was owned by Peter Walsh and run by Barry Perkins. Peter Walsh managed and acted as agent for Hot Chocolate, and Marmalade, amongst a whole host of cabaret acts. Barry Perkins was the stereotypical entertainments agent sitting in a dark, back room office in his oversized pinstripe suit with an over-flowing ashtray on his desk. He was short and stout and wore thick-rimmed glasses. Quite a nervous character, he spoke very quickly. He was put in charge of looking after The Bay City Rollers.

To celebrate signing to the agency Barry took us out to a London club. Of course Tam wasn't too happy about the fact there were a lot of very attractive girls in the club, or that Barry Perkins was buying us all drinks. Every time I got the taste of alcohol I didn't know when to stop, so Tam was watching me like a hawk. The night got out of control. We were all very drunk, with the exception of Tam, who was like the teacher on a school trip. Barry was completely pissed, and Archie Marr recalls, "I was standing next to Barry Perkins when he was admiring a girl on the dance floor. When she came closer he asked her for a dance and got a refusal. When he asked her a second time and got a refusal he said to her, slurring his speech, "I was admiring you from afar and thinking you were very nice, but I see now that you're arrogant and blunt to the point of ignorance. Now I'm imagining you going to the toilet for a shit." It was time to leave.

Our diary was full of gigs up in Scotland and Barry Perkins was trying to juggle dates to get us into clubs in England. Some of our Scottish gigs had been booked months ahead, starting with the RAF base in Thurso (right up at the very northern tip of Scotland) then on to Lossiemouth and Elgin, where we played the famous dance club The Two Red Shoes, followed by Nairn, and then down to the J.M. ballroom in Dundee.

We did all of this in a Vauxhall Viscount car with Tam driving, three members of the band in the back seat and two in the front seat. Somehow the dates had all got mixed up, and we drove from Dundee at one o'clock in the morning, followed by the van with two roadies and all the gear, overnight, all the way to Bournemouth on the south coast of England. To make it worse, Davie Gold, who was our driver and roadie at the time, was so tired he got onto the M6 motorway going the wrong direction and drove sixty miles back up north before he noticed.

After Bournemouth we headed for Andover, where we met Reg Presley from the Troggs. He had booked us for a gig which he'd organised in Andover. I liked him, he was a really nice guy, very forthright, and invited us all back to his house for a meal. It was really two semi-detached houses knocked into one, with an indoor swimming pool and large games room with a snooker table. His name had been associated with mysterious crop circles appearing in fields in and around Somerset. "And what's this about the crop circles?" I asked him. "It wasn't me," he replied, with a smile.

It had been a ridiculously tiring run of gigs that probably did us more harm than good. The whole time up till now, regardless of who was in the group, we'd all got along well. But now there was a tension between Archie Marr and Neil Henderson, while Tam Paton and I were at each other's throats constantly. The Rollers were unknown in England at this time. It was hard coming from the hysteria in Scotland to relative obscurity while trying to promote the new single, *Keep on Dancing*.

We played at the New Century Halls in Manchester, where there was no dressing room so we had to get ready in the long, thin corridor behind the stage. We had the drums all set up ready to be lifted onto the stage when the opening act came off. Alan was searching for a socket to plug in the hair dryer, but couldn't find one and decided the only thing to do would be to wire it straight into the light pendant. He climbed up onto my shoulders and said, "Don't let anybody switch that light on." Just as he said that an argument broke out and Archie threw a cymbal stand at Neil who was standing on the other side of me. Alan was balancing on my shoulders, with bare wires hanging out of the light socket. Neil took a kick at Archie, who was on the opposite side, and kicked me in the leg then Archie stretched across my back and tried to grab Neil, while Alan was shouting, "When I come down I'll batter the two of you!" He was just connecting the wires together when Davie Purdie, our roadie, came in and switched the light on. "Bang!" There was a bright flash and Alan fell right off my shoulders onto the floor. We had to go on stage with smiles, and messed up hair, and pretend everything was just great.

My mother had kept all the newspaper clippings, magazine articles and photographs that documented the history of The Bay City Rollers right from the start. I would collect them for her when I was away and give them to her when I got home. She put them all into scrapbooks in date order and updated them regularly. Every so often I would look through them and remind myself how far we had come, and it would give me a boost when times were hard.

Down in London Dick Leahy was still trying to get our single off the ground, but three months had passed and it was looking less and less likely. So they brought in a guy called Chris Denning who was a friend of Jonathan King, and had worked at the BBC. He was now a freelance plugger, which was someone who went to meetings with radio show producers and plugged records in order to get them played.

Bell Records re-launched *Keep On Dancing*, and with Chris Denning on board it started to move. The first Radio One DJ to pick it up was Johnny Walker, and from there it made it onto the playlist, which meant it was guaranteed a certain amount of plays over the week. Radio Luxembourg (208) also liked it and played it every night. It entered the charts at number 37 and quickly jumped to 26 then 17. It was September 1971, nearly four months after the initial release date.

Dick Leahy took us all out for a slap-up meal in one of London's most expensive restaurants to celebrate. He said, "Have anything you like, lads, it's on Bell Records." So we did—we ordered champagne and steaks and lobster and had a fabulous time. Little did we know it would be charged to our account and set against any royalties.

Chris Denning lived in Weybridge, Surrey, south of London. He was one of the first Radio One DJs, before working with Bell Records. As well as his promotion work he ran a disco club in Weybridge for teenagers. He invited us down to stay for a couple of nights at his house which was a very unusual, hexagonal-shaped building. It looked to me like a gatehouse at the entrance to a large estate. All of us, including Tam and Chris, went out to a restaurant for a meal then, having consumed a few bottles of wine, we headed back to Chris's house. It was all very jolly and friendly until Tam suggested that Chris would probably do more for us if one of us slept with him. I freaked. I pulled Alan aside and said, "Well, it definitely won't be me!" and he replied, "It definitely won't be me." I don't know what else happened that night, we didn't ask, but Alan and I slept on the floor with one eye open. I was beginning to see Tam in a completely different light—I felt we were becoming pawns in his game.

The following night we were invited down to Chris Denning's disco club, The Walton Hop. It was full of young boys and girls, and looked almost like a school disco. I didn't like the man. I felt uncomfortable in his presence.

Chris Denning was later convicted of paedophilia, serving jail sentences in 1974, '85, '88, '96, '98 and four years in a Slovakian prison in 2008. Both he and Jonathan King were said to have preyed on young boys at the Walton Hop. In 2002, Jonathan King was convicted of a string of sexual offences against young boys and served three and a half years of a seven-year sentence. He was also placed on the sex offender's register.

CHAPTER SEVEN

We were back in Edinburgh having a couple of days rest when the phone call came from Tam saying, "We've got Top Of The Pops." This was the most exciting moment of my life! After all these years of hard slog it was finally beginning to pay off.

Top Of The Pops was the longest-running, and most popular, music chart show on television. It was presented by Radio One DJs of the time, and each week they would do a run down of the singles chart.

We flew down to London a few days before the show for a photo shoot and some magazine interviews before heading for Bell Records offices for a meeting with Dick Leahy.

When we arrived at the office there was a very attractive blonde girl sitting at Dick Leahy's desk. He introduced her as Dinah Knight and said she was going to be our publicist. I don't think any of the group were too unhappy about that. She was gorgeous, tall and slim, and wearing a tight-fitting, black, pinstripe trouser suit. The focus was on Top Of The Pops and, the next thing we knew, we were whipped off to Selfridges on Oxford Street to buy some new stage clothes. Dinah Knight picked out suits for us and suggested red for me, and various colours for the other guys. She bought and paid for them herself.

Archie Marr was a car freak, so when Dinah Knight drove up in her white Mercedes 250 SL Sport with the concave roof, he was all over it saying, "This is my all-time favourite car."

The following day she put it into a garage for repair and someone broke into it and stole her briefcase, so she borrowed her daddy's white T-Series Bentley to get her around London.

Dinah Knight's father was chairman of Lombard Banks, and she lived in a penthouse flat in Park Lane where she invited me up on my own a few times. Tam Paton hated her.

Everytime we went to London we stayed at the Royal Norfolk Hotel in Paddington.

That Wednesday morning, when we were getting ready to go to the BBC studios, we were in and out of each other's rooms, talking nonstop because we were so nervous and excited.

Top Of The Pops was always recorded on a Wednesday and then broadcast at seven thirty on the Thursday night. We arrived early for the rehearsals and were shown down the long corridors of BBC Television Centre to our dressing room, where we hung up the suits and got ready for the first rehearsal. In fact there were two rehearsals, the sound rehearsal and the dress rehearsal, then the recording of the actual show.

On the way to the rehearsal we met Rod Stewart and the Faces playing football in the corridor. Well, I say met... I brushed up against Rod Stewart and he said, "You alright?" By the time we were ready to record the show, Rod Stewart and the Faces had obviously been at the vino and were having a party.

There were four live artists on the show that day: The Bay City Rollers with *Keep On Dancing*, which had jumped from number 17 in the charts to number 9; Rod Stewart and the Faces were at number 1 with *Maggie May*; Mungo Jerry were singing *You Don't Have to be in the Army to Fight in the War*; and Bruce Channel was singing *Keep On*. Shirley Bassey was on film singing *For All We Know*, and Pan's People danced to the other previously recorded films.

Chris Denning had turned up to give us support and accompanied us along the corridor to the studio. On the way Alan Longmuir stopped me and said, "You've still got the sellotape on your face!" I used to tape my hair down so it would dry straight and I was so nervous I had forgotten to take it off.

Chris Denning bumped into Bruce Channel's manager, and there must have been some history between them as we heard Bruce's manager saying, "Hey Chris, you'll be alright if that jacket comes back into fashion!" and Chris shouted back,

The Bay City Rollers.
Top Of The Pops 1971.

"Yeah, and you'll be alright if Bruce Channel comes back into fashion!"

We recorded the show, had a fantastic time doing it, and the following morning we were off again, back on the road. Desperate to see ourselves on Top Of The Pops that evening, we stopped off at a hotel in Cheshire and watched it on the television in the bar. All the boys in the band were going round the bar telling everybody, "Look up there, that's us on the telly! Look see, that's us!" We were on a high.

Back in Edinburgh, by the way, Davie Paton had met up with Billy Lyall, purely by chance. (There's a famous story about their meeting at the library on George IV Bridge, which Davie later documented in his song *Library Door* on Pilot's *Two's A Crowd* album.) After leaving the Bay City Rollers, Billy Lyall had started working as a sound engineer at Craighall Studios, so he invited Davie Paton down to do some recording.

Davie had written a song called *Magic*, and that was the first song they worked on together. The demo of *Magic* was sent to EMI who loved it, so the result was they formed a band called Pilot. The original line up was Davie Paton on lead vocals and guitars, Billy Lyall on keyboards, flute and vocals, and Stuart Tosh on drums. They were later joined by Ian Bairnson on lead guitar. *Magic* was released on the EMI label and became an international hit. They followed that success with *January* (another of Davie's compositions) which reached number 1 in the UK charts in January 1975. The producer of Pilot's first album, Alan Parsons (who had previously engineered *Dark Side of the Moon* for Pink Floyd), recognised their musicianship and asked them to play on The Alan Parsons Project's albums.

Both Davie Paton and Ian Bairnson played on the Kate Bush album *The Kick Inside,* which included the song *Wuthering Heights,* and Davie also played with Paul McCartney on *Mull of Kintyre,* before going on tour with Elton John and playing at the Band Aid concert in London.

Davie never publicised the fact that he was a member of the Bay City Rollers, but he admitted to me recently that he had a great time in the group and enjoyed the hysteria whipped up by the fans. I can't help but feel if it hadn't been for Tam Paton's obsessive and controlling nature, and ridiculously strict rules, we may have been working together for longer. Who knows?

Bell Records was now looking for the follow up to *Keep on Dancing* and we were soon in Trident Studios this time, with Jonathan King, recording *We Can Make Music* and *Jenny* (one of his compositions, again). There was an opportunity here to put up an argument for getting one of our own songs on the B-side, but Tam did nothing and let them walk all over us.

Any delusions of grandeur we had were quickly dashed when *We Can Make Music* was released as the second single. It was given a blanket release in Britain and ten other European countries and we made our first appearance on ITV's Lift Off With Ayshea, along with the actor Jack Wild and The Real Thing from Liverpool. We did a lot of promotion for *We Can Make Music* and it sold a fair amount of copies in Europe, but it flopped miserably in Britain.

It transpired that after *We Can Make Music* flopped, Jonathan King put forward *Hooked On A Feeling* as a potential song for us but Dick Leahy wouldn't agree his terms, so King recorded it himself and put it out under the pseudonym The Piglets, and had a massive hit.

I had long been an admirer of Tony Macaulay—his past history as a successful songwriter spoke for itself. The incredible list of songs he wrote and produced included *Baby, Now That I've Found You* and *Build Me Up Buttercup* for The Foundations; Long John Baldry's *Let the Heartaches Begin*; The Paper Dolls' *Something Here In My Heart*; and *Love Grows Where My Rosemary Goes* for Edison Lighthouse.

You can imagine my excitement, then, when told he was asked to write a song for The Bay City Rollers. Tony Macaulay invited us to his penthouse flat in Kensington, a beautiful place with a sunken floor in the living room. We sat in a row on a long couch at one side of the room while Tony sat at the other side on a chair, with his guitar on his knee. He said, "I've got a rough idea for you. I'm still working on the lyrics but here it is, it's called *The Rhythm of a Big Bass Drum*. He sang the song and I was blown away, absolutely loved it.

We didn't spend a lot of time on it that day, I just learned the melody using the draft lyrics.

I got on great with him and asked a lot of questions about his songs. He was very candid, as I actually said to him, "You must have made a lot of money with all these hits you've had?" and he replied, "I'm just about to pass my first ten million."

Within a couple of weeks the studio was booked. Tony Macaulay went in first and recorded the backing tracks with session musicians. I came in and recorded the lead vocal and put on the harmonies with Alan, Archie and Neil—it sounded fantastic, I was so excited.

We waited for Dick Leahy's response, which didn't come. I didn't understand it—the whole thing went cold. No explanation, nothing. The next thing I knew we were going to work with Howard and Blaikley.

Again, these were guys who had written a whole host of hit songs for The Herd with Peter Frampton, The Honeycombs, and Dave Dee, Dozy, Beaky, Mick and Tich. They wrote a song for us called *I'd Do It Again*.

We were staying, as usual, at The Royal Norfolk Hotel where Alan Blaikley came in to meet us and take us to their house to listen to the song. Archie said to him, "What kind of car do you have?" and Alan Blaikley replied, "Oh, I don't know, it's a blue one." Parked outside was their metallic, blue Rolls Royce Silver Shadow, with Ken Howard at the wheel. Of course Archie was mesmerised. (He was mad about cars.) The irony is we were surrounded by wealth while we were skint.

We got to the house where they both lived, in a gay relationship. It was a strange little house that reminded me of a doll's house: very low doorways that I had to stoop under, and small rooms with low ceilings. An open staircase in the corner of the living room passed up through the three floors. The walls were covered in gold, platinum and silver discs, and there was also a basement where the music room was. Up against the wall was an old-fashioned Farfisa organ. Ken Howard sat down in front of it to play and sing the song. It was like listening to someone doing a party piece, on an organ they got for Christmas—I couldn't concentrate on the song for wanting to laugh. All I heard was, "Wouldn't you like it baby, baby. Wouldn't you like it?" I thought, "Oh my God, what have we got now?" But I was very polite. We recorded the song, but it was rejected by Dick Leahy and they went back to the drawing board.

While that was going on, someone, I think it was Peter Walsh, had the idea that it would be good experience for us to play working men's clubs in the north of England. Good experience? We had been on the road for over four years, so the last thing we needed was experience in working men's clubs. We protested, but Tam insisted that we do them.

The cabaret circuit was made up of social clubs, or working men's clubs, as they were called. We were a group of young guys, with a massive following of young girls in Scotland and down in the south of England—we had never played in the Midlands, had no experience of social clubs, and were not a cabaret act. The Rollers were sold to them only on the basis of *Keep On Dancing* being a top ten hit.

The first on the list was The Top Hat Club in Spennymoor, just south of Durham. They had a poster up on the wall in the entrance of the club when we arrived that said: ***The Bay City Rollers appearing at The Top Hat Club following their smash hit "Keep on Dancing."*** Also on the bill were comedian Norman Collier, and Sylvia and her Performing Poodles.

The club itself was laid out with tiers of tables that had a red light on each one. The crowd arrived and soon the place was full of older men and women, with blank expressions on their faces, who just sat there as if to say, "Go on then, entertain us." So we played our set, and it went down like a lead balloon.

We left Spennymoor the following day depressed and despondent, and headed for the Fiesta Club in Stockton-on-Tees, where we were to appear for a whole week. It was a disaster. The club manager phoned the agent, saying if we didn't start playing some songs that the audience knew they would get someone else to replace us. Tam Paton got the message back in Edinburgh and phoned Derek, telling us to rehearse some new songs. But, to be honest, we were pretty pissed off and we spent most of the spare time playing pool. Tam was furious when he heard this, and jumped in the car to speed down to Stockton. About an hour before we were due on stage he stormed into the dressing room. I was standing in the adjoining room with the door open, drying my hair in front of the mirror and I listened to Tam rip all the boys to shreds, one by one, with personal insults, as they stood there with their heads down. Then he turned on me shouting, "And as for you, Nobby..." I turned on him before he could say any more and screamed back, "Don't you fucking dare start on me! Who the fuck do you think you are ripping people to shreds like that?" He was caught off guard and just stood for a second, then stormed out of the room in the huff and drove back up to Scotland.

Archie Marr had had enough—he told me he was thinking about leaving the group. I think his final decision was made on the way from Liverpool to the Isle of Man in the middle of winter, on a freezing cold ferry on a stormy sea. We played the Royal Lido in Douglas, the capital of the Isle of Man, to packed audiences and went down a storm because we were back to a young crowd again. But it wasn't enough to keep Archie in the group, and he left when we got back to Edinburgh.

We made up with Tam Paton and brought in John Devine to replace Archie. John was from Tranent, the location of the Town Hall battle, and he had played with Eric Faulkner in a local group by the name of Kip. He wasn't the world's greatest guitar player, but he was an extremely handsome guy. Very tall and very slim, with long dark hair, high cheekbones and dimples that drove the girls wild.

We got sent off on a whistle-stop tour of Northern Ireland. The first gig was in Belfast at the height of the Troubles. I really didn't like it. The atmosphere was tense everywhere we went. The van was searched at every army checkpoint and armed policemen escorted us to and from the hotel. The promoter who brought us across to Ireland took us down the Shankhill Road to see the murals on the ends of the buildings and it was very surreal, eerie and intimidating. When we got to the hotel where we were playing, the people could not have been nicer—we were the only live band who would agree to perform there. The place was packed and it was a fantastic night. They were so grateful that we had come.

Then we headed down over the border into the Republic of Ireland, to the city of Cork. We played at the town hall there along with Thin Lizzy, with Phil Lynott on bass and vocals, and Gary Moore on guitar.

But our "troubles" were still on going. Shortly after John Devine joined us, Eric Manclark left with his girlfriend, followed by Neil Henderson, and we were falling apart at the seams. It was all to do with the rules set by Tam Paton. He was absolutely obsessive, and jealous of us even talking to girls.

The bond between Alan Longmuir, Derek Longmuir and myself was still there, despite the fact we had lost our way. We had been through so much together and supported each other through bad times. But I honestly didn't know if we could pull this back together again—it had happened so many times now, that even we were getting weary from the battle. It was a roller

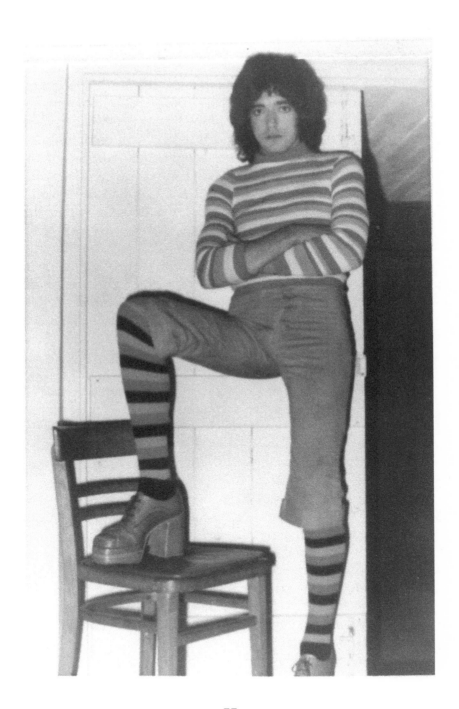

coaster of extreme highs and extreme lows, and we desperately needed something to boost our spirits.

Tam Paton was searching for another guitarist for us, and he found Eric Faulkner to complete the new line up of the group, which was now: Nobby Clark, lead vocals; Alan Longmuir on bass; Derek Longmuir on drums; John Devine on rhythm guitar; and Eric Faulkner on lead guitar. Eric lived in Edinburgh, had a great image and, apart from not being able to tune his guitar, fitted nicely into the group. We were ready to go again.

In the background, Howard and Blaikley had been working away, writing songs, unaware of the troubles within the group. They came up with four new songs. Three of them were *Mañana*, *In Love's Dominion* and *I'd Do It Again*, but the title of the fourth one escapes me, so obviously it didn't make an impression. I heard the songs for the first time in that basement in the Wendy House but, honestly, I couldn't keep a straight face. I couldn't imagine them writing such greats as *From The Underworld* and *I Don't Want Our Loving To Die* for The Herd, and *Hold Tight* and *The Legend Of Xanadu* for Dave Dee on that old Farfisa organ.

But when we got into the studio it was a different matter— they had a full thirty-piece orchestra, and when they played the rough mix of the backing tracks for *Mañana* I said, "Wow! That's impressive!" *In Love's Dominion* with a full orchestration was even more breathtaking. *I'd Do It Again* was very good too, but had less of an impact.

Of course, all the backing tracks were recorded with session musicians, but it took a long time to record all the vocals as there were a lot of harmonies and double tracking. I recorded ten tracks of vocals and the end result was a big full sound—this was the boost that we needed.

Mañana was chosen from these sessions to be the next single. However there was still the decision to be made about the B-side. I presented a demo of one of my songs, *Because I Love You*, to Dick Leahy and he said, "Let's do it." So we did.

Howard and Blaikley produced *Because I Love You* and we were set up and raring to go. It's hard to describe the feeling of

fulfilment and achievement now, having been through uncertainty about our future when things were all falling apart, to be sitting with a new record and about to embark on a journey of adventure that releasing a new single would activate.

I was offered a publishing deal with RAK Music Publishing, Mickie Most's company, but Tam Paton was going ballistic. He was against the idea of me signing a separate publishing agreement for *Because I Love You* as he said everyone in the band should get a share of the royalties—I protested because no one else had contributed to the song. In the end I got so sick of arguing about it that I agreed we'd set up our own company called Bay City Music. I signed an agreement with RAK Music, with a clause added stating all royalties for *Because I Love You* would be paid directly to Bay City Music. We got the lawyers to prepare an agreement whereby all the members of the group would be directors and equal shareholders. When it came back for signing, Tam Paton's name was also on the contract as an equal shareholder. This meant that not only would he get his 15% management fee from all the group's earnings, he would also get a share of royalties from any songs written by members of the group. I didn't like that at all, and neither did Alan or Derek. When we confronted him with it Tam got aggressive and abusive, calling me everything under the sun—we were bullied and blackmailed into signing the agreement.

In the early seventies London was buzzing, the music business was thriving and the music scene was vibrant. There seemed to be record company or publishing company offices on every street and recording studios were everywhere.

Carnaby Street was still the place to buy stage gear. It was colourful, exciting and new to us. We were from Scotland where everyone wore grey, black or blue, and the shops catered for, let's say, the more "conservative" tastes.

The Marquee Club in Wardour Street was the place to go and be seen, if you could get in the door. Everytime we were there it was full of well-known faces, everywhere you turned there was another famous person. I would be standing next to Keith Moon from The Who, and pretending to be blasé about the whole thing. But it was hard to relax with Tam Paton breathing down your neck the whole time. He never let us out of his sight in case we got up to something he didn't approve of.

We went out shopping to Carnaby Street and I bought black, embroidered, bell-bottom trousers. I cut holes in the legs and put silver studs around them. All the boys in the band bought platform shoes, which were all the rage at the time. Eric Faulkner was the first to wear tartan and had it sewn onto a short tight jacket. We got ready for the launch of *Mañana*: each day was filled with photo sessions, interviews for magazines and news-papers, meetings at Bell Records offices, answering fan letters and signing autographs. It was a whirlwind.

Dinah Knight was left in charge of the publicity while we went off again, round the country, with the new line-up. It was a non-stop tour of Top Rank ballrooms and dance halls, where we shared the stage with top groups at the time—like Showaddy-waddy, Sweet, Mud and Slade—ending up in Newcastle, abso-lutely exhausted. The band needed a break just before *Mañana* was released, so Tam Paton suggested we take a trip to Hamamet in Tunisia for a week.

There was a chance we might get an appearance on Top Of The Pops, in the New Releases spot, so the BBC agreed to make a film of us performing *Mañana*. I got on my black embroidered bell-bottom trousers and platform shoes, and painted the top half of my body with gold paint. Alan Long-muir bared his skin too, and painted it with silver paint. We performed the song in front of the cameras and then went off on holiday for ten days.

It was the middle of summer 1972 and Tunisia was scorch-ing hot. The coach that took us from the airport to the hotel wasn't air-conditioned so Tam Paton moaned all the way about the heat, "Open the window, I can't breathe!" He was going on and on about it till everyone was sick of hearing it.

The hotel was grand and palatial. At the reception we went through the ritual of who would be sharing rooms. Tam didn't like anyone sharing a room for too long in case they struck up a close friendship. Alan Longmuir and I liked to share whenever possible because he didn't want to share with his brother Derek, and to be honest we could have a more mature conversation, and we also had a similar sense of humour.

That first night in the hotel, Tam slept with his feet hanging out the bottom of the bed and got severely bitten by mosquitos. In the morning both his feet were swollen up like balloons, so he couldn't get his sandals on and couldn't walk. This meant free-dom for the boys while he was confined to his room, although every so often he would come hobbling along with his big swollen feet to see what we were up to, then he would moan and complain about everything and go back to his room.

One afternoon, three days into the holiday, while Tam was still indisposed, Alan and I went down to the bar for a drink. We were contemplating the meaning of life over a glass of rotgut rum when a scantily clad waitress came up and stood next to me. Alan said quietly, "She's gorgeous," and I turned to him and whispered, "Look at the size of her boobs, never mind her lovely face." But I didn't know that Tam was standing right behind me. "What did you say?" he asked suspiciously. I replied, "I was just saying what a lovely place." Alan burst out laughing and spat his drink over the bar. That started me off—I couldn't stop. I was doubled up holding my stomach, then brought my head up just as the waitress was lifting a tray full of champagne and glasses off the bar, and I knocked it out of her hands. It smashed all over the floor and Tam stood on the broken glass and cut his foot open—there was blood everywhere. He hopped about on the other swollen foot shouting, "Are the two of you off yer fucking heeds?"

It looked like a war zone. The blood mixed with the champagne and was all over the floor amongst the broken glass. He wrapped a towel around his foot and went off to his room to get it bandaged, mumbling and swearing as he went. Alan and I defiantly carried on drinking.

They didn't use measures at the bar, they just filled up your glass with the cheap, white rum that had a Bacardi label on it. Someone at the bar told us they filled the bottle up from a barrel round the back. By late afternoon we were legless.

I left Alan embroiled in a conversation with a gorgeous girl at the bar while I went off to buy a pack of cigarettes, but I didn't go back. I had stopped smoking years earlier, but I must have bought them out of pure devilment because I knew it would annoy Tam.

When he found out I had gone AWOL he rounded up the rest of the group, including Alan who had to be prised away from the love of his life, and went out searching everywhere for me. They trekked up and down the road, and into all the bars of the nearby hotels. Alan said, "Eventually we found you on the beach, talking to a camel." Tam was standing there with a huge bandage on his foot, pointing at me and yelling, "Look! He's smoking. I'm having nothing more to do with him!" and stormed off in the huff, limping up the beach, mumbling angrily.

I never heard the last of it. He went on and on. He was like a spoiled kid sometimes, when he couldn't get his own way. I just tried to enjoy the rest of the holiday amongst the fragrant smell of jasmine and poor sewerage.

I had been considering my position with the group for a while. Tam Paton was a genius when it came to publicity and promotion, of that I've no doubt, but when it came to business he didn't have a clue and he lacked any mettle when it came to standing up for us. The arguments between Tam and I were becoming more frequent, and I was beginning to dread being in his company, but mainly it was a feeling of emptiness. This shallow, commercial pop industry was only interested in our image and nothing else—it had precious little substance, meaning all the hard work we had put in was of no consequence. Yes, we could sell records, and yes, we could become famous, but it was becoming more and more obvious to me that we were just a vehicle to drive Tam Paton's ego and it was all really about making Tam Paton famous.

I didn't know if I wanted it anymore, so I spoke to Alan and Derek about it. They were also deflated, and slightly disillusioned, but wanted to fight on. "We can't give up now, we've come so far," Alan said. It felt horrible. This was all I knew. I loved these guys, they were my friends—we shared everything together—so I decided to give it another six months.

When we got back to London, we found out that Ken Howard and Alan Blaikley had entered *Mañana* into The Radio-Tele Luxembourg Grand Prix International, a competition to find the best produced songs in Europe. And *Mañana* had been selected as one of the twelve songs in the final.

An extract from a special report by Andy Gray read:

The Luxembourg Grand Prix is becoming more and more important to producers and artists alike. Each record selected for the final gets many plays on Radio Luxembourg and will be performed on a massive TV show, seen in twelve countries via the Eurovision link. It will be networked on radio and TV to most of Europe and beyond, to an estimated audience of 40 million listeners (but not in Britain for some reason) and, in addition to introducing the twelve contenders, "Star of the Year awards" will be given to six acts including Slade, Vicky Leandros and Israel's filmstar singer, Daliah Lavi.

The organisers chartered a Luxair Champagne flight for all the performers, writers, producers and record company representatives. The list of names on the plane was straight out of a Who's Who of the music industry: record executives included Colin Burn (EMI) Wayne Bickerton (Polydor), Dick Rowe and Don Wardell (Decca), Johnny Wise (Pye), Geffrey Everett (MAM), Dave Most (RAK), Muff Winwood (Island), Don Percival (Phonogram), Dick Leahy and David Bridger (Bell), Gerald Black and Jan Olofson (Young Blood), Eliot Cohen (Red Bus), Glyn Evans and Dave Margereson (CBS), and Lyndon Holloway (RCA).

Amongst the writers and producers there were Eddie Blackwell, Roger Greenaway, Bill Martin, Ken Howard, Alan Blaikley, Tony Hiller and Johnny Mercer.

The British artists that would perform in the Grand Prix were The Bay City Rollers, Slade, Steve 'n' Bonnie, and Yellowstone and Voice, while other seats on the plane were taken up by Chas Chandler (Slade's manager), Tam Paton, Barry Perkins and a whole host of press.

We arrived at Luxembourg and were taken in a luxury coach to the Holiday Inn where we all piled into the reception area. There was laughing and singing, and a lot of noise and confusion, but I noticed that Chas Chandler and Slade had got to the check-in desk first and were already on their way up the big wide staircase. When they got to the landing, they stopped, dropped their trousers, and mooned to an appreciative audience below, with the exception of the Hotel Manager who blew a gasket and threatened to throw everybody out of the hotel. Only the intervention of the more sensible among us prevented that from happening.

The live competition took place in the Nouveau Theatre in front of a packed audience. We were met by the hosts and introduced to the Radio Luxembourg DJs (Tony Prince, Kid Jensen, Paul Burnett, Mark Wesley, Bob Stewart and Dave Christian) and afterwards directed to our dressing room where we prepared for the show. Alan and I had brought the gold and silver body paints with us and we asked the makeup girls to apply it, then we were called on stage, ready and waiting for the red light.

We performed *Mañana* with a full, live, thirty-piece orchestra, then stood back and watched Yellowstone and Voice, and Steve 'n' Bonnie perform their songs, along with the entries from all the other European countries. There was a long wait after this while the judges made their decision. When the announcement came nobody could believe it... top honours went to Howard and Blaikley for *Mañana* performed by The Bay City Rollers! Second spot went to Miki Dallon for his production of *Eyes of Tomorrow* sung by Steve 'n' Bonnie. Third place went to Ellis Elias and Roberto Danova for *Days to Remember* sung by Yellowstone and Voice: a British first, second and third.

The reporter Andy Gray wrote in his article:

The result of the fourth Radio-Tele Luxembourg Grand Prix International left hopeful German, French, Belgian and Dutch producers stunned as judges from their countries voted Britain's three entries 1st, 2nd and 3rd—an unheard of, never-before feat in this annual contest to find the best produced records in Europe.

It was a great night for Slade too. They broke into their current European tour to be honoured with a special Golden Tower trophy for the Act of the Year, and performed two storming songs. Vicky Leandros and Daliah Lavi were given TV awards.

Champagne corks were popping that night and the party back at the hotel went on until daybreak. I ended up so drunk I crashed out on a lounger at the side of the swimming pool. The following morning, the whole crowd of us (nursing hangovers) got back on the plane and the party started again.

I hate flying at the best of times and, when I looked up the aisle to the cockpit, the door was wide open and the captain was sitting side on in his seat, with a glass of Champagne in his hand, having a conversation with a passenger who was standing beside him holding a bottle in one hand and a glass in the other. I thought, "This isn't right."

We were crossing the English Channel when it started to get a bit bumpy. I was already tensed up and hanging onto the arm rests, but it was quite surreal because everyone else was relaxed. Some were very drunk, and some were singing up at the front end of the plane, when we hit an electric storm and the whole plane started to shudder. There was a huge bump and the plane tilted sharply to one side then the other. I could hear the engines revving really fast then slowing, then revving again. People standing in the aisle got thrown around, and glasses were smashing. Suddenly we went into a nose dive and I thought, "Oh my God, this is the end!" Then we levelled off and it gradually calmed down. Everything was quiet for a few minutes, then I heard singing coming from the front of the plane: (to the tune of *When The Saints Go Marching In*) "The captains pissed… he nearly missed…"

Mañana was released in most European countries and as far afield as Israel, where it reached number 1, and overall it sold around 1.5 million copies. But it didn't make the Top 30 in Britain.

I expected to work with Howard and Blaikley on a follow up single, but the next thing I knew Dick Leahy was talking to Bill Martin and Phil Coulter about writing some songs for The Rollers. Bill Martin and Phil Coulter were hugely successful song writers, having written many hit songs including the 1967 Eurovision song contest winner *Puppet on a String* for Sandie Shaw, *Congratulations* for Cliff Richard, and *Back Home* sung by the England World Cup Squad in 1970.

Off we went back on the road. This time it was a tour of Europe, with Glasgow band Middle of The Road who had a massive hit with *Chirpy Chirpy Cheep Cheep*. The lead singer of the band, Sally Carr, told me that the composer of the song

(Lally Stott) set out to write the most simple and commercial song ever written—I think he achieved that. Middle of The Road were later joined by Neil Henderson, a former member of The Bay City Rollers.

The tour was enjoyable, but way out of our comfort zone. No screaming fans this time—instead it was seated audiences, staring at the stage, waiting to be entertained for an hour and marked with smatterings of unenthusiastic applause between numbers. All they knew about The Bay City Rollers was that we won the Luxembourg Grand Prix with a song called *Mañana*. The problem for us on stage was reproducing a song that was recorded with a thirty-piece orchestra when we were just five guys with guitars, bass and drums. Having a hit doesn't always make it right.

When we got back to London, Bill Martin and Phil Coulter had been recording the backing tracks for four songs written specially for The Bay City Rollers. We were invited round to Mayfair Studios to hear the songs for the first time. I knew a bit about Mayfair Recording Studios having heard the stories and read the articles in the Musical Express—it was said to have the magic touch. Many successful artists recorded there, and wrote some of their best material. The list is so long but included Paul McCartney, Robert Plant, Elton John, Queen, and Jeff Beck, to name a few. (It closed in 2008 due to the worldwide recession and implosion of the music industry, but its presence lives on.)

I was buzzing as we walked into the studio. Phil Coulter was sitting in the control room and introduced himself saying, "We're just working on the tracks, but you'll get the idea." He handed me a copy of the lyrics for the first song called *Remember*, and I read: "*Shimmy shammy shong—we used to make up songs, remember. Hidy hidy ho—we used to kiss hello, remember. We would hum a lum, to the beating of a drum, remember.*" I wasn't exactly over-excited by it, but when Phil sang it over the backing track I loved it and thought we could be on to something here.

The second song was *Saturday Night* and immediately I thought this has to be a hit song. It was a rocker, had bags of energy, and an instant hook in the chorus. What more could you ask for? The other two were *Hey C.B.* and *Bye Bye Barbara* which didn't do a lot for me, and I assumed they were potential B-sides. By now we were resigned to the fact that there was no chance of playing any instruments on the songs, much to the disappointment of the guys in the band, so we set a date the following week to record my vocals over the previously recorded tracks. We hadn't had a hit in the UK since *Keep on Dancing* over a year and half ago, so there was a lot riding on this.

The recording session went really well. The vocals sounded great and, as usual, I put down a lot of layered voices to build up the chorus, and some falsetto ad-libs towards the end. The whole band got round the microphone to record hand claps, but Phil wasn't happy with the sound. He said it was too thin and needed something else. The sound engineer came up with a suggestion, "I think The Glitter Band's drums are still set up in the studio below," he said, so everyone followed him downstairs. The drum kit was there behind the glass panels of the drum booth, and lying on the floor beside it were the two flat pieces of wood that were used to create the heavy hand clap sound that was on all the Gary Glitter records. They set up a microphone and Derek Longmuir clapped the two pieces of wood together on the drumbeat… and that's the sound you can hear on all the Rollers' records through to *Shang-A-Lang* and *Bye Bye Baby*.

Bill Martin appeared at the studio, along with Dick Leahy from Bell Records, and they listened to the rough mixes of the songs. I heard Dick Leahy say to Bill, "I think we have a couple of hit records there, let's talk business". The deal was done and *Saturday Night* was chosen to be the first single from the sessions with *Hey C.B.* on the B-side. We had tried again to talk to Tam Paton about getting one of our songs on the B-side but he refused to bring the subject up.

Saturday Night (Bell Records 1319) was released in May 1973 to critical acclaim. I didn't read one negative review. The Record Mirror said it was a chart cert. and all the teenage magazines loved it—we were convinced it would take off like a rocket. It entered the top forty for one week, then disappeared into oblivion and flopped miserably.

The band had worked extremely hard on publicity, doing newspaper and magazine interviews all over the country. Commercial radio stations played it occasionally but BBC Radio One, which was essential at the time, gave it the thumbs down. It just didn't click.

The record company didn't seem to be behind it and we found it difficult to get any information as Tam Paton seemed to be cut out of the loop. It was all very cold and non- responsive. I became completely detached from it.

CHAPTER EIGHT

That was the breaking point for me. I told Alan and Derek first, then Tam and the rest of the boys, that I was leaving. I told them it wasn't my intention to do them harm and I would give them the chance to find another singer.

It was the hardest and saddest thing I had done in my life. It was all I had known for six years. I didn't have anything planned, but I just knew it was time for me to go even though it was very frightening. I don't think Tam told anyone outside of the group, I think his intention was to bring in a new singer before announcing the change.

A meeting was called at Bell Records offices in London. Dick Leahy called Tam in Edinburgh and requested his presence. He jumped on a plane expecting to be confronted with the bad news that Bell Records were pulling the plug on The Bay City Rollers, and that their recording contract would be terminated. Instead he was given an ultimatum: Dick Leahy made it very clear that they were prepared to give it one last shot—the label would release *Remember*, but if it wasn't successful it was curtains for The Bay City Rollers.

Alan seemed to take it quite badly. He was prone to depression, and had once confided in me that, not long before we met, he'd stuck his head in the gas oven and turned it on... but the meter ran out before it was too late.

Tam hurried back to Scotland with the news, knowing that he had to throw everything at this one. So every waking moment was spent drumming up publicity. He sent out flyers to all the fans, informing them of the imminent release of *Remember* and he even got a hold of David Cassidy's fan club addresses and sent them flyers and photographs too. It was all go. His mind was fully occupied in the process, and he forgot that I had set a date for leaving the band. That date had been moved forward several times, but I'd had enough and told them I was finished and would leave the band at the end of 1973.

What I didn't know was that Tam had his eye on a young singer from Edinburgh by the name of Les McKeown. He was the lead singer with a local band called Threshold, and Eric Faulkner took Tam to their gig one night, where he pulled Les straight out of that band into the Rollers. The situation left them with no option but to move fast.

Remember was released, with my voice on it, and was immediately picked up by the radio stations, including BBC Radio One where it made the playlist and quickly entered the top 40. It climbed up the charts over the next two weeks and reached its highest position at number 6.

Since it was being played on the radio and distributed round the shops, and had become a big hit with my voice on it, I made an arrangement with Tam Paton to make my last appearance with The Bay City Rollers on Top Of The Pops. It was still being recorded on a Wednesday for broadcasting on a Thursday evening. So I flew down to London on the Wednesday morning, as arranged, and arrived at the BBC studios to be told they had made a special arrangement and had already recorded the Rollers performing *Remember* on the Tuesday…

When I watched the show, there was Les McKeown singing my song. They had a track of my voice in the background, with my harmonies, and a live track of Les McKeown's voice over the top. I'm no lawyer, but I would say that comes under fraudulent use of my performance, and misrepresentation.

Remember was a hit before I left the band and all the records sold had my voice on them, so I headed back to Scotland with a promise from Tam Paton that all royalties due to me would be paid, and I got on with putting together my solo career. (Thinking about it at this precise moment it is now almost forty years since that day—as yet, I have not received one single penny.)

It was rumoured by Tam Paton that I had met a girl in Edinburgh, fallen in love, and that was the reason I left the group. Yes, I had met a girl, but it had no bearing on my decision. I had to lick my wounds, look forward, and fight for what I believed in.

A new dawn, a new day. Where would I go from here?

During all the time I'd been shrouded in the ethos of The Bay City Rollers, it never occurred to me that one day I would be standing alone, on my own two feet. How would I go about it? I had no direct experience of talking to the record company executives, or trying to sell myself as a solo artist. Where would I start?

I was back at my mother's house at Drum Brae Drive. I had a piano in my bedroom and a head full of song ideas. So the first thing to do would be to write new material. What direction do I want to go in? My influences were from the west coast of America because I had been listening to Crosby, Stills and Nash, Neil Young, Joni Mitchell, Linda Ronstadt—all of them way outside of the pop music world I had been involved in.

The day that I left the BBC studios to head back north I'd had some time to spare as my flight wasn't till later that night, and so I took a walk through Regents Park. Purely by chance I ran into Andy, the Scottish roadie working with Slade when we'd met them on tour. He invited me back to the house that he shared with another five Scottish roadies. They worked with various bands at the time, including Nazareth.

It was a roadies house all right—there were open speaker cabinets lying around with wires hanging out; posters stuck up all over the walls; plenty of joints being passed around; and lots of booze. It felt a bit alien to me, having never been in this sort of environment. I accepted the offer of a joint, took a couple of draws and passed it on thinking this stuff does nothing for me. Within five minutes I could feel the effects, and when it came round again I took some more. My head was spinning to begin with, due to the nicotine, but when that wore off I liked the experience of being stoned for the first time.

In the house that day was a guy called Jim McKenna from Armadale in Scotland. We just sort of clicked and got into some meaningful conversations. I told him I was heading out to the airport shortly, to fly back to Edinburgh. He told me he was catching the bus up to Scotland in the morning, so I cancelled my flight and stayed overnight in the house. With an invitation of a place to crash anytime I was down in London, I left in the morning and got the bus with Jim.

I really enjoyed that trip—we talked all the way to Edinburgh. During the journey I told him about my experiences with the band while he enlightened me about a world I knew nothing about, involving recreational drugs, parties and music. I was intrigued. On arrival at Edinburgh Bus Station we shook hands and went our separate ways, having agreed to be in touch with each other.

Being released from the oppressive regime imposed by Tam Paton for six years was like being a caged animal released into the wild. A euphoric sense of freedom combined with an overwhelming fear of the unknown. All I'd got, financially, with The Bay City Rollers was £10 a week spending money and a verbal agreement that all royalties due to me would be paid along with my share of the group's assets—none of which materialised. So I went to the bank and borrowed some money. I bought myself an old banger of a car and worked out my next move.

I didn't know very much about my recent girlfriend, Margie, as we hadn't spent much time together. To begin with, she never spoke much about her past and avoided my questions. All I knew about her was she followed the group when we were first starting off, and was related to one of the early members. I suppose if I had known everything about her at the beginning I would have run a mile, but it all happened gradually. Her best friend Leana, whom she had known since her school days, was living with a guy called Billy Steel, and Margie took me down to their flat in Leith to meet them.

I knew of this guy from my younger days growing up in Clermiston. He was from the top end of the scheme and I was from the bottom end, and never the twain shall meet. You had to side with the gang from your own area. But I had come across him, and heard of his reputation as a hard nut although, when I met him at his flat, he came across as being a friendly, likeable character.

Within minutes of us sitting down Billy was asking Margie if she had any mandies. I had no idea what they were talking about and watched her take a small bottle out of her pocket and empty some white pills into her hand. "I've got six left, but I get my script on Wednesday," she said. (What the hell's going on here? I was asking myself.) "If you give me half of what you've got, I'll give you them back when I pick mine up," said Billy, quite casually. It seemed to be just a normal conversation between them.

It turned out that all three of them were on this prescription drug called Mandrax, an extremely potent, hypnotic drug that came under the heading of barbiturates. Its medical name was Methaqualone and in the USA they were known as Quaaludes. They were extremely addictive, and responsible for many fatal overdoses.

In the midst of conversation, Billy pulled a white packet from his pocket and put it on the table. "Do you want a line of sulf?" he asked, like asking if I wanted a cup tea. I responded, "What is it?" hoping I didn't sound completely naïve. "Just Amphetamine Sulphate," he replied. Just! Amphetamine Sulphate! What the hell have I got involved in? I wanted to get up and get out, but I didn't know how this guy would react, so I tried to act all streetwise and cool. I refused the offer of a Mandrax, but accepted the offer of a small line of Sulphate, knowing it was the wrong thing to do. He put some white powder onto a mirror, rolled up a five pound note and snorted it up his nose, then handed it to me. Obviously gentlemen first, I thought. So I tried to mimic Billy. I put the rolled up note to my nose but, instead of inhaling, I exhaled and blew down the tube. A puff of white powder went up in the air and all over the table. "For fuck's sake!" he shouted, "What's that all about?" "I'm sorry," I said sheepishly, "I've never done it before." It was like being up in front of the headmaster at school. Then he burst out laughing and I knew it was alright. He chopped out another line and I had my first taste of speed.

I had other concerns about Margie. She drank a lot. Not falling down drunk or anything, but she liked a good drink. I should have paid heed to all the warning signs but I had no other friends in Edinburgh. For the last six years or so all my time was taken up with the group and I'd lost touch with my friends from school days. I had enough concerns about my own drinking, which past experience had taught me that when I started I couldn't stop, so I had tried to leave it alone.

Meanwhile down in London there were a lot of loose ends to tie up. My recording contract with Bell Records had just under a year to run. I had some new songs on the go so I needed to speak to Dick Leahy. He agreed to meet me at his office and I flew down to London, heading for Wardour Street. There was something about arriving in London that always excited me. It gave me a feeling of anticipation and expectation. Although I was apprehensive this time, I felt quite confident it would all work out. I kept telling myself, the next door I walk through will start the next chapter in the Nobby Clark musical experience! Dick took me for lunch at a nice restaurant... and I talked and I talked. I felt he needed to know just some of the reasons why I'd left the group. After I finished Dick gave me a look of enlightenment, false or otherwise.

I was about to start talking music, but it was Dick who opened the subject. "So what are you planning to do?" he asked, relaxing back in his chair, leaning slightly to the side, holding one hand up as if holding a cigar. "I want to talk to you about my plans for a solo career. I've got a demo here of new songs I've been working on," I said, handing him the tape. "Leave it with me—I'll have a listen to it and get back to you," he replied, with a slightly dismissive tone. I picked up an air of indifference about his body language, the feeling you get when someone is saying one thing but thinking something else. The lunch was cut short with the statement, "I have to get back to the office." He paid the bill, we shook hands, and he departed with the words, "I'll be in touch".

He never was. I heard nothing for weeks so I called him. "I'm still thinking of the best way forward for you, leave it with me. I'll get back to you." But it was me who called and called. Sometimes he would take my call, other times I would be given all kinds of excuses from his secretary as to why I couldn't speak to him. In the end I got the message—he was making sure I was kept out of the way.

I tried one final time. I thought, if he's not impressed with the songs I presented to him, I'll hit him with another proposal. I called his office and made an appointment saying, "I'm coming to London and would like to speak to him about an idea I have."

I arrived at Bell Records office and was told he would be with me shortly. I sat there for ages trying not to stare at his secretary, fidgeting with my rings and attempting to appear relaxed but failing miserably. I looked around for a camera thinking he might be watching me from his inner office. He eventually appeared in his usual dark green, velvet suit with the Robin Hood-style high collar at the back, short jacket with silver buttons up the front, and frilly white shirt that overflowed his lapels and burst out of his jacket sleeves covering most of his hands—like Errol Flynn in a swashbuckling movie. Oh! And bell-bottomed trousers over black, silver-buckled shoes. His thick, dark wavy hair was combed forward in a fringe. This is the man who had at one time questioned my taste in up-to-date fashion!

The purpose of this meeting was to put forward a proposal. Thinking back over all the recordings I'd made with The Bay City Rollers, one thing always puzzled me. The song *Rhythm Of A Big Bass Drum,* written for us by Tony Macaulay, had been rejected and never heard of again. Why? I thought it was potentially a hit song, so my proposal was to revive it and release it as a solo single. The idea was met with a short silence and a blank stare. "Let me think about it," he said, with false enthusiasm. We sat and talked for a while, having quite a mundane conversation about music in general. We touched on the subject of the Rollers without him giving away too much, and I left feeling empty, knowing in my heart that nothing would come of it.

I was right. My proposal was rejected. I waited another few weeks, then put it to Dick Leahy that if he wasn't intending to allow me to pursue a solo career he should release me from my contract.

Meanwhile, The Bay City Rollers were storming the charts in the UK. They had a number 1 with *Shang-A-Lang*, a top ten hit with *Summer Love Sensation*, and were currently in the top twenty with *All Of Me Loves All Of You*. The papers were full of their success story and I was sick of reading about it.

Dick Leahy had no intentions of releasing me from my contract until he was sure I couldn't harm the success of Rollers. It took a long time. He kept stalling. I hounded him for months. In the end, with approximately four months to go, and almost a year after I left the band, he agreed to terminate my contract and release me from any further obligations to record on the Bell Records label.

It was a relief on one hand, and a sad ending on the other. I'm a very loyal person and expect others to be the same, but we're talking the music business here and they take no prisoners. However, I was not easily defeated, and I believed in myself. "I'll make this work, I can do this," are the things I was telling myself, because I had no one else to talk to. What a strange, disconnected feeling it was.

Back in Edinburgh, I took some time out to consider my next move. I was still living at my mother's house in Drum Brae but spending a lot of time with Margie.

She took me to a top flat at the corner of Ardmillan Terrace and Gorgie Road in Edinburgh and introduced me to a whole bunch of people, all sitting around in the living room and kitchen smoking dope. I wandered around for a while, with no one paying me much attention, then sat at the kitchen table where all the conversation was taking place and watched what was going on. I saw substances lying in open packets on the table and I asked a guy, known as Johnny, who was sitting next to me and seemed quite friendly, what these substances were. He, in a proud and patronising manner, happy to impart his superior knowledge to the uninitiated, pointed to each packet and said, "That's a piece of Temple Bowl, that's a bit of Lebanese and that's opium oil." A joint was passed over to me, so I smoked it and passed it on. Another one came round the other way, so I smoked that and passed it on. Then I ran to the loo and spewed up violently. Once it all settled down I actually liked the feeling.

The doorbell rang and in walked a tall, skinny guy with a long, grey beard, by the name of Pete. He had with him a huge black Doberman Pinscher, which growled at everyone who tried to touch it. Pete looked a lot older than the others. I watched some quiet talking go on in the corner before someone left the room and came back a few minutes later. A packet changed hands, so I assumed some dealing was going on.

I noticed Margie pulling out a bottle from her pocket while talking to a short, stocky, fair-haired Glaswegian. She took what I presumed was Mandrax out of the bottle and exchanged them for a piece of cannabis. While this was all going on I could hear some incredible music blasting from the living room down the hall and into the kitchen. It was *Sailin' Shoes* by Little Feat— I had to go through and listen. I nodded to those amongst the sprawling bodies that showed any interest and sat down. I was handed another joint but was already out of it, so just took a short drag before passing it on.

This scene was a real eye-opener for me. I hadn't experienced much like it before and, although it was frightening and strange, I found myself inexplicably attracted to it.

Back at my mother's house I was searching through my address book for any London contacts and came across Howard and Blaikley's phone number. I called them and asked if I could come down and see them. I'm not even sure why I called them— maybe I thought they would write me a hit song.

I left Edinburgh at three o'clock in the morning and drove down to London in my clapped-out Austin A40, with an out-of-date tax disc and no MOT. Fitted to the car was a second-hand, four-track stereo that I picked up from the scrap merchants, with two large speaker cabinets I fixed to the back shelf behind the rear seat. I only had two cassettes, big clunky things, both with the Todd Rundgren double album *Something/Anything* on them, and I blasted it all the way down the motorway.

By the time I arrived in London I was shattered. Ken Howard had invited me to the Wendy House for lunch at one o'clock.

I sat with them both at the table and told them about my situation. I played them the songs that I had given to Dick Leahy and they liked them, or at least they said they did. "We're not really producers, we only write and produce our own songs," Ken responded, quite forthrightly, "You should really be looking for a manager." They leaned over to each other and had a quiet talk before Ken said, "You should speak to Charles Armitage from Noel Gay Artists, he might be able to help you."

I took a note of his phone number, thanked them for seeing me and headed over to Regent's Park to see if I could get a bed for the night. The guys in the house were taking the piss and singing *Bye Bye Baby*. The Bay City Rollers were currently at No.1 with it and it stayed there for six weeks.

I called Charles Armitage first thing the following morning, using Howard and Blaikley's name as a reference, and over the phone I gave him a brief history of The Bay City Rollers and told him I was only in London for another day. He agreed to see me that afternoon.

It all happened quite quickly after that. Noel Gay Artists offices were in Denmark Street in the Soho area, known as Tin Pan Alley, where all the music publishers were. The entrance to their office was like a shop front but with the bottom half of the display window blanked out. The reception area was very small, with an attractive older woman looking over an old-fashioned reception desk, and talking to someone through a telephone headset.

I was taken through to the back office and met by a very well-spoken young guy, not much older than me. He shook my hand saying, "I'm Charles, come in." He had reddish fair hair and a slight beard, which looked like that was as much beard as he was going to get. His stout build suited his enthusiastic personality.

I wanted to know more about him and the company so Charles very proudly obliged me with his family history: a music publishing company had been formed by Charles's grandfather, Reginald Armitage, in 1938, in order to protect his business interests as a prolific songwriter. He'd changed his name to

Noel Gay after reading a sign on a London bus that read "**Noel** Coward and Maisie **Gay** in a new review". The list of songs penned by Noel Gay is vast, and includes the wartime songs *The Lambeth Walk, Run Rabbit Run*, and *Leaning On A Lamp Post*. Some of these hits were also in his musical *Me and My Girl,* which originally opened in the West End in 1937, and included the song *The Sun Has Got His Hat On*. The side of the company known as Noel Gay Artists represented such household names as David Frost, Esther Rantzen, Rowan Atkinson, John Cleese, Russell Harty, and The King Singers, to name a few.

Nothing of the above, impressive as it was, related to anything I was trying to do. But I liked Charles Armitage. He was a young guy with new ideas and I got the impression he wanted to put his stamp on things. The office didn't match the image in front of me. Here was a dynamic character, surrounded by dusty bookshelves and framed photographs of past performers in their stage costumes hung up all over the walls. He was either using someone else's office or had just moved into this one. I told him my story. "Can you hang around till five o'clock? There's someone I'd like you to meet. I'll see you at the Red Lion at the bottom of Denmark Street," said Charles, not giving me a chance to respond. I left and wandered round the streets of Soho for an hour or so.

The Red Lion was a pub used by all the music industry representatives to meet and discuss business. I got there early and walked into a mass of people, mainly in suits, talking very loudly. I made my way right through the crowd to the other side of the bar just to get a feel for the place and soak up the atmosphere. I was excited and apprehensive at the same time. Keeping an eye on the door, I saw Charles come in with another guy and make his way to the bar. I made my way over and caught him just as he was about to order. "Ah! Nobby, I would like you to meet Mike Smith." I turned round and shook the hand of a guy wearing a short, tan-coloured leather jacket and very tight jeans over cowboy boots. He had a patterned shirt with the collar out over the top of his jacket and long, messy hair hanging down to his shoulders. He was wearing large thick-rimmed glasses and was smoking a miniature cigar.

Mike Smith was a record producer. Originally hired by Decca Records as a studio assistant, he'd worked on Billy Fury's *Half Way To Paradise* before being upgraded to producer. At Decca he worked closely with Dick Rowe (an A+R manager). Mike told me later that he was given the final decision on whether to sign either The Beatles or Brian Poole and the Tremeloes—he'd turned down The Beatles in favour of the latter. He'd gone to see the Beatles at The Cavern in Liverpool in 1961. "I thought they were wonderful, but when I got them into the studio, they weren't so good," he said. "I met them subsequently and they gave me the two-fingered salute!"

Brian Poole and the Tremeloes did have a string of hits with Decca, including *Do You Love Me?* which went to number 1 in the charts, and *Twist And Shout* taken from The Beatles first album. Mike also produced The Applejacks and Dave Berry. When Poole split with the Tremeloes, Mike moved with them to CBS and produced their songs, including the number 1 hit *Silence is Golden*, a cover song originally released as a B-side by The Four Seasons and written by Bob Gaudio and Bob Crewe in 1967. Mike's other successful productions included *Yellow River* by Christie, *The Ballad Of Bonnie And Clyde* by Georgie Fame, *Everlasting Love* for Love Affair, and Marmalade's version of *Ob-La-De, Ob-La-Da*.

He was great company, and funny stories about the people he had worked with came pouring out, although not in a bragging way. He just seemed to love being a player in the game and my first impression was that he was an honest guy who wore his heart on his sleeve. We hit it off immediately and, after telling him a bit about my history and the songs I had written, Mike said, "Have you got somewhere to stay?" He gave me his address in Southgate, in north London, and invited me to stay the night. I stayed for three.

Mike lived in a large, semi-detached house with a huge garden in a quiet suburb of Southgate. He had bought the house when he got married but was now divorced, his son was living with his ex-wife but staying with Mike at weekends.

His interest in me was apparent right from the start. He liked my image and my voice, and he wanted to start working on songs immediately. Over the years, Mike had collected songs from publishers that he thought had hit potential, so most of our time together was spent listening to his collection as well as the demos of my own songs. One in particular caught his attention, a new song of mine called *Steady Love*. The demo was very rough, just me strumming guitar and singing into a cassette player, but he got quite excited about it. I picked out two songs from his collection and we started making plans—it was that fast.

Only one thing concerned me, he seemed to drink an awful lot.

On the 9th September 1975, the day before my 25th birthday, I signed a management contract with Charles Armitage, and a publishing deal with Noel Gay Music Publishing. Both Mike and Charles had taken the package to CBS to negotiate a recording contract.

While all the negotiations were going on I was back in Edinburgh. Out of the blue, I decided to call Jim McKenna, the guy I'd travelled back to Scotland with on the bus. He wanted me to come through to Armadale for the weekend to meet all his buddies. I was at a loose end anyway and, since it was only about twenty-five miles from my house, I drove through on the Saturday afternoon and met Jim at The Highlander pub in the centre of Armadale. There I was introduced to a bunch of guys who looked like leftovers from the hippy period of the late sixties, dressed in tie-dye T-shirts and Indian kaftans. One guy they called Groovy had on a Mexican poncho and pointed cowboy boots. It was all love and peace, man.

There was some serious drinking going on and I joined in. By early evening we were all well oiled and invited back to Groovy's house. Everyone was way over the limit, but those with cars, including me, drove to Whitburn where he lived. Their preferred vehicle was a Volkswagon Caravanette, which two of these guys had—there was a definite sense that I had walked into the past.

Groovy was a dealer in curios and antiques. The large flat he lived in was full of old furniture, with Indian rugs on the walls and floors. A miniature castle, lit up from the inside, sat on a small dark table and there were many other interesting pieces lying around. I liked the atmosphere in the place—it was fascinating.

We sat around in a rough circle and at least three people started rolling joints. I got completely out of my tree and was lying back on the couch, incapable of holding any meaningful conversation, when somebody put Jackson Browne on the stereo and turned the volume up. I had no idea who he was but it blew me away. The lyrics and the melodies were out of this world. I heard: *"Don't confront me with my failures, I've not forgotten them,"* and *"These days I sit on corner stones, and count the time in quarter tones to ten"*. Apparently he was seventeen when he wrote these lyrics. The album was *For Everyman* and contained the song *Take it Easy*, later recorded by The Eagles. This was the start of my love affair with Jackson Browne's music.

Through these guys I also got my introduction to Robert Palmer, Dr John, Ry Cooder, The Ozark Mountain Daredevils, and Tom Petty and the Heartbreakers. Living in this backward, out-of-the-way place didn't seem to fit with their worldly-wise knowledge of music and their love of life. I had been caged up for years, out of touch with reality, and I learned a lot about what's important in life, about friendship and doing what makes you happy. We sat up in the Bathgate hills playing guitars, singing and getting stoned. Many weekends were spent in their company at a time when I was lost, and I'm grateful for it.

I got the phone call that the CBS recording contract was ready for signing. It meant that I would receive a substantial advance, which would keep me financially secure for a while. I booked a same-day return flight and caught the early morning shuttle down to London. I signed the contract in Charles's office and we went out for lunch with Mike Smith to celebrate and to discuss a timescale for booking the studio. Everything seemed to be in place. When we were getting ready to leave the restaurant, and while Charles was distracted paying the bill, Mike handed me a small piece of cannabis he had produced from his pocket. We shook hands on the way out and went our separate ways.

It was a beautiful, hot, sunny afternoon and I had the rest of the day to waste as my flight back wasn't until the evening. I had left my guitar at Charles's office on a previous visit and now I was carrying that, and my bag, as I wandered around the London streets. I decided to go to Hyde Park to sunbathe for a while and I found a nice, sheltered spot beside some bushes. I thought, "I'll roll a joint and just chill out", so I put the guitar case up on end and laid my bag alongside it to give me some protection. I'd just got the cigarette papers together and was heating the cannabis, breaking it into the tobacco, when a policeman, in full uniform with nipple helmet, climbed out of the bushes not twenty yards from where I was sitting. I quickly pulled my guitar down over the half-finished joint and lay back pretending to be sunbathing. He walked right over to me, crouched down and lifted my bag up saying in a deep, cynical voice, "You know what I'm looking for?" I replied in a shaky voice, "No, what's the problem?"

He lifted my guitar and exposed the offending object. He took the unfinished joint and put it in a plastic bag, lifted my guitar in one hand and my bag in the other saying, "You'll have to follow me to the police station." I didn't know there was a police station in the middle of Hyde Park, and I couldn't run away because he had all my stuff. I walked behind him like a man going to the gallows. You know that walk when you try and walk normally but your knees don't bend when you expect them to. He strode across Hyde Park carrying my bag and guitar, in front of all the people walking round and sunbathing and staring at me from all directions. I kept my head down trying to hide my face.

At the police station they emptied my bags, strip-searched me, went through all my pockets, found the very small piece of hash, and charged me with possession of a controlled substance.

When the case came up a couple of months later I flew back down to London for the court case. The judge asked the police if they knew the value of the cannabis found. The policeman said, "Between five and ten pounds." The judge looked at me and asked, "Have you come all the way from Scotland?" I answered, "Yes, your honour." He glanced sideways at the police, as if to say what a waste of everyone's time. "I have no choice but to give you the minimum fine of twenty pounds," he said, almost apologetically.

I stayed overnight at the roadie's house by Regents Park, and Andy told me that some of the guys would be going with Noddy Holder to the matinée showing of the film *Cabaret* starring Liza Minelli. He was laughing when he told me that it was the twelfth time Noddy had seen it. Andy said, "If you fancy coming along I'll phone him and tell him." So the following day, eight of us, including Noddy Holder, arrived at the Odeon cinema in Leicester Square. We bought tickets for the balcony and got seated in the front row. We had a few minutes before the film started while the lights were still up, so Noddy decided to go down to the foyer and buy cartons of Kia-Ora orange juice for everyone. He got to the top of the balcony steps, carrying the eight cartons of juice, just as the lights went out. He missed the top step and tumbled all the way down the stairs! The Kia-Ora cartons went flying up in the air and he landed in a bundle at the bottom of the aisle—it was hilarious.

I was getting excited—it was the first day of recording. The plan was to record three songs: two of my original compositions, *Steady Love* and *Give Me The Heart,* and a song Mike came up with called *Oh, I Love You.* I'd spent a few days at his house beforehand, going through the arrangements of the songs, while he set up the musicians. I was excited and nervous, but also concerned about the amount of alcohol Mike was consuming. This was a big thing for me and I wanted his full attention and commitment.

CBS Studios in Whitfield Street (just off Tottenham Court Road) was a four-storey building with two sixteen-track studios, cutting room, dubbing suite and studio leisure area. Mike had contributed to the design and layout so he proudly gave me a guided tour and introduced me to the people working there. Everybody knew Mike, and he was obviously well thought of, being welcomed in every room or studio we walked into, and he left everyone with a smile on their face—he had that effect. Later I discovered he was being considered for the Managing Director's job at CBS Records, London, and that he expected to be offered it. I just loved being in recording studios, amongst the creative vibes. I was like a kid in a candy shop. I wanted to know the names of every artist who had recorded there.

We had the studio booked for three days. All the backing tracks were done on the first day, which included a long pub break at lunchtime. I had my concerns about some of the sounds Mike was using, but I left it in his experienced hands. That evening Mike wanted to stay up town with his drinking pals, but I was tired and headed back to Southgate.

The following day was for recording overdubs and vocals. I could see Mike was a bit the worse for wear in the morning, but I didn't say anything. I sat in the control room and listened while a wonderful session guitarist by the name of Nigel Jenkins put down some tracks, and then we added a keyboard. I wanted a pedal steel guitar on the song, but Mike suggested I put the vocals down first so they could hear where the spaces were.

I went into the main studio to do the lead vocal on *Steady Love* and, after a couple of takes, I looked over to the control room window. I saw Mike taking a half-bottle of whisky from his jacket pocket and drinking it straight down... I went into the control room for a listen, but I wasn't happy with what I had done so I went back out to do it again. Halfway through, I looked into the control room again and there was Mike asleep in the chair. I was so angry I put my jacket on and walked out of the studio.

I was wandering around the streets, in two minds about what to do. I still had Tam Paton's voice ringing in my ears about the evils of drink. Should I go and speak to Charles Armitage? That might ruin everything. I decided, now that I had calmed down, to go back to the studio. Mike apologised, but he was in no fit state to continue so we cut the session short.

The following day I completed the vocals, added pedal steel guitar, and Mike mixed the tracks. I wasn't a hundred per cent happy with it as it didn't seem tight to me—the mixes were a bit sloppy. But when we played them to Charles he liked them, especially *Steady Love*, so I bowed to their better judgement.

At CBS Records, Nicky Graham was assigned as my A+R (Artist and Repertoire) man. Nicky was a musician in his own right and had played keyboards with David Bowie throughout most of 1972, on *The Spiders From Mars* tour. (He later went on to produce the Nolan Sisters and also, when head of A+R at CBS Records, he was recognised as being the guy who signed The Clash.)

Nicky was hooked by *Steady Love* right from the start. As soon as he heard the three songs he said, "That's the single!" It was later announced that they were going to release it on the Epic Label, which CBS used mainly for rhythm and blues and country music, so I was delighted.

Mike took me round to meet more people at CBS Records. He was so well-liked and respected that he could just walk into all the offices, and at the press office he grabbed me by the arm, pulled me in, walked over to the stereo, put on *Steady Love* and pointed at me saying, "He wrote that!" It was a proud moment.

The day we got the first pressing of the single with *Steady Love* on the A-side and *Give Me The Heart* on the B-side was a day for celebration. Mike, Charles and I went out for a wine-soaked lunch then ended up at Mike's private club in Soho. It was a seedy little private men's club with a sliding panel on the entrance door behind which two eyes appeared. Of course they recognised Mike and in we went. I stood for a minute looking around. It was dark and noisy with a low ceiling and a small bar at the far end. A circle of rowdy men stood in the middle of the floor shouting and pushing each other. When I got closer I saw two girls on the floor completely naked, having some girl-on-girl action. A drunken guy in a dark suit shoved his way through to the front and was touching the girls. The bouncers immediately jumped in, grabbed him by both arms and gave him the bum's rush right out the door. As they passed me I was shocked—it was Hughie Green, the man I had seen many times on television presenting Opportunity Knocks!

The following day at Mike's house I was standing in the kitchen making a cup of coffee when Mike walked in and produced two LSD tablets, asking me if I'd ever tried it. Well, I hadn't, but had always wondered what it would be like. "Just take a half to begin with," he said. I replied, "You go first." He swallowed his and I swallowed mine. Just then the phone rang. Mike answered it and spoke to someone for a while before saying, "Just pop round anytime if you need to talk," and put the phone down. The guy was a friend of his who had called to tell him he had just split up with his wife after finding her in bed with another man.

As the drug began to take effect we were talking more and more. It was a beautiful sunny day and I was looking out into the back garden. I began to see extremely vivid colours and had a very strange feeling, but I wasn't frightened by it. I felt really good. I could see every blade of grass and every individual petal on the flowers—it was amazing. Just then the doorbell rang and it was the guy who had been on the phone. He'd just popped round.

"Oh my God!" Mike exclaimed before letting him in. I had to try and act normal while Mike introduced me to Ken, whose face was moving in a wave as I looked at him. Mike sat him down in the living room and we both disappeared into the kitchen where we burst out laughing. "Listen," Mike said, "this guy's dead straight. He doesn't know anything about drugs. Don't tell him anything." I couldn't stop laughing. Mike was going, "Shhhhhhhh!" but he couldn't talk for laughing himself, all while the poor guy was sitting distraught in the living room.

I gathered myself together and went through. Mike suggested we sit out in the garden and have a glass of wine, so we sat outside on the large stones at the bottom of the rockery. Mike was talking to Ken and I was looking up at the rear of the house when I saw a lion, a male lion, roaring out of the bedroom window. I looked back at Ken who had his head in his hands and had burst out crying. I burst out into a fit of the giggles. I couldn't help it, it was the LSD. Mike looked at me and that set him off. I had to excuse myself.

There were French doors at the back of the living room and I thought, "I'll open them and put on some music as a distraction." I just put on the first album that came to hand and turned it up loud so it could be heard in the garden. Out of the speakers came *What Becomes Of The Broken Hearted*—I ran to the stereo and whipped it off! Then Mike came in. He was in hysterics with laughter—the tears were running down his face. It was terrible... we weren't doing it deliberately, but the LSD and the situation just got out of hand. Thank goodness Ken left shortly afterwards. The following day I phoned him up and apologised for my behaviour, blaming it on too much wine.

There had been no contact between me and the members of the Rollers since I left, so imagine my surprise when, out the blue, I got a phone call from Alan Longmuir in America. He told me, "You better get a hold of your lawyer... *Saturday Night* has just gone to number 1 with your voice on it." I looked it up and there it was: No.1 in the USA's Billboard Hot 100 chart!

He also told me he was leaving the Rollers. He'd had enough and couldn't stand it anymore. Inviting me up to his house in Dollar, Perthshire, the next time I was back in Scotland, he said, "I'll tell you all about it when I see you," and we left it at that. Soon after I came across an article about Tam Paton and the Rollers in which Tam alleged that Alan had tried to commit suicide and I thought, "Things must be bad."

The wheels of publicity started turning as soon as CBS set a release date for my single. Both the publicity department at CBS and Noel Gay Artists arranged for hundreds of photographs to be taken and I was in my element in front of the camera. Interviews, meetings, image consultants: it was all starting to happen. We set up a fan club too, which Charles's girlfriend wanted to run. I was on top of the world.

We still had a few weeks before the release date and I needed to sort out some things back home. When I got there Margie was getting more and more into speed and other substances, and I found myself being dragged, willingly, into it. I was concerned she was becoming addicted and tried to speak to her about it, but was met with denial. It seemed that every time I met her we would end up either at the Ardmillan flat or at Billy Steel's in Leith.

One day Billy asked me if I could help him out with something and, wanting to please everybody, I said, "Yeah, what is it?" "You just need to follow me in your car," he said. So I did, I followed him all the way to Muirhouse. It was known as the seedier side of town—not somewhere you would want to go on your own. There was a long dual carriageway there, and about halfway along it Billy pulled up at the side of the road. He came over to my car and said, "Hang on, I'll be back in a minute." I watched him walk across a grassed area and disappear into the woods. After about fifteen minutes he reappeared carrying two plastic carrier bags filled with something, I didn't know what. He opened the back door of my car and put them on the back seat saying, "Just follow me back to my flat." I had a bad feeling about this.

When we pulled up outside his flat, he took the bags and I followed him upstairs. Margie and Leana were sitting in the living room drinking cheap wine. Billy emptied the bags onto the table and out poured hundreds of pills and capsules, and packets of drugs of all different kinds. He told me some guys had broken into a chemist shop, stolen all the drugs, and he had followed them and seen where they'd buried the stuff. I was absolutely shocked—it began to dawn on me what I'd done, and it was way over my boundary line. I was up for a good time but was no crook. I told Margie, quietly, that I was feeling sick and needed to get out of there, so we made an excuse and left. That was the last time I saw Billy Steel. I heard a few years later that he died of a drugs overdose.

I had to get out of this relationship with Margie—it was dragging me down. I tried to call it off but she started screaming and chasing my car up the street. I felt sorry for her and eventually went back a few days later, but I knew it was near the end.

CHAPTER NINE

The date was upon us, 18th June 1976, and *Steady Love* was released. I was back in London doing more promotional stuff and answering the fan letters coming in thick and fast in response to all the teenage magazine coverage. I had a number of TV appearances lined up, and CBS were also in the process of arranging a tour round all the commercial radio stations, up the west side of the country and down the east side. I had a few free days with nothing on, so I suggested to Mike that he come up to Scotland with me for a long weekend. He was up for the idea.

Rosko's Roundtable was on BBC Radio One, early on a Friday evening. "Emperor Rosko", to give him his full title, was the Radio One DJ hosting the programme. He'd invite other DJs and artists to sit round the table and review the week's new single releases.

It was a very powerful show. It had a large audience because people were keen to know which records were coming out, and a good review could help a song along its way, but a bad review could do some damage.

Steady Love was scheduled to be reviewed the next Friday, the same day as Mike and I were planning to go to Scotland. We talked about it and Mike wanted to take his car, which was a beauty, right enough. He drove a Ford Capri MK2, with a vinyl roof and a 2.8 turbocharged engine. I persuaded him to leave mid-afternoon on Friday in order to miss the rush hour traffic, but it would mean we'd have to listen to Rosko's Roundtable in the car. Off we went with a big bag of sweets (and I mean a carrier bag of them), loads of music and happy hearts. We got to somewhere between Birmingham and Manchester when the programme started. We pulled over immediately onto the hard shoulder, turning up the radio to listen.

Steady Love came on and my heart was in my mouth. It sounded good on the radio. The fade out came and there was a short silence before the talking started. As it passed from one critic to the next it went something like this, "I like the song but the production's terrible." "The tune is very catchy and the lyrics are nice, but they don't match the messy production going on in the background." We drove off and hardly said a word all the way to Edinburgh.

I could see that Mike was really down the following day. I said to him, "Listen Mike, I like the song the way it is. I like the production. Lots of songs get bad reviews and become big hits. Forget about it and have a good weekend."

We did have a great weekend. My sister, Margaret, put Mike up in her spare room and they had a fantastic time—she was just the best fun to be with. I took Mike everywhere: to Holyrood Palace, up to Edinburgh Castle, and down all the closes in the High Street. He was having a great time because we stopped at nearly every pub on the way. We even had lunch under the Forth Bridge. Of course, he met Margie too, and within an hour of meeting him she was asking him if he wanted a line of speed. She said it like everybody took a line of speed. In the end, we all did and were up all night.

The plan was that Mike would drive back down to London, and I would stay in Edinburgh for another couple of days. When he was leaving he came up close to me and said, "You need to get away from her." Eventually I did, and never saw her again.

Over the next couple of weeks all the interviews, photographs and press releases started coming out in the magazines and newspapers, and there were lots of them. Charles's wife, Diane, did a great job of cutting them all out and filing them. The problem for me was that every single article was headed: "EX- LEAD SINGER OF THE BAY CITY ROLLERS, Nobby Clark, tells why he left the band to pursue his solo career," and somewhere buried deep in the text it would say, "…releases his first solo single *Steady Love*". I didn't like that, but there was nothing I could do.

Nobby Clark

Meanwhile, I was conveniently dismissing the fact that drinking was creeping up on me again. I would have to beware.

CBS Records had a network of representatives around the country who looked after the artists when they were on tour, set up the publicity and promoted the new records. I had interviews set up with all the major commercial radio stations around England, and up into Scotland as far as Glasgow and Edinburgh. It was going really well. I would get the train from one place to the next and the reps there would pick me up in a limousine and take me to the local radio station. From Bristol, to Birmingham, to Bolton... I was full of chat, laughing with the DJs, talking about *Steady Love* and my plans for the future.

Then we got to Manchester. I was to do a radio interview and then I was to go on to a huge dance club, full of teenagers, to do a live interview. I booked into my hotel and was going up in the lift when I felt disorientated. My head was spinning, and when I got out of the lift the floor was moving under my feet. I called Simon, the rep for the area, and he called a private doctor. When he arrived at my hotel room, he went into this big long speech about all the big stars he had treated, including Frank Sinatra, The Beatles, Tom Jones and Shirley Bassey. I'm not sure I believed him, but he was an interesting character.

His diagnosis was that I was suffering from anxiety and nerves. He prescribed Valium (Diazepam), 5mg tablets, which definitely calmed me down. So much so, that I sounded slightly drunk at the radio station, but no one really noticed at the dance club because it was so loud you couldn't hear me speak anyway.

My next stop was Liverpool's Radio Merseyside, a BBC radio station, and then on up to Carlisle. Each stop meant a different hotel for the night, and each night I would sit in the bar and have a few drinks. I kept it pretty well under control, until I reached Glasgow. There I was to go to Radio Clyde for a piece on a programme called Stick It In Your Ear, presented by John MacCalman. I took a Valium in the morning, as the doctor had prescribed, then at lunchtime I sneaked off and had a couple of drinks before going into Radio Clyde to record my interview. It was a Friday afternoon and John MacCalman just opened the mike while I rattled on about The Bay City Rollers' early days in Scotland and my solo career. I think they quite liked me talking nonsense and having a laugh. It was that kind of show.

When I finished recording, the CBS rep told me he had to go and take care of business and would pick me up in Glasgow early evening. That meant I had four hours to waste and stupidly went into a pub in Glasgow city centre. I sat there drinking one after the other, saying to myself, "You shouldn't be doing this," but the little devil on my shoulder was telling me, "It'll be alright, go on have another one." By the time Simon picked me up I was drunk as a skunk. On the way through to Edinburgh in the limo, I was hanging out the window being sick.

In Edinburgh I was booked to appear on the Radio Forth Road Show at the Cavendish Ballroom. Simon attempted to sober me up with some food, but I was still pissed. As soon as the producer saw me and spoke to me, he looked at Simon and said, "I can't let him go on like that, it's being recorded for the radio," and he cancelled my appearance. Simon passed that information back to CBS the following day, and they cancelled the remaining stations.

Charles Armitage was summoned to attend a meeting with Nicky Graham at CBS to discuss the event and he managed to persuade Nicky that the problem was due to the medication the doctor had prescribed me. Amongst his other talents, Nicky Graham was also a songwriter, so when he asked me to sing one of his songs, which he planned to enter in The Eurovision Song Contest, I knew everything was alright with him. I recorded the song and it was entered in the competition. We made it into the last twenty but it was never heard of again. However, it meant that Nicky liked my voice and that was something.

We got a break when *Steady Love* was chosen as the "Power Play" on Radio Luxembourg's Tony Prince show, being played on the hour, every hour.

I also had some TV appearances lined up, and appeared on the Saturday morning show Tiswas, with Sally James and Chris Tarrant, and the Basil Brush show. Then, strangely, the other three shows I had been booked for cancelled, one after the other. Charles Armitage asked me if I knew anything about it. I said, "Not a thing. The other shows were great."

A few years further down the line I met Ray Cotter, who was Tam Paton's partner and gay lover throughout the Bay City Rollers' success years. When I met him, this particular time, he and Tam had split up, and I asked Ray about some things that had happened when I left the Rollers. He informed me that Tam had employed a guy by the name of Dave Eager and given him explicit instructions to make sure I didn't appear on television. Dave Eager had worked at the BBC's Radio One, and also had close contacts in television. He was told to contact the producers and tell them that if they put Nobby Clark on their show, The Bay City Rollers would not be appearing on any of the shows. Since they had the power, they called the shots.

It had felt like I was running through a swamp sometimes.

Back in 1976, despite all the efforts of everyone involved, *Steady Love* only made it into the Top 50 in the British singles chart. However, at the beginning of 1977 it was released on the Mercury label in Sweden where it was a big hit, followed by Germany and Japan on the Philips label. In all three countries we sold a lot of records, over a period of time. It made it all worthwhile. But we could not get it to move in the U.K.

I discovered through Charles Armitage that Mike Smith had been passed over for the job as Managing Director of CBS Records, in favour of an American executive. I spent a lot of time with Mike, going round the publishers, listening to new songs. We always had a laugh, and Mike always had too much to drink, as did I, in his company.

Charles thought it would be a good idea to make a new start. In the background he had been talking to his contacts at Phonogram about me because the first year of my CBS contract was coming to an end and he suggested it might be better for both parties if they didn't pick up the option on it. They agreed, so negotiations began with Phonogram instead.

Mike and I had a night out and got pissed. I told him I was going to move on and try something else. He got very emotional and so did I—I felt like a traitor. After that night I never saw him again.

While I was writing this chapter, I looked up the internet to see if Mike had a website or anything, and I came across his obituary. Mike Smith died on December 3rd 2011, aged 76. It was a very sad day for me.

I was privileged enough to work with, and learn from, some of the best music producers in the business over the years, one of the most memorable being Christopher Rainbow. Chris had written and produced mainly his own songs in the past, most notably *Give Me What I Cry For* and *Solid State Brain*, both held in high regard by DJs, producers and musicians alike.

He was not the easiest of producers to work with. It took three different drummers and two full days to get the drum sound he wanted, and a full day to record the vocal harmonies. In total, it took a full week of studio time to complete a song. *Love Will Save The Day* was the only song I recorded with Chris, but it turned out to be quite outstanding in its production and was released on the Phonogram label in Germany, Holland, Belgium and Sweden. Chris and I became good friends and I hoped we would work together on more material, but other people had other ideas.

We were still looking for that elusive breakthrough hit in the U.K. I had some new songs, which Charles wanted me to make proper demos of, and he brought in Don Gould to work with me on the musical arrangements. I had met Don before when I was recording *Steady Love*, when he had written out all the parts for the session musicians.

We booked into a small studio in southwest London. We had a drummer, bass player and guitarist while Don played the piano himself. The tracks came out really well but, as had happened in the past, the song that I thought had the most commercial appeal was not the one they picked.

Steve Lillywhite was an in-house producer with Phonogram at the time and Charles was keen to get him on board. A meeting was set up at Phonogram Studios so that I could meet him and play the demos of the new songs. However, when we got there, Steve Lillywhite was sitting at the mixing desk, working on a track for Siouxsie and the Banshees. Sitting beside him was a young guy he introduced as Steve Brown. Steve Lillywhite said he had too much on his plate right now as he was producing the Boomtown Rats as well as the new album for Siouxsie and the Banshees, so he suggested that I work with Steve Brown. Steve

Brown was Mr Lillywhite's prodigy and had worked as his assistant before moving into production in his own right. We shook hands and arranged to meet at a later date to discuss the songs.

All four songs were re-recorded at Phonogram Studios and the one they picked out as the single was *Shake it Down*. I didn't think it was the strongest song, but I didn't want to make any waves.

I had rented a flat in Dalston, northeast London, in the borough of Hackney. It was a basement flat with a large garden to the rear and the rent was £75 a month, which was quite reasonable, but in 1977 Dalston was not a nice area to live in. Most of the surrounding flats had no curtains, and when you looked in the windows you saw bare light bulbs with no lampshades, while the front gardens were full of old furniture and mattresses. I didn't feel safe walking back there at night, but it was a base to work from.

It was going to be a couple of months before *Shake it Down* would be released, so I went back to Edinburgh for a while. When there I called Alan Longmuir and he invited me to come up and stay at his house for a few days.

Alan lived in a country house called Shelter Hall. It was located in Perthshire, approximately two miles to the east of Dollar, and surrounded by beautiful countryside. It was an extended farmhouse with stables and a bit of land. Alan's retired father also stayed at the house and helped Alan to look after his horse and chickens.

We just picked up where we left off—the bond between us was still strong, and it felt good to be friends again.

Alan's girlfriend, Julie, lived in Glendevon Castle. She was very much into horses and he'd first met her when she was seventeen, while he was looking to buy a horse for himself. He drove me up to Glendevon Castle that weekend, and I met Julie's father and mother, Danny and Dot, and her older sister, Karen, a very attractive girl who spoke her mind—I liked that. The family name was Macnee and their great-grandmother's portrait hangs in the National Gallery of Scotland on Princes Street, Edinburgh.

The castle was built in the 17th century but also had more recent extensions and additions. The old dungeons below the castle were converted into a bar and a modern extension to the rear was used for functions and dances. The family owned the land and the hills as far as you could see, divided only by the River Devon, with the castle on the north side and a beautiful mansion, Glendevon House, on the south side where the girls' grandmother lived. The gardens around the house were spread out with lawns and tennis courts, a glazed summerhouse and a wooden gazebo.

I spent many extended weekends at Alan's house or at the castle, and eventually got into a relationship with Karen which lasted about a year and a half. This is when the drinking really started: every time I was up there, Alan and I spent most of the day in the Dollar Arms pub or in the bar at Glendevon Castle.

Alan had an ex-racehorse that had been taken off the track because it was too highly strung. He used to ride the horse down to the Dollar Arms and tie it up outside while he was in having a drink. If he got too drunk, he could just get on the horse and it would find its own way back to the stable. One night, riding the horse up Dollar's high street, it spooked and threw Alan off, then took off at full speed, galloping down the main road. It was stopped eventually at the far end of the town by a car. When Alan got to it, its two front hooves were buried in the bonnet of a brand new Range Rover.

I rode that horse a few times through the fields around Alan's house. It was frighteningly fast and uncontrollable.

Karen invited me up to the castle for one weekend as there was a big wedding being held at the nearby Glendevon Hotel on the Saturday night. I drove up on the Friday and arranged to meet Alan at the Dollar Arms, before we headed up to the castle together. Karen's father Danny liked to have an occasional gamble on the roulette tables at a casino in Dundee, and when we arrived, Danny and his wife Dot were just getting ready to leave. Alan and I went down to the dungeon where Karen was working behind the bar and found Julie sitting having a drink.

By the time they closed the bar we had all had a lot to drink, while Danny and Dot were off having fun in Dundee.

The castle had a turret with a stone spiral staircase leading to Julie's bedroom, on the first floor, and to the spare bedroom on the second floor where Alan and I were to sleep. Further up, on the top floor, was Karen's bedroom. Of course, Alan disappeared into Julie's room while Karen and I headed up to her room on the top floor.

About an hour later I heard a car coming up the driveway and across the stones in the car park. Karen looked out the window and saw her dad's car at the front door. "Quick, you better get down the stairs!" she shouted. So I jumped out of bed and ran down to tell Alan, but it was too late... I heard the door to the turret opening and the footsteps of the mother coming up the stairs. Alan had heard it too and had jumped out of Julie's bed and stood behind the bedroom door, stark naked. The door opened and the light went on. A bank of mirrored wardrobes ran right across the far wall. Julie's mother just stared at Alan's nude reflection for a minute, then said, "Goodnight Julie," and shut the door. The following morning the atmosphere at the breakfast table was not pleasant, but nothing was said.

That night we all got dressed up and went to the wedding reception at the Glendevon Hotel. It was a freezing night. The snow on the ground had turned to ice and cars were sliding all over the place. I didn't know anyone at the wedding, but they were all buying drinks and Alan and I were having a great time knocking back the whisky and dancing around the floor to the piper blasting out highland jigs. As usual, I didn't know when to stop and, by the end of the night, I was drunk and loud and making a fool of myself.

When we were leaving, I staggered out to the top of the stairs leading to the car park. I unfortunately had my hands in my pockets when I slipped on the top landing and fell right down the stone stairs, head first, landing with my face straight into the packed ice on the ground. I couldn't move. I just lay there until I felt someone pulling me up from behind, and then saw all the blood on the ground and running down my face. Someone got a towel and held it against my face to stop the bleeding.

The nearest hospital was miles away in Dunfermline and some of the roads were closed due to the bad weather, so they drove me back to the castle instead. I had deep cuts all over my face, but Karen cut up small strips of plaster and knitted them together. The following day I went to the hospital and the doctor said, "I'm not going to touch them, you've done such a good job." but I also had two horrendous black eyes and my face was severely swollen. I had to phone my mother to warn her before I went home.

I needed to get myself together quickly because *Shake it Down* was going to be released soon. The bruising cleared up within a couple of weeks and, luckily, I didn't have any pronounced scars.

There were a lot of good things happening. *Steady Love* was released in Japan and I was in all the pop magazines, getting hundreds of letters from fans each week. *Shake it Down* was then released in the UK, Scandinavia, and all over Europe on the Mercury label.

My manager, Charles Armitage, was also acting as agent in the United Kingdom for a very famous French singer songwriter called Claude François. Although he was fairly well known in many countries, in France he was a megastar with his own TV show. During his career he'd sold more than seventy million records and he had also written the original version of *My Way* (as *Comme D'Habitude*). The original song had been sent to several publishers in London and New York, and was even given to David Bowie to write English lyrics, but had been rejected until it landed on the desk of Paul Anka's publisher. Anka was given the song to translate into English lyrics, and then it became the legendary *My Way* made so famous by Frank Sinatra.

Claude François later had a major hit with another of his compositions, *Parce Que Je T'aime, Mon Infant* (Because I Love You, Child) which was covered by Elvis Presley under the title *My Boy*.

121

I was asked to perform on the Claude François Christmas Special television show in Paris, in December 1977. Amongst the other artists on the show was a very young Jodie Foster who was on a promotional tour of Europe, accompanied by her parents.

At the start of the show I lined up with her and sang *I'm Just A Day Dreamer*, then performed my own song *Shake it Down* with Les Claudette dancers all dressed in white behind me. It was a massive show, with a huge audience, and it put *Shake it Down* into the French charts.

The next time I met Claude François, he was preparing for a show at the Royal Albert Hall and wanted to go there to see Paul Anka, and to get a feel for the place. I sat up in the balcony with Claude and Charles, and we listened to Paul Anka introduce *My Way* with the words, "Here is a song I wrote for my friend Frank Sinatra." Claude François stood up and walked out.

I was booked to appear on four more of Claude's TV shows in Paris, to start shortly after his concert at the Royal Albert Hall in front of six thousand people. Then, on the 11th March, he was at his house in Paris, taking a bath, when the light went out. He reached up and touched the light fitting and electrocuted himself. The whole of France went into mourning.

In the standard music-publishing contract there was a clause, which stated that each year of the contract, the writer must provide a certain number of songs. Not just any songs—they had to be accepted by the publisher. I was coming up to the end of the second year of my contract with Noel Gay Music and had not yet fulfilled my quota. I was frantically writing and sending down songs that I hoped would be accepted.

In amongst them was an instrumental piece that I had composed on the piano. Out of the blue, Charles phoned me and said, "What's that piece of music called?" I didn't even have a title for it. He said, "A French producer wants to orchestrate it and use it in a French film." On the spot I came up with the first thing that came into my head and said *"The Big Sky."* It was subsequently orchestrated, used in the film, and gave me my first break as a writer away from pop music.

There were another three songs that I had submitted at the last minute that Charles really liked and he sent a copy over to Steve Brown at Phonogram who immediately responded and asked me to meet him at the studio. We played through the demos and he said, "I've got an idea. There's a group we've been working with called Clover—I think we should let them hear the songs and see if they would be interested in playing on them." I liked the sound of that.

He set up a meeting at their hotel so I arrived there with my acoustic guitar and my demos, and was introduced to four American guys. We listened to the songs and they immediately started playing along with the tracks and coming up with ideas. I thought, "I really like this." Then they sat down and talked with me, "Look, we're a group in our own right called Clover. We've just finished playing on an album for Elvis Costello called *My Aim is True*, and we told him the same thing—we'd be happy to play on your songs, but we don't want to advertise that we are session musicians." I had no hesitation replying, "Doesn't matter to me, I just want you to play on the tracks." So Steve Brown produced them, Clover arranged and played on them, and the tracks were fabulous.

It was pure ignorance on my part that I didn't know who these guys were: the guitar player was John McFee who later went on to play with the Doobie Brothers; the singer was Huey Lewis who, of course, went on to form Huey Lewis and the News (I was honoured to have him sing harmonies and play harmonica on my songs); on bass was John Ciambotti who went on to work with John Prine, Carlene Carter and Lucinda Williams; on keyboards was Sean Hopper who later became a member of Huey Lewis and the News; and on drums was Micky Shine who did sessions with many successful artists.

There's no greater thrill for me than working with talented, enthusiastic musicians and singers. Watching and listening to them play was such a pleasure. I've had too many experiences with clock-watching session musicians. It's different when you're talking about a thirty-piece orchestra where cost is of the utmost importance, but when you're trying to capture a moment and the pianist is telling you that you only have fifteen minutes left, it's not the best creative environment.

My contract with Phonogram was for one year, with options for a further two years, but not long after we recorded these songs a new Managing Director took charge at Phonogram. Charles was informed that due to financial difficulties they were looking at the contracts of all the artists who had not sold over a hundred thousand records in the U.K. I was devastated when I was told they wouldn't be picking up the option on my contract. But I still have the tapes of those recordings, and they are a treasured possession of mine. Maybe someday I'll make them available.

Behind the scenes, Charles was quietly negotiating a deal with RCA, but I was heading back to Scotland with my tail between my legs.

This was a very low period in my musical career. I felt like packing it all in. Just when I had success within my grasp, it was snatched away. To make matters worse every time I indulged in my favourite pastime of sifting through records in record shops, I came across lots of Bay City Rollers albums with my songs and vocal performances on them, and I wasn't being paid a penny. Whenever I tried to contact Tam Paton, or Dick Leahy at Bell Records, they wouldn't take my calls. There was obviously a big cover-up going on.

Back up at Glendevon Castle, one day, Alan Longmuir and I were sitting having a drink together when he told me he was going back to the Bay City Rollers. During his year or so away from the group he was replaced by Ian Mitchell, who then left the group within eight months of joining, followed by Pat McG-lynn who was asked to leave after six months. Both members have spoken about the terrible pressures of being on the road, and the lack of financial reward for the work they put in. Alan had been asked if he would rejoin the group and, after some consideration, he agreed.

However, he was concerned that he had put on a bit of weight and was unfit. Jokingly, I suggested that we hitchhike up to the Isle of Skye. I said, "That would get you fit!" not thinking for a minute that he would give it serious consideration. I was really surprised when he said, "That sounds like a good idea."

So we got the map out and hatched a plan, a plan that expanded the more alcohol we consumed. The end result was that we marked out a route that would take us right up through the Isle of Skye, over the water to the islands of Harris and Lewis and up to Stornoway. I was getting excited about it—I had never been to the Isle of Skye before, but had wanted to for a long time.

We decided that if we were going to do it, we would do it properly. We would camp out in a tent instead of sleeping in hotels and take waterproofs, walking boots and rucksacks, but otherwise we'd take as little with us as possible. We'd stop shaving and grow beards, partly so we wouldn't be recognised. It's amazing how sensible it all sounded after eight pints of lager!

Alan suggested we take the car up to Fort William, park it there and make that our starting point. The following week everything was in place and, before we could change our minds, we were on our way.

Alan drove us to Fort William, where we parked up in a hotel car park and headed west out of town towards Mallaig ferry port, a distance of approximately forty-five miles. We took off with an excited spring in our step and, once we got on the open road, we were singing Harry Lauder songs like *Roamin' In The Gloamin'* and *Keep Right On To The End Of The Road*, and having a right laugh.

After three miles and one hill we could hardly speak. Our legs were aching and we had to lie down at the side of the road. Everytime a car came passed, one of us would jump up and get the thumb in the air, but no one would stop. Eventually we didn't even get up, just lay there with the thumb up.

I said, "We better start walking again," so off we went with a renewed vigour. After trekking another three or four miles, a van pulled up and a burly workman-type rolled down the window and asked where we were going. He said, "I'm not going all the way to Mallaig but I'll get you near enough." I looked at Alan and said quietly, "You can get in the front—he looks like an axe murderer to me."

We survived the ride and he dropped us off outside a pub about five miles from the ferry port, so in we went for a pint or two. A bunch of local guys were playing darts, and I said to Alan, "Do you fancy a game for a laugh?" Neither of us had much experience playing darts, but after a couple of pints we were up for anything. The spokesman for the locals said, "We're playing for money," obviously thinking we were an easy touch. "We're playing doubles," he said, "and its five pound a game." That meant Alan and I against two of them. We put the money on the table and the game started. I've no idea how we did it, but we won the first game. They were looking at us suspiciously saying, "You'll be staying for another game, double or quits?" "Yeah, of course. I don't know how we won that, we're not really darts players," I said, trying to keep it friendly.

In the next game I was somehow hitting all the high numbers, so we were in the lead but needed a double eighteen to finish. I said to Alan, "Don't worry, I'll never get it!" The first dart flew straight out my hand, and I swear it was possessed, as it went straight into double eighteen. They were staring daggers at us. I whispered to Alan, "We better get out of here!" "Don't worry," he said out the side of his mouth, "I've already asked the barman to get us a taxi." We grabbed the money, got our bags and left, just as the taxi arrived.

I asked the driver what time the ferry left for the Isle of Skye. He said, "You're cutting it tight, the last one leaves at seven o'clock." It was twenty minutes to seven. We arrived at Mallaig just in time to see the ferry leaving the dock—just missed it. "You'll have to wait till the morning," the taxi driver informed us, stating the obvious. "But there's a ceilidh on at the fish market tonight, you'll enjoy that."

Alan and I walked down to the pier and looked out across the water. It was absolutely beautiful. The fishing trawlers had just come in and were lined up along the dock, tourists were quietly strolling around in the sunshine enjoying the views. Nearby there was a large building with open sides, which we assumed was the fish market as the sides had been closed off with fish boxes piled on top of each other, and at the front they had created an entrance with fish boxes on either side.

We went off to find a quiet place to pitch the tent, and to get something to eat. That night we headed down to the dance in the same clothes we had been walking in. I thought they probably won't let us in, dressed like this, but when we got to the pier there was a crowd of people, mainly men, hanging around drinking out of bottles and all dressed in wellies and waterproofs looking like they were straight off the boats. They couldn't have been friendlier, and told us,"If you're going to the dance you better get a carry out, there's no bar." So we headed to the nearest pub and got some booze. By the time we got back they were all inside this huge open building. A ceilidh band was at the far end with a fiddle, an accordion and a set of drums. I looked around and saw that the people were sitting along the sides on fish boxes. This'll do for me, I thought.

We found a spot and sat down. Next thing I knew, a bottle of whisky was passed up the line. I took a swig out of it then passed it on to Alan, who in turn passed it to someone beside him, and then it came back down the line. We returned the compliment, and this went on all night while everybody was up dancing and singing. It was a fantastic night—I'd never laughed so much in ages. All the fishermen were throwing their hats in the air. By the time it finished we were both absolutely steaming drunk.

The tent was pitched up on the hill, somewhere amongst the heather and gorse bushes. Neither of us had considered that it would be dark later, or that there was no path or landmarks to follow, let alone taking into account the condition we might be in. All I remember is us both climbing half way up the hill and falling on top of each other all the way back down again. The torch we had was running out of battery and, by now, we couldn't do anything for laughing anyway. After another couple of attempts we said, "Oh, fuck it!" and spent the night under some bushes.

The following morning when the sun came up, both of us (still half-drunk from the night before) wandered down to the pier to find out what time the next ferry was, and to get some breakfast. Once our heads had cleared a bit we climbed back up the hill, packed up our stuff and got back down in time to see the ferry arriving at the dock.

Most Scots have at some time sung the words "*Speed bonny boat, like a bird on the wing, over the sea to Skye*" from *The Skye Boat Song,* which recalls the escape of Prince Charles Edward Stuart (Bonny Prince Charlie) from the Isle of Uist in the Outer Hebrides to the Isle of Skye, after his defeat at the battle of Culloden in 1746. Other Scottish folk songs describe the outstanding beauty of the Isle of Skye, but none of them prepared me for the sight of the Cuillin Hills rising up from the mist as we approached from the sea—it was breath taking.

We got off the ferry at a port near Armadale and had a long hike to the island's capital, Portree. Surprisingly, the lifts were coming thick and fast and we got there quickly. This time we pitched the tent in a more accessible place on a hill overlooking the harbour. In amongst the trees on the side of the hill we came across a waterfall cascading down the rocks into a pool of clear water. We stripped off and jumped in for a well-earned wash. It was wonderful. We gave the clothes a wash too, and hung them over the rocks to dry. That evening was spent in the pub in Portree before crashing out in our tent, which was really too small for two people in sleeping bags.

In the morning, when I woke up, the floor of the tent was covered in ticks (small blood-sucking insects). I panicked and jumped up, pulling all the tent pegs out in the process, and the tent came down on top of us. If anybody had seen it from the outside, it must have been hilarious, two people fighting each other to get out of a collapsed tent.

It's strange looking back now. This was 1977 when there were no mobile phones, or computers, and we were cut off from the world. Telephone boxes, if you could find one that worked, were our only means of communication and were few and far between. But that's what this was about—getting back to reality and friendship.

A guy by the name of Linnie Paterson once said to me, "You know you're with a true friend when you don't feel you have to make conversation." Alan and I had hours of silence, and also hours of talking about where we came from, going back to the humble beginnings of The Bay City Rollers and the fun we had. We reminisced about the youth clubs and dance halls where we learned by our mistakes, all the hard work and dedication we put in over those early years to achieve that elusive success, and how it all got messed up, and mixed up, by outside influences. There was sadness too that it hadn't worked out as we had planned it when we were teenagers. But both of us agreed we wouldn't change a minute of it.

Leaving Portree and heading north, I had that feeling you get when you've been somewhere that leaves an imprint, and you know you'll be back some day.

The walking was getting much easier, which was just as well because we had a long way to go on narrow, single-track roads and there weren't many cars around. We met some of the nicest people as we were passing by their country cottages. One little old lady had no hesitation in inviting us in for tea and scones. It was heart-warming.

When we reached the top end of Skye, we caught a ferry over to Tarbert on the Isle of Harris (where Harris Tweed originally came from). It was far more remote than the Isle of Skye, but by now we were really enjoying being out in the wilds with the mountains all around, taking turns at walking in front to give each other encouragement. It wouldn't have been the same without the midges and the bites and the drizzle.

The Isle of Harris is connected to the Isle of Lewis, and it was our goal to reach the port of Stornoway on the northeast side of the island. Even with a few lifts along the way, it took us two full days of hard walking. I had a slight sense of disappointment when I caught sight of the town. It meant that our adventure was nearing its end.

We reached Stornoway with a heavy growth of bum fluff on our faces, and a warm feeling in our hearts that we had achieved the status of teuchter. Only when we arrived at Stornoway, gasping for a drink, did we realise that it was Sunday and everything was closed! It was quite normal, back then, for all businesses on the islands to be closed on a Sunday because the population was very religious, in comparison to the mainland.

Wandering up and down the High Street, we looked at every hotel and pub, but we were sorely disappointed to see they were all locked up tight. The streets were deserted, with the exception of one man coming towards us. I stopped him and asked, "Is there nowhere we can get a drink around here?" "Aye, only one place," he said. "Follow me," and he took us round the back of a pub that was all boarded up at the front, and he knocked on the door. When we got inside the place was heaving with people, and they were singing and dancing—it was a real party atmosphere. They made us very welcome and wouldn't even let us buy a drink.

The following morning, hung over and feeling rough, I said to Alan, "I better try and phone my manager in London and let him know where I am." I found a phone box down by the harbour and had a pocket full of change ready.

I got through to the office in London and Charles Armitage answered the phone saying, "Where the hell have you been? I've been trying to contact you for days! There is a meeting set up with the managing director of RCA Records tomorrow. You need to get yourself down here fast. Where are you?" I had to think for a minute before I answered, "You won't believe this, Charles, I'm up in Stornoway in the Outer Hebrides." I came off the phone and explained the situation to Alan that I needed to get myself down to London the following day.

I went down to the ferry ticket office and was told that normally the ferry would be in by now, but due to bad weather a lorry had overturned on the lower deck and they were holding out at sea until the wind died down. Where we were standing it was blowing a gale and the waves were crashing over the harbour wall. It didn't look likely we would get to the mainland that day.

Later on the weather calmed down and the ferry finally arrived, looking a bit battered. The people coming off were a sorry-looking bunch, pale faced and not at all happy. It must have been a hair-raising journey. I don't like sailing much, so I wasn't looking forward to it and, as it was taking a while for them to upright the overturned lorry in the hold, we went for a drink and discussed how I could make it to London for lunchtime the following day.

That ferry trip across from Stornoway to Ullapool was one of the most frightening experiences I've ever had. We were thrown about all over the place, and I honestly thought we were going to sink... we were both so relieved when we caught sight of the mainland.

The plan was to get a bus from Ullapool to Fort William and pick up the car. We would then drive to Alan's house at Dollar, get cleaned up and have a sleep. In the middle of the night I would drive down to my house in Edinburgh, grab some clothes and a suitcase and get out to the airport in time to catch the first shuttle flight to London Heathrow.

Problem was, there *was* no bus to Fort William at that time of night. The only option we had was to get a taxi from Ullapool to Fort William and it cost £35. This was a lot of money in 1977 (approximately £150 in today's money). It was heavy going—we hadn't been working to any time schedule and all of a sudden I was rushing to make a deadline. I got to Alan's house in Dollar, then on to my house in Edinburgh, packed a case and prepared myself for meeting the managing director of RCA.

I got to Edinburgh airport in plenty time, only to find that all flights were cancelled due to gale force winds. I had to phone Charles and cancel the meeting.

I did eventually sign a recording contract with RCA, but I started working on some new material of my own which they had decided wasn't commercial enough for them. They had wanted me to sound more like the Bay City Rollers, who were still selling millions of records around the world, but if I'd wanted that I would have stayed in the band. I recorded a number of songs that the record company presented me with, but my heart wasn't in it. I thought they were rubbish and told them so.

As a separate arrangement altogether with Noel Gay publishing, I had an ongoing songwriting partnership with Don Gould. We were coming up with some really good stuff and we wrote and produced an album for Clodagh Rodgers who had been best known for her hits *Jack In The Box* and *Come Back And Shake Me*.

But that was the only good thing that was happening. My solo career seemed to be going nowhere and my drinking was getting out of control. I was becoming increasingly depressed and thought maybe it was time to get away from the London scene. I was even considering giving up music all together. It had been a very lonely existence working as a solo artist, after having been in a band for so many years. So I decided to move back to Edinburgh, to my mother's house where I felt safe.

I was still in regular contact with Alan Longmuir. We kept each other informed about what was going on and I went to stay with him in Dollar one more time before he rejoined the Rollers on tour. One day that's very clear in my memory is when I was at Alan's, looking round his house at all the gold, silver and platinum records on his walls. Reading the labels, they were for all the songs that I had sung on. It really annoyed me, since I hadn't been credited for any of the songs and not one of the group played on them.

That same morning Alan told me the record company wanted him to release a solo record. He'd told them he had written some songs, but Alan hadn't written a song in his life. Song publishing was worth a lot of money, as you could make as much being the writer of a B-side as you could for an A-side.

I told Alan that I'd been working on a song that would be ideal for him, called *I've Got Songs To Sing You*. I played it to him on the guitar and he loved it. We did a rough demo and he sent it off to the record company. The next thing I know, it was being recorded and produced for Alan by Russ Ballard who most famously was the guitarist and lead singer in the band Argent. His voice can be heard on the hit single *Hold You're Head Up*.

After Ballard left Argent to concentrate on writing and producing, he wrote many hit songs such as *So You Win Again* for Hot Chocolate, *Since You've Been Gone* for Rainbow, and *I Don't Believe In Miracles* for Colin Blunstone.

Some months later I found out that my song *I've Got Songs To Sing You* was released by Bell Records, and on the label it stated "words and music by Alan Longmuir". The song was in the charts in Japan, Germany and other European countries and he never paid me a penny...

I still have the original demo I did of that song.

One of the last things Alan Longmuir said to me was, "We're getting ready to take Arista Records to court for unpaid royalties, and I'm going to make sure it's done right this time. Everyone who is due money will get paid."

CHAPTER TEN

It wasn't long before I was back mixing with the guys in Armadale, outside Edinburgh, but it wasn't the same. Some of them had moved on and there wasn't that feeling of closeness that I had felt before. I was looking for something new in my life.

Even the Edinburgh scene was changing. The sudden impact of heroin arriving on the scene had devastated the lives of some of the people I had known when we were experimenting with cannabis and amphetamines, when it was all good fun. I was hearing stories of friends who had died from overdoses or from injecting bad gear, and others who at one time would have stood back to back, were now stealing from each other. I stayed well clear of it.

There was an American-style bar and restaurant in George Street, in the centre of Edinburgh, called Madogs. I first went there to meet an old friend of mine, Linnie Paterson. He was a popular and respected character in the uptown Edinburgh scene, and I'd met him away back, when I was singing with the Rollers round the clubs and dance halls. He was the lead singer with a group called The Jury who later became the Writing On The Wall. Linnie was one of the best front men and stage performers I've ever seen.

Madogs was the "in" place to go at the time, for those who had money and those who wanted you to think they had money. It was there that I was introduced to cocaine, and the people who supplied it. I loved the place—it was exciting and always full of interesting people. It was frequented by top hairdressers, fashion shop owners, club owners, designers, lawyers, musicians, gangsters, conmen and, most importantly, beautiful women. If you were one of the chosen few you could drink and eat till early morning behind closed doors.

Just around the corner from Madogs, and down a little back street, was a pub called Marr's Bar. It was owned by Archie Marr, the keyboard player with the Rollers when we recorded *Keep On Dancing,* and he'd also appeared on the first Top Of The Pops show we did when the song reached number 9 in the UK charts.

I hadn't seen Archie since he left the band so I was really pleased when I walked in and saw him there. I started to go to Marr's on a regular basis, and Archie and I became good friends again. In fact, it became far too regular, and after closing time in the pubs a crowd of us would usually go on to Buster Browns nightclub till the early hours of the morning.

We even created The Marr's Bar Gang—a whole bunch of people who drank as much as I did and liked to party. Archie had the best jukebox in town, every song was especially chosen by him, and he had impeccable taste and played it very loud. Most of the guys I hung out with were oilrig workers who earned loads of money. They worked two weeks on the rigs followed by two weeks off, which they would spend throwing their hard-earned cash across the bar.

We had some outrageous parties after hours in Marr's Bar, when the doors were locked. There was a crowd of women in the Marr's Bar Gang and quite often we all headed down to the beach at Cramond for a so-called barbecue. We would get there in taxis with no food, just lots of alcohol, and it was all about sex on the beach or in the bushes.

For a long time it was a vicious circle of Marr's Bar, Madogs, Buster Browns, booze, drugs and women. I had a good bit of money at that time, but I was spending far too much. It was in the days before debit cards, and I cashed so many cheques behind the bar I lost count.

Many mornings I would fall out of someone else's bed and head round to Madogs at 12 noon, opening time, looking terrible and feeling hungover. Dave behind the bar would fill up a glass with Jack Daniels and say, "Breakfast is served." They never used measures in Madogs, just poured it into the glass. If you were one of the crowd you were well looked after.

135

But it was starting to get to me. I was getting a reputation as a drunk and my personality was changing, I was becoming aggressive when I had too much. One guy I had become very friendly with, by the name of Charlie, pulled me aside and said to me, "Listen, you're a really nice guy when you're sober, but I don't want you around me when you're drunk." Apparently I had been abusive to his friends. It was beginning to frighten me. I didn't know which drink would be the one to put me over the edge into blackout where I wouldn't remember anything that happened afterwards.

It was about this time that I met Sheila. I had met her before, way back in the early days of the Rollers, as she was a friend of Keith Norman's, our first keyboard player. I was at a club called Tiffany's when I met her again, after all these years. She was there with Linnie Paterson's wife, Alison.

We just met up a few times to begin with, and sometimes she came to Marr's Bar for a drink. I had been seeing another girl, off and on, for some time. Mandy worked in one of the top hair-dressing salons in Edinburgh and knew a lot of the uptown set.

I wanted to call it off, but I hadn't had the nerve to tell her.

Meanwhile, I had arranged to have a drink with Sheila in Charlie Parker's, a bar opposite Madogs. It was a Friday night and the place was heaving. The bar was in the basement and had an open staircase coming down from the ground floor, where you could look right over the people below to the bar at the far side. It was so busy, we had to fight our way through the crowd to get to the bar. I managed to get us a drink, and had just turned round to hand it to Sheila when I saw Mandy coming down the stairs. She looked right across at me, and it was like the parting of the waves as she pushed everybody out the way, heading towards me. She slapped me hard across the face then walked away. Everybody saw it. I turned to Sheila and said, "Who was that?" She just gave me a dirty look.

It wasn't the best start, but I worked on it over the next few weeks.

One of The Marr's Bar Gang was a guy called Tommy Hall. His family owned garages in and around Edinburgh and were extremely wealthy, before Tommy gambled and drank away most of the money. He would walk into the bookies and put a £1,000 on a horse without even thinking about it. Tommy always had wads of cash in his pocket, and lots of hangers-on ready to spend it. He was a loveable rogue, an interesting character, with a mischievous smile on his face. But, as time went on, his family cut him off before he lost all the money and Tommy got himself into difficulties.

His solution to the problem was to become a drug dealer. He disappeared for a while, then one afternoon I was in Marr's, talking to Archie, when I looked out the window and saw Tommy in a doorway on the opposite side of the street with another guy. Tommy had a carrier bag between his legs, bulging at the seams, with KLM printed on it. He had another carrier bag in his hands that he was holding open, showing the other guy its contents.

He finished his discussion and walked across the road with his two large carrier bags. The bar was busy with the regular crowd of people and Tommy, in his usual fashion, walked in and shouted "Archie—let's get the party started!"

His two KLM carrier bags had shoeboxes in them, full up with blocks of cannabis. Tommy planted them on the bar and pulled out a large slab, holding it up for everyone to see as if it was a bar of chocolate. Then he started biting bits off and handing them round. I couldn't believe my eyes. I grabbed him, "Tommy, don't be so stupid. Policemen drink in here! You're going to get caught." He was so full of the drink, and wallowing in the attention, that he just turned back to me and growled, "I don't give a fuck." A few days later I heard he was banged up in Saughton Prison.

Some time later that year I was in Marr's Bar as usual, hanging out with the gang, when Linda Rivers came in one afternoon. She was a regular—a crazy mixed-up kid who could drink like a fish. I met her in the bar and she said, "I hear Tommy Hall is out of prison." Just as she said it he walked in the door. "Archie—let's get the party started!" were his first words, and off it went. He had a crowd around him all afternoon, laughing at his stories of prison life, but I could see that something about him had changed. He tried to rekindle the old spirit but he looked old and tired. He might have still been making people laugh, but he wasn't the same person.

Tommy told us a story about a real hardened criminal that he met and befriended on the exercise yard. He said, "This guy was doing life for raping and murdering an eighty-two year old woman, but a nicer person you couldn't meet."

Tommy was only out a matter of weeks before he was arrested again in possession of a large quantity of drugs and, convicted of drug dealing for the second time, he died in Saughton Prison, on the exercise yard, of a massive heart attack.

Meanwhile, Sheila and I got into a full-blown relationship. She was staying in a flat above the Greek Embassy in Regent Terrace, at the east end of Edinburgh city-centre, with two other girls while I was still staying at my mother's house at Drum Brae.

The girls decided to have a party so, of course, I spread the word around all my drinking pals. I arrived at their address straight from the pub and rang the bell. Someone let me in, without asking who I was, and I walked into a large hallway with a wide, ornate staircase winding all the way up to the third floor. I could hear loud music and made my way up the stairs. When I got to the second floor I heard cheering and singing. Opening the double doors I walked into a party where guests dressed in colourful clothes were dancing round in a circle to loud music, so I joined in.

I had gate-crashed a Greek wedding in the rooms of the Embassy. People were handing me drinks and food before an official-looking man (in what I thought was fancy dress) asked if I was a relative. "No," I said, "I just walked in." I was very eloquently asked to leave.

I made my way up to the party on the top floor, but could hardly get in the door. The girls had expected around twenty to thirty people to turn up, instead it seemed like hundreds of people were crammed into the flat, and down a back staircase as well. The party went on until the early hours and Sheila and I spent most of the next day in bed.

The following morning, on the front page of the newspapers, was a photograph of a red bucket on the top of the Greek Embassy's flagpole with the headline, "Anti-Communist protest at Greek Embassy." The truth, though, was that two of my drunken friends found the bucket in the street, climbed up the flagpole, and stuck it on the top.

Sheila and the other girls' tenancy agreements were terminated shortly after.

Davie Paton, who had at one time been a member of the Rollers, had gone on to have worldwide success with his band Pilot. He'd married his longtime partner, Mary, and moved to London where they brought up their two daughters Sara and Katie. I hadn't seen him since those early days at Craighall Studios so I was really surprised to get a phone call from him saying he was back living in Edinburgh and it would be nice to meet up. I was delighted. He came and picked me up in his silver convertible E-type Jaguar, my favourite car at the time.

We became friends again and he introduced me to a guy called John Turner. John was a classically trained pianist who had been working with a Manchester band called Sweet Chariot around the cabaret clubs, before joining Demis Roussos and touring around Europe. John met his future wife, Ann, while on tour, when she was one of Demis's backing singers. (Demis Roussos was a Greek singer who had had some success with his band, Aphrodite's Child, in which Vangelis and Loukas Sideras were also members. Demis' solo career took off with the song *Forever And Ever* when it hit the top of the charts in many countries.)

John Turner's father owned the Palladium Theatre in Edinburgh's Fountainbridge area. His circle of friends included Rikki Fulton and Jack Milroy (Francie and Josie), Chic Murray, and Stanley Baxter. When I first met John, the theatre was closed to the public and John had a recording studio set up in one of the rooms. John wasn't a singer, and asked me if I would put the vocals on some of his songs. We've been friends ever since.

Through John I met Mike Hood, a businessman selling stationery and office equipment, and in his spare time he played keyboards with a band in a social club. His ambition was to start up his own recording studio but had no idea how to go about it, so asked me to get involved.

We started with a small studio in the extension on Mike's house and opened it up commercially. It did so well that we looked for bigger premises and found a suitable, disused warehouse in West Saville Terrace on the south side of Edinburgh. We split up the building into eight rehearsal rooms and a recording studio, the very first of its kind. I designed the studio and fitted all the equipment. The idea was that Mike would deal with all paperwork, accounts and bookings, while I would run the studio.

We had a good relationship for a long time and the studio was very successful. I recorded and produced a lot of great music there, including all the original demos for Billy Mackenzie of The Associates before they hit the big time in London. (Sadly, Billy took his own life in January 1997.) Simple Minds rehearsed and recorded at the studio, and we even had The Bay City Rollers rehearsing there in preparation for a tour! The place was rocking with young musicians—if they weren't rehearsing or recording, they would meet up and play pool or just sit around soaking up the atmosphere.

Mike had a young assistant working in his stationery shop. Callum wasn't a musician but he loved music and asked if he could sit in on some sessions. He soon became my assistant in the studio, and also my drinking partner. I introduced him to Marr's Bar, and Madogs, and the gang... Because I spent so much time in these places Callum became a good friend to Sheila, and he would accompany her when she came to meet me, in case I was drunk.

Sheila witnessed my alcoholism spiralling out of control, and began to talk to me about getting some help. I admitted, for the first time, that I couldn't stop and was ready to talk to someone about it. So I phoned up Alcoholics Anonymous and went to my first meeting in Cockburn Street.

I was quite shocked by it. There were a lot of ex-seamen at the meeting, telling stories about when they had no money for alcohol they would drink methylated spirits and even swallow shoe polish that had alcohol in it. It was clear that some of them were suffering from wet brain syndrome (brain damage caused by long-term excessive alcohol consumption). I read the Twelve Step programme and the Twelve Traditions of AA which were displayed on two large posters pinned to the wall on either side of the top table, where the chairperson and the alcoholic (sharing his story) were sitting. What made me most uncomfortable was the word God all over the walls.

As it went round the room everyone spoke about God and a higher power and I thought, "This isn't for me, it's a religious organisation." I came out of the meeting and went straight to the pub. I remember standing with a drink in my hand talking to a stranger and telling him all about this place I had just been to, and giving every excuse under the sun why I wouldn't be going back. I wasn't as bad as these people. I told Sheila about my experience, emphasising the religious aspect, saying it was only for people who believed in God.

Sheila came up with another idea, The Council for Alcoholism, which was an organisation run by the local authority. You had to make an appointment to see someone who was not a recovering alcoholic their self, but was trained to give counselling to people who had a drink problem. So I made an appointment, and sat with a very nice woman who listened to my story and said, "You definitely have a problem. We can help you deal with the reasons why you're drinking, and teach you ways to become a social drinker again." I liked the sound of that. I went to three of four sessions with that nice lady, who did everything she could to help me—but I was still drinking in between.

I wanted to be told I could become a social drinker because I was terrified of being told I couldn't drink again. Off I went with the knowledge I had gained, and a promise to Sheila that I would not drink any spirits. From now on I would stick to beer, and life would be a lot better. I know now that an alcoholic can never become a social drinker. I'd never understood how anyone could go out for a drink and have one glass or two then say, "That's it, I've had enough, I'm off home now." I could never get enough because one drink set up the compulsion to have more. There's an old saying in AA: one's too many and a hundred's not enough.

The studio was still doing a roaring trade. I turned up for every recording session and Callum remained a loyal friend. He and I spent a lot of time together, and he knew I was in serious trouble with alcohol. I felt I was leading him down the wrong path.

Mike Hood and I discussed having a holiday. He suggested that we go away somewhere together, meaning Mike and his family along with Sheila and I. We looked at places abroad and settled for the Greek Island of Corfu. We decided Jacky Garcia could look after the place while we were on holiday. A Spanish drummer, Jacky already helped us out at the studio, sometimes staying in a makeshift room above the control room as a night watchman.

We booked the holiday and in no time were flying off to Corfu. I was terrified of flying, so to get me on the plane I sneaked off and had a few large ones at the airport. Then on the plane I had a few more. When we eventually got to our apartments, sitting just back from the sea front and looking out over a beautiful bay, the landlord was waiting with the keys. Sheila and I got our cases into the apartment and unpacked our clothes, then went down to Mike and Louise's apartment where Sheila helped their two boys sort out their stuff.

While she was busy, I went out for a wander and found a bar hidden away between the trees in a back street. The place was empty and the barman was standing leaning on the bar. The first thing I noticed was a bottle of Gold Tequila staring at me from the shelf. I got talking to the barman and we both started knocking them back. Then a couple of guys on holiday came into the bar and joined in, buying round for round.

It went on until late that night, and I ended up so out of it I couldn't find my way back to the apartment. Instead I found myself down at the beach, walked along a boat jetty and fell off the side into the deep water. I could easily have drowned. I remember being in the water and not knowing which way was up. I had no idea what time it was, but it was dark. I pulled myself out of the water, crawled onto the beach, and fell asleep.

I woke up when it got light and found that I had both keys for the apartment in my pocket. Sheila had had to spend the night on Mike and Louise's couch. I had spoiled the holiday for everyone because after this Sheila was on edge the whole time and was watching my every move. I didn't drink again until the day we were coming home. Or, at least, they thought I didn't… but I had some hidden away.

Shortly after we got back from the holiday, Mike was told by the owners of the warehouse, where the studio was, that they had sold the building for development. He had two months to find other premises. By this time I was getting tired of the erratic hours at the studio, and I think Mike was ready to do something else too. We'd had a good two years at it and it was time for a change.

Sheila's grandfather lived in a flat in Bruntsfield, and when he passed away her uncle James inherited the property. He lived abroad at the time, but wanted to keep the flat for his retirement, so we rented it from him and moved in together.

When we moved in I was worried that it wouldn't last very long. I was kidding myself on that I could control the drinking, but in reality it controlled me. I had treated her very badly in the past and wanted to make it up to her, so I asked her to marry me. As expected, she wasn't going to make a commitment right away and said, "I'll have to think about it." She took her time, but in the end said, "Yes."

I wanted to make the wedding a bit different and suggested we get married in period costume. I really liked the style of dress from the late 1700s, the Robert Burns era. The guy I was closest to at the time was Jim from Armadale, so I asked him to be my best man. The first thing he said to me was, "Are you sure you're doing the right thing?" I was quite taken aback by that.

An important thing to do was to organise the clothes. I had a friend who worked at the Lyceum Theatre's costume department and there I found exactly what I was looking for: Robert Burns-style outfits with knee high leather boots to fit both Jim

143

and I. Sheila found the perfect dress in a period style. Off-white, high neckline, tight fitting to suit her slim figure, with a bonnet to match the dress and a parasol fashioned in the same material.

For the ceremony we chose the Haymarket Registrar's Office, and the date would be the 25th April 1981. The wedding reception afterwards would be held at the Turnhouse Golf Club, where Sheila's father Harold had been a member for many years.

The next thing I had to do was to introduce my best man, Jim, to Sheila's family. I arranged to meet Jim and take him to Harold's house, but Jim turned up the worse for wear, having been on the sauce all day, and was quite drunk. I took him to the house anyway. At first the meeting was quite jolly and light-hearted, but soon it descended into a heated argument with Jim insulting my future father-in-law. Harold retaliated, and I had to ask Jim to leave.

One week before the wedding, I got a phone call from Jim saying he couldn't be my best man. I didn't say anything, just put the phone down. What was I going to do now? Everything was organised. I already had the costumes but now I had no best man and only a week to go. I put Callum on the spot, and asked him if he would step in at the last minute... I was so relieved when he said he would do it. One problem though—he was a completely different size to Jim, who was tall and slim, while Callum was shorter and bulkier. The clothes didn't fit him. We had to pin them together as best we could.

On the day of the wedding everything was going smoothly— the ceremony at the Registrar's Office was just lovely. Sheila looked amazing, and happy, and we headed off to the Golf Club for the reception. I had invited a lot of people, mainly involved in music, but also some friends from Marr's Bar and Madogs whom I thought I could trust. I was unaware that they were smoking cannabis round the back of the building, and snorting cocaine in the toilets. Some of my so-called friends were feed-ing the photographer with booze until he was out of his face. To make things worse, we had planned to have the photographs taken on the 18th green, but it started snowing. It was April— that wasn't supposed to happen.

After the speeches and the meal were finished the tables were cleared away and, as I was walking about talking to people, I looked round to what was going to be the dance floor. Linnie Paterson was in the middle of the floor, completely stoned, with Sheila's wedding bonnet on his head, the matching parasol fully opened, doing some crazy dance in front of everybody. I just thought, "This whole thing is turning into a farce."

When we got the photographs back a few days later they were all out of focus and squint, with some so dark you couldn't see who was in them. Harold was not happy at all, and I felt so sorry for Sheila, so we decided the best thing to do was to get the costumes back, get dressed up again and take new photographs with a different photographer.

Sheila's mother, Phia, did her best to make light of the whole thing, bless her. She was a wonderful woman. One of the best things that happened on the wedding day was during the speeches, when Phia stood up and insisted on making her own— and it was the best of the day. She said nothing else matters: the only important thing is that you find happiness. Her wedding present to us was two tickets to Benidorm in Spain for our honeymoon. The flights weren't until the following week, which was just as well because my friend John Turner was getting married to Ann, the girl he met on tour with Demis Roussos.

We attended their wedding and I asked John what he was doing about their honeymoon. He said, "We're not having one, we've been living together for ages. We don't need a honeymoon." John was well known for being very tight with money, even though he wasn't short of a bob or two. I used to wind him up about it all the time. I said to him, "Don't be so tight. You need to take Ann away somewhere. How about coming to Benidorm with us?" He relented and I got them booked onto the same flight, and into the same hotel—we all went on honeymoon together!

Nearly the whole time we were there it poured down with rain, the beaches were deserted, and the hotel food was terrible. We were stuck in the hotel most of the time. Benidorm was everything I hate about a holiday resort, but we did try to make the most of it.

Back home, I started up a small building business, hoping that it would keep me out of the pub and change my life, and it did for a while. I built the business up and got on the "approved contractors" list with Edinburgh Council. I started out with one employee and before I knew it I had ten employees, as well as sub-contractors, all working flat out. With Sheila being the manager of Dorothy Perkins (a ladies' fashion shop) on Princes Street we were doing well.

With Harold's help we'd bought our first flat, a small one-bedroom, second floor flat in Roseburn. We had a belated house-warming party, with far too many people crammed into the living room and kitchen, but it was a great night nonetheless, and went on till the wee small hours. Callum stayed the night and slept in the boxroom on a camp bed. In the morning Sheila and I were wakened by smoke belching along the hall and into our bedroom! I jumped out of bed and ran through to the kitchen, choking with the smoke and hardly able to see. Opening the window to let the smoke out I found the curtains were gone—all that was left was blackened remains on the curtain pole. Lying in the sink, in front of the window, was a burnt out grill pan, still smouldering.

There was no sign of Callum... he had got up to make some breakfast, managed to set the grill alight, thrown the burning grill pan into the sink, set fire to the curtains in the process, and then run away.

Callum was very accident-prone. He once invited Sheila and I, and his girlfriend Fiona, to a "fondue" dinner party at his parent's house in Murrayfield, while they were away on holiday. His parents had some very nice antique furniture, and Callum placed the fondue set on top of a beautiful mahogany cabinet. I had never seen a fondue set before. It had a burner underneath a metal dish, which Callum was topping up with methylated spirits while the burner was alight. He didn't notice that the spirit was running down the bottle and onto the cabinet, then down the front of the cabinet onto the Axminster carpet. I watched in disbelief as a blue flame trailed all the way down the cabinet and set alight to the carpet!

I had never been a gambler, in fact I despised it—the most I would do was put some coins in a fruit machine. A young painter called Chris was working for me, and he was addicted to horse racing. Everytime I dropped him off after work, it was outside a bookie's shop. "What are you doing losing all your hard-earned money in there?" I said to him. "It's a mug's game." He laughed and replied, "You should try it sometime, you might like it." "No chance," I said emphatically, "I'm not that stupid."

But, one day, I went into the bookies out of curiosity. The punters were shouting at the screens when their horses lost, frantically writing out other bets to try and get their money back. I didn't even know how to put a bet on, so I asked Chris how to do it. On discovering that if you put money on a favourite the odds were very small, I said to Chris, "That's no good. There must be a way to win more than that!" So he explained how to put on a "roll-up" by picking three or four horses in different races, and if the first one wins the returns are put on the second horse, and so on.

So I picked three horses, got Chris to write out the line for me, and I put £5 on it. I watched each horse come in first, and I won £360. I declared, "This is easy!" Chris laughed and said, "That's just beginners luck."

I wasn't really drawn into the bookie's shops again, until much later. But with my addictive personality, it wasn't long before I was putting more into fruit machines than I was ever going to get out of them.

It was now 1982 and I hadn't had any contact with Tam Paton for six or seven years, although I had heard in 1979, through the jungle drums, that he'd been sacked as manager of the Bay City Rollers.

So when I read in the papers that he had been convicted of gross indecency with young boys, and given an eighteen-month jail sentence, I really was stunned. I'd heard so many stories about Tam Paton, some quite shocking, but I assumed they were gross exaggerations and gossip, and I never listen to gossip—I prefer facts and evidence. I'm reminded of a story my father used to tell about being in the army during the war: a message was sent from the front line saying, "Send reinforcements. We're going to advance." By the time it got back to the base it said, "Send three and fourpence. We're going to a dance."

With the success of my building business and Sheila's salary we bought a house at Riversdale in Edinburgh, looking onto the Water of Leith. I really wanted us to have a baby now, and spoke to Sheila about it. She was scared, as she knew I was unstable, and she said I would have to stop drinking first.

Around this time I had a big, blue, open back truck that I used for carrying building materials. Quite often, when I finished work, I would drive it to Marr's Bar and park it outside. The gang used to call it The Ferrari. One night, after a few hours in the pub, a crowd of us were heading to Buster Brown's nightclub and I stupidly said, "Come on, jump in the truck, I'll drive us up there." Three people were in the open back of the truck, while four of us were in the cabin. I drove all the way through the town and didn't even notice there was a police car following me, but when I stopped outside Buster Brown's they pounced. I was breathalysed and found to be three times over the limit, arrested, and charged with drink driving. In court, I was fined £200, and banned from driving for three and a half years.

Consequently, in order to keep the business going, I employed a driver to take me round all the building works. Some mornings I was so ill that Jimmy, my driver, would just run me quickly round the jobs to make sure the men were out working, then I'd give him his instructions for the day and get him to drop me off in Leith where the bars were open early in the morning.

My tolerance for alcohol had gone up the hill and was now coming down the other side. I was so dependent on it, now, that I had to keep topping up or I'd go into withdrawal. There was no fun in it any more, it was just survival. I never set out for oblivion, but I'd keep feeding my addiction until I went into blackout. I would be found unconscious in doorways, or I'd get arrested and locked up in police cells, more often than not for my own safety, and I wouldn't remember anything about it. I lost days on end, sometimes. But when Sheila was upset and crying, and threatening to leave, I would be saying to myself, "It can't be that bad," although I had very little recollection.

Callum and Fiona were members of the Murrayfield Tennis Club and Sheila wanted to be a part of that social scene too. To become a member you needed to be introduced by someone else who was already a member, so we were invited to a wine evening at the club. Sheila asked me to be on my best behaviour and I arranged to come home early so that we could all go round to the Tennis Club together—but I spent the afternoon in a bar somewhere and, by the time I got home, Sheila had already left with Fiona and Callum.

I got cleaned up and walked round to the club on my own. When I walked into the clubhouse I saw the lady members all dolled up in Laura Ashley dresses, holding wine glasses delicately between their fingers, their pinkies sticking out, while the men stood around in grey suits with striped ties, talking business, and all looking down their noses at this long-haired, casually dressed, drunken lout—yours truly.

I walked to the middle of the floor, took all my clothes off, and proceeded to streak around the tennis court. When I came back in they were all putting their coats on and leaving. Sheila was mortified, Callum thought it was hilarious. Needless to say we didn't receive an invitation to join.

Shortly after that it was our wedding anniversary and Sheila begged me to stay sober so we could have a nice dinner together. But I just couldn't stop myself—on the way home that day I picked up a bottle of Champagne, but I was late arriving back and was well-oiled, as usual. By the time I got home she had already packed her bags and gone to stay with her parents.

I couldn't find my key, so I smashed the front window with the Champagne bottle—that's all I can remember. The next morning, when I came downstairs, I found the living room trashed. Broken glass was everywhere. Furniture had been thrown all over the place. My Pioneer stereo, my pride and joy, was smashed all over the floor.

Someone must have broken in during the night, I thought, so I phoned the police. I let them in and they looked around, found the empty Champagne bottle on the floor, discovered that nothing was missing, and deduced that I had done it myself. I can only assume that at the time I was punishing myself by destroying something I treasured, but it was erased from my memory.

It was the same cycle over and over again. Every day I faced the challenge of supply and demand. I had hidden bottles in various places around the house although, one day, when I went looking for them, I found I had already used them all up. Then I remembered I'd stashed a bottle in the bushes on the other side of the river, strategically hidden near a bench on the footpath. I walked along the road, over the bridge, and down the path to the hiding place. I was so relieved when I saw the bag was still there, until I reached under the bush and pulled the bag out to discover it was empty. Someone had found it and taken my bottle of vodka.

Eventually, I had an experience that really made me accept I was in the gutter…

I'd woken up flinching from a sharp pain in my side. It was dark and I could feel the rough hairs of a blanket over my head. My right arm and leg were completely numb, and the side of my face was pressed hard against a concrete floor. I slowly pulled back the blanket and screwed up my eyes against the light—I could just make out the words "Ernie was here" scratched into the surface of grey-painted brickwork. A plank of wood ran along the full length of the wall, sloping down towards the floor to make it uncomfortable to sit on for any length of time, and I recognized the small, barred window that was too high up the wall to see out of. I muttered to myself, disgusted and defeated, "Oh no, not again… police cells."

What had I done this time? I had no memory of how I got there, nor why, and had no idea of the time, day or night. The blue, padded jacket I had on was filthy and my trousers were wet. When I exposed my feet I was wearing old, worn sandals with no socks. I was cold, very cold, and started shaking uncontrollably.

I crawled over to the door, hardly noticing the other two bodies in the cell: one was propped up against the wall, beside the exposed toilet bowl splattered with vomit; the other was lying comatose in the corner, wrapped in the familiar grey, horsehair blanket. I reached the door and banged as hard as I could, but no one came. A loud voice was shouting down the corridor, "Turnkey, turnkey!" over and over again, interlaced with, "You fucking bastards!" and deep, resonating thuds that sounded like a boot against a door. I found a button on the wall to the right-hand side of the steel door, and I pressed it repeatedly. There was a distant ringing but it got no response.

My shaking was getting so bad that I couldn't control my hands, and my clothes were already soaked through with sweat that stank of body odour and alcohol. I kept banging the door and ringing the bell for what seemed like eternity until, eventually, a small sliding panel opened at eyelevel and a face appeared. I could see a white shirt and black epaulettes with raised silver numbers across the top of his uniform. He looked angry at being disturbed and growled impatiently, "Yes?" "I'm an alcoholic," I said begging for sympathy, "I've got to have a drink... Please... I need to have a drink." The panel slammed shut in my face.

By now I was familiar to the police, and as usual, when I was sober, I was very ashamed and apologetic for my abuse and behaviour. This time there was to be no court appearance, how-ever. Instead, they took me to a room where a police doctor was waiting to talk to me. He told me about a Doctor Chick at the Royal Edinburgh Hospital's alcohol dependency unit and said I should see my own doctor about a referral as soon as possible.

When they released me that morning they gave me back all the personal belongings they'd taken away before locking me up—these included my socks and belt, and also a half bottle of vodka.

The police station was in the High Street. I left it and walked round the corner to a doorway. I hadn't even bothered to put my socks on, I still had them in my pocket. I stuffed the vodka bottle into a sock, so that no one could see what I was drinking, and swallowed the whole lot down as quickly as I could.

How my life had deteriorated so quickly. It didn't seem very long ago that I was singing in front of thousands of fans and making hit records with The Bay City Rollers, appearing on Top Of The Pops and other television shows, touring all over Europe, doing radio interviews, photo shoots and taking part in recording sessions with world-class musicians.

I walked around the streets for what seemed like hours, completely lost in despair. When I found myself in Morrison Street at Haymarket I nearly walked right into a guy washing the pavement outside a chip shop—it was Eric, an old drinking pal of mine. He saw the state I was in and said, "Why don't you come to an AA meeting with me? I'll be going on Wednesday to one at Palmerston Place." He wrote down all the details on a piece of paper and handed it to me.

I hadn't seen Eric for a long time, and didn't know he had been sober for a year or so. I phoned up Sheila and told her what had happened. She said that if I could show her I was really determined this time, she would move back to our house.

CHAPTER ELEVEN

The Alcoholics Anonymous meeting was in the basement of Palmerston Church. I got there about an hour too early and walked back and forward, up and down the street until it was time. I watched people arrive one by one and go down the stairs, but before I could go in I had to make sure there was no one in the street, as they might have recognised me. How crazy was that? I was more concerned about being seen going into an AA meeting than I was about being found lying in the street or in a doorway.

I was surprised to find that I already knew some people at the meeting, people I had drunk with many times. One of them actually said to me, "I wondered how long it would take you to get here!"

I'd had quite a lot to drink that day, and wasn't really in a fit state to take it all in, but I did remember meeting a man who had been two years sober with the help of AA. I couldn't wait to tell Sheila about it, but she seemed more interested in Coronation Street on the TV. I told her about the man who was two years sober and she replied, "Two years? I was hoping you would meet somebody that was ten years sober." I shared this exchange at the next meeting. The response I got was, "Why should she believe you this time? You've probably told her a hundred times before that you're going to stop, that you'll never do it again." They were absolutely right.

During my first AA meeting I met Alec, an older gentleman who immediately took me aside and said, "If you're an alcoholic, this is the place for you. It's kept me sober. All you have to do is come regularly to meetings, shut your mouth, and open your ears." As it turned out, Alec was over twenty years sober. He was a very small man, with a slightly hunched back and a bald head, smartly dressed in a suit and tie, but almost crippled with osteoarthritis. The fingers on his hands were bent and twisted, and he had trouble walking. He took me under his wing, and in time I got to know him very well. Sometimes I could see he was in a lot of pain, yet he was one of the funniest people I have ever met. I remember being at a meeting one night when some people were moaning about how terrible life was since they had stopped drinking. Alec stood up and said forcefully, "If you're not happy coming to AA, just you go out and get pissed—then come back and tell us how good it was! Otherwise, stop moaning, and get on with the business of getting sober!"

I had only been to a few meetings when Sheila announced that she was pregnant. Of course I was delighted. Maybe this would be the turning point.

It was the hardest thing I've ever done, but I was doing okay. I went to a meeting every day and sometimes even twice a day. They had them all over the town at lunchtimes and in the evenings. The common saying in AA is "a day at a time". Well, for me, when I was struggling, it was an hour at a time! Having the phone numbers of other members I could speak to helped me, and I stayed completely abstinent for six months, everything around me getting better.

But, mentally, I seemed to be getting worse instead of better. I had no concentration. When I tried to read a book I would get to the end of a line and forget what I had read, and have to go over it again. I was disorientated a lot of the time and could hardly hold a conversation—I really thought I must have done some irreparable damage to myself.

One Wednesday night, at my regular meeting, an American guy walked in and was asked to share his story at the top table. He spoke about how his life was before he drank when he was a doctor by profession. Then what life was like after he drank and he'd lost everything. He'd had the same problems as I was experiencing and had discovered he was suffering from Post Acute Withdrawal symptoms. He told us severe alcohol abuse can cause lesions in the brain, which take time to heal, and it would take a long time to get over it. What a relief it was to hear that I wasn't going crazy after all. I now had a hook to hang it on and within another couple of months I started to feel a lot better.

Sheila and I were getting on well, the bump was developing nicely and I had just managed to pull my business back from the brink of bankruptcy, when I picked up a drink and all hell broke loose again.

Why did I do it? I had dropped off going to as many meetings and had stopped speaking to people on the phone. I was telling everyone that I was fine, when I wasn't. It didn't last long, just a couple of weeks, but it took everything right back to the start again.

I struggled off and on, right up to when Sheila went into labour and was rushed into the Western General Hospital. It was a long labour, right through the night, but I was there the whole time, and present at the birth. I have to say that most of it was extremely unpleasant, but when I finally held my daughter Sarah in my arms it became the most wonderful experience, and something every father should go through.

She was born on the 1st September 1985, a Virgo like her dad. Regrettably, I used it as an excuse to go out and celebrate. I turned up drunk at the hospital the following day and was escorted out of the building.

The following year is a bit of a blur. I had gone back to AA and told my story. I was never judged by anyone there—we were all at the meetings for the same reasons. I got nothing but support, but I still couldn't manage to stay sober for more than a few weeks, after which I'd be off again on a drinking binge.

It got really bad when Sarah was about a year old. Sheila just had enough. On top of the drinking, I had started gambling quite heavily, and she noticed large sums of money coming out of our account. She needed to get away from it and one day I came home to an empty house. I phoned round everyone we knew but no one would tell me anything. Eventually Sheila's dad Harold let me know where they had gone—Sheila had taken Sarah with her down to London, to stay with a close friend she'd known since her school days.

155

The next day I jumped on a train to King's Cross in London. On the way down I hit the buffet car and bought a dozen miniature bottles of vodka. I went back to my seat and shared them with a bunch of guys sitting beside me and when I got to King's Cross I went straight into the nearest pub.

Sheila's friend lived in Beaconsfield with her husband, Jack, and two adopted children. I had been there once before, so I thought I would be able to find the place easily enough. Beaconsfield was in Buckinghamshire, some twenty-five miles from London, and all I had to do was to catch a train. But by the time I left the pub the last train had gone, so I jumped in a taxi instead. When we got into Beaconsfield, the taxi driver asked me for the address, which I didn't have, but I had a rough idea where it was from the town centre. We drove around for ages, until eventually he said, "Look, I've got to get back to London," and he dropped me off in the town center.

Then I did something I would never have done had I been sober… I phoned the police and made up a story about my daughter being ill and needing to find the house she was staying at. A police car arrived at the telephone box with two policemen in it. I described the house and its surroundings and at last they dropped me off at what I thought was the right house.

It was dark. I walked up a long driveway to the door of the house and rang the bell. A very irate man answered the door in his dressing gown and told me the house I was looking for was next door. As soon as I walked up the right driveway I recognised the house, but all the lights were out. I pressed their bell and a sound like a loud, old-fashioned clanger was surely going to wake the whole neighbourhood! I saw lights come on upstairs, then downstairs, and Jack opened the door in his dressing gown. Looking past him, into the hallway, I saw Sheila in her nightdress, halfway down the stairs, with a terrified look on her face. Jack said, "You'd better come in." They didn't spend any time on niceties, they just showed me straight to the spare room.

The following morning, when I sobered up, I was full of remorse and apologies but they seemed to fall on deaf ears. I could feel I wasn't welcome. They had arranged a garden party that afternoon for all their friends and everyone, including Sheila, was running around preparing food. I offered my help to set up the tables in the garden, but got no response.

It was a very hot summer day, not a cloud in the sky. Walking around the garden it was immaculate, just as I expected it to be. The grass was cut to perfection with the edges perfectly defined. This was the kind of people they were—a place for everything, and everything in its place.

As the morning progressed, I was sinking fast. This addiction knows no bounds and gives no favours. I grew more and more desperate for a drink. When I started shaking and sweating I withdrew to the lounge and sat there on my own.

Two-by-two their guests began to arrive, and were shown straight out into the garden. I wasn't in a fit state to meet anybody, and sat on a couch at the far end of the room looking out through the French doors thinking, "I'm an alien, I shouldn't be here. Maybe I'll just disappear and leave them alone."

I noticed a drinks cabinet, full of bottles, against the wall beside the French doors, and I decided to try and get to it without anyone seeing me. I crawled along the floor as close to the wall as I could, and opened the glass door of the cabinet. I didn't care what was in the bottles, I opened each one in turn, and drank just enough out of each one so as not to be too noticeable, then crawled back along the floor and sat back down on the couch.

When the alcohol got into my system I started to feel normal again and ready to go out and introduce myself. Sheila knew right away that I had found alcohol somewhere because I was a different person and ready to join the party.

Sheila's friend (also called Sheila) had completely ignored me all day and had gone upstairs to get changed. She and Jack were real snobs who loved to impress, and most of the people they had invited were very wealthy. When she came back down from her bedroom, all dressed up in a floral blouse and yellow, knee-length shorts, I noticed she still had a label hanging out the back. I was about to tell her when I noticed that it said "Oxfam" on it—she must have bought them out of the charity shop. I let her walk around amongst her guests with the label in full view until Sheila pulled her aside and told her. She was mortified.

Sarah was only a year and nine months old and, thankfully, oblivious to what was going on. The next day, I suggested taking her out in her buggy down to the shops to get the papers. I found a pub with a beer garden and quickly threw down a couple of straight doubles, then went into the shop and bought the papers, along with a bottle of vodka. I stopped at a park bench on the way back to the house, with Sarah sitting in her buggy, and drank straight from the bottle, then hid the rest of it in the bushes. This was a step too far... even for me. To be in charge of my one-year-old daughter, and not be in a fit state to look after her—I couldn't live with that.

As soon as we got back to Edinburgh I went straight to an AA meeting and threw myself right into their Twelve-Step programme. I had a shaky start, and I fell off the wagon a couple of times, but once I got the message, I didn't drink again for ten years.

My business was in serious trouble due to my neglect. I needed to work hard to get it back on a stable footing.

Sheila's mother and father lived in a bungalow further up the street from where we lived in Riversdale. It was a strange mix of houses around there. On one side of the road were a number of prefabricated houses built just after the war, while on the other side, between conventionally built bungalows, were two experimental houses, one of which was up for sale. These two houses were of a timber frame construction, with pressed steel panels fixed to the external face of the timber frame, and as this was not a recognised construction technique, the houses were difficult to sell, being un-mortgageable.

I persuaded the bank to lend me the money to buy the house at a knockdown price, and I re-built it to comply with building regulations. It required stripping off the metal cladding, extending the foundations and building a new brick wall all the way around the property. To help finance the project, I did exactly the same for the owner of the adjoining property and also built a large extension right across the rear. We had been still living in the smaller house along the road, but when the new house was finished we sold it and moved into the larger one.

I then landed some big contract work with architects and developers, and along with the Edinburgh Council contracts I was, at last, turning over a lot of money. I took on more men and bought another van. On the face of it, it was going really well.

Then I hit a problem. Cash flow was getting tight. I was sometimes waiting two months to get paid by the council, and my overdraft was going over its limit. More than once it got to the stage where I had to go to the bank manager, cap in hand, and ask him if he would allow me to extend the overdraft to cover the wages and payments to sub-contractors. The weekly outlay on wages was running at approximately £3,500, my overdraft was already over £40,000, and this was on top of the money I had borrowed to build the new house. The bank was getting worried. I had credit accounts with all the suppliers, but some months I couldn't make the payments.

I had taken on a large contract converting offices into a public house in McDonald Road, and it was nearing completion when the client's own business ran into financial difficulties, owing me a lot of money. That was enough to tip the balance. I was unable to supply the building materials for other contracts, and it gradually got worse and worse.

At home one Sunday my bank manager came to our house unannounced. He had allowed me to borrow much more than he had security for, and came to talk to me unofficially about how I was planning to pay it back. When we did the sums, including all the outstanding credit accounts, I was in debt to the sum of £120,000.

I struggled on for another two months but we were in too deep. Sheila's father had loaned us some money to keep the business afloat, but in the end we had to declare the business insolvent. We decided it would be better for us to sell the house and clear some of the debts rather than have it repossessed, and as soon as it was sold we filed for bankruptcy.

It meant that I couldn't own anything for three years, and anything I earned would have to be declared so that a percentage could be taken by the administrator and put towards the outstanding debts. I think in the end both Sheila and I were relieved. The amount of pressure we'd been under was unbearable. It would be hard, but after three years we could start afresh. Meanwhile, it wasn't worth Sheila working any more because all her earnings would have been taken from us, but I carried on for a while working as a joiner although it proved hard without any transport.

We then had to stay in rented accommodation and therefore we moved a number of times—some places were good and some were bad. Sarah lived in seven different houses before she was five years old. The last rented house we lived in was the happiest one of all. It was a ground floor flat in a block of four, with gardens to the front and rear, in Featherhall Avenue in Corstorphine, on the west side of Edinburgh.

The owners were a brother and sister whose father had recently died and left the property to them. We got on well with the neighbours, and found out through them that the father had kept racing pigeons in a loft in the back garden—every time he cleaned it out he would spread the droppings all over the garden.

The man upstairs was a grower of prize flowers and specialised in chrysanthemums. When he found out we were not particularly interested in gardening, he asked if he could take over our section of the garden to grow his flowers as the earth was well-fertilized with the pigeon droppings. It made no difference to us, so I gave him the go-ahead, and during that summer he produced some beautiful flowers. He watched like a hawk every time Sarah was playing in the garden anywhere near his prize chrysanthemums.

Once, on a Saturday morning, I was sitting with Sarah watching television, when someone passed by the front window. I didn't think much of it at the time, but later that afternoon the man from upstairs came to our door. He was very angry, "Your daughter has thrown soap powder all over my flowers!" "Don't be stupid," I replied," why would she do that?" I walked round the back with him and, right enough, there was a white powder scattered over the garden and over his chrysanthemums.

I licked the ends of my fingers and dipped them in the offending substance to taste it and see if I could identify what it was. It didn't taste of anything, and certainly wasn't soap powder. Sarah swore that she knew nothing about it, so we left it at that. Later, I discovered that the brother and sister who owned our flat had decided that, since their father loved his pigeons so much, the best place to put his ashes was to spread them on his garden…

My driving ban had now expired, but before I could have my licence back I had to sit another driving test. I had been off the road for three and a half years, and had no chance of passing without some refresher driving lessons. It also was difficult finding an insurance company willing to insure me to drive Sheila's Fiat Uno in order to take the test. If it was hard the first time, it was a lot worse the second. I was a gibbering wreck sitting in the test centre waiting for my test to start, but I passed with flying colours.

The only way to improve our situation was for me to find a good job. I picked up the papers and searched through the job ads. I didn't even look at the job descriptions—I just looked for one that would pay enough to give my family the life they deserved. The position I decided to apply for was as a specialist surveyor in the preservation field, with a Glasgow-based company. The job came with a good salary and bonuses, a company car, and pension benefits. Maybe I was punching above my weight, but I had nothing to lose! I had no idea what the job entailed, let alone any experience, but I went for it. The company had an office in Edinburgh and the interview took place there.

I had never been for an interview in my life before. When I'd completed my joiner's apprenticeship, all those years ago, I'd become a professional singer, and self-employed ever since then. So I was very nervous, and kept repeating the Serenity Prayer in my head. Not that I'm religious, but it has a calming effect. In preparation for the interview I had read up as much as I could on the subject of wood-decaying fungi and insect infestations, and I must have persuaded him that I was the right man for the job because he offered me the position.

It was much more involved than I had imagined. After a settling-in period I had to study hard and take exams at the Institute of Wood Science, which allowed me to use the letters CTIS and CRDS after my name.

I also had a nice, new, shiny company car with a fuel allowance. The only downside was the office was in Glasgow, so I had to drive back and forward from Edinburgh every day. I would get up in the morning at 6.15am, put on my suit and tie (which I hated), hit the motorway and get to Glasgow before the rush hour traffic built up. I didn't get back at night till around 7pm, then after dinner I would have paperwork to sort out... but it was worth it.

Now that we were on a firm footing, financially, we scraped up enough money to have our first family holiday abroad, on the island of Majorca, near the town of Alcudia. In a complex called Bourganville we had everything you could need on a family holiday, including a kid's club for Sarah, as well as shows and entertainment around the pool in the evenings. One night they had a singing competition, but I was keeping well out of it. However, a couple from Scotland joined us at our table and Sheila let it slip that I was a singer. The guy had obviously been at the vino, and was drawing attention to us by shouting, "Come on, give us a song!" so I agreed to take part in the contest for a laugh. I got up and sang *Lady in Red* to rapturous applause, and was well ahead in the competition until a drunk guy got up on stage, stripped off to his underpants, and sang *Wild Thing* while pouring a pint of lager over his head. Now that's entertainment.

My bankruptcy still had nine months to go before I could apply for discharge, but it seemed crazy to me that we were paying more in rent than we would be if I took on a mortgage and bought a house. I spoke to my administrator and he saw the logic in my argument. He said, "If you can find a company willing to lend you the money, and as long as there's no equity on the property, I don't see why not." So off I went on the search of a lender who would take me on under the circumstances. I found one through a broker, but I got the feeling he was a little economical with the truth when it came to declaring my bank-ruptcy—however, he did manage to get us the loan.

We bought a nice semi-detached house in Drum Brae, not far from my mother's house. It had two bedrooms, a front and back garden, and a small extension at the rear that I could use as an office and music room. It also had a garage, which the previous owners had built onto the side of the house.

Sarah was seven when we bought the house and she attended Fox Covert Primary School, as I had done over thirty years before, although it was now in a new modern building. Living close by meant my mother could meet Sarah after school and take her back to her house. I got into a routine of going to regular AA meetings twice a week, and this was probably the happiest period in our married life.

I really liked my job and I was good at it. I had the responsibility of surveying historic buildings and churches all over Scotland and writing up reports and preparing documents for any large-scale remedial works. I was in my element.

I hadn't told anyone in the company about my background—it felt nice to be anonymous, and it's how I would have preferred it to stay. The company's offices were open-plan, with forty or so people working in departments sectioned off by chest-high partitions. I was sitting working at my desk when I was distracted by a loud conversation going on. As I looked up to see who was doing all the talking, the guy recognised me and shouted "Nobby Clark! What the hell are you doing here?" Looking round at the other company employees beside him, he pointed at me and said, loudly, "That's the original singer with the Bay City Rollers!" All of sudden, there were heads popping up across the whole office.

The guy had been the guitar player in a band I had met many years ago. Everything changed after that. I found it quite uncomfortable that our Managing Director started introducing me to clients by saying, "Gordon used to be the singer with the Bay City Rollers..." Thankfully, after four years working in Glasgow, I took over the Edinburgh office to manage the preservation business, so it was worth putting up with a bit of stick.

We lived at the Drum Brae house for approximately three years, and in that time I took Sarah everywhere with me. During school holidays I would say to her, "Pack a bag, we're going off on an adventure!" and we would get in the car and head north to wherever the road took us, booking into bed and breakfast places along the way. Once we came back down from up north and booked into the Crieff Hydro Hotel, where we went horse riding through the woods and, in the evening, danced around the Winter Garden ballroom to a Ceilidh band.

The next morning I asked Sarah, "What would you really like to do next?" She said, "I'd like to stay in a log cabin." So we drove off to Glendevon Castle where I introduced her to Karen. We went gold panning in a stream in the hills above the castle, and stayed overnight in a log cabin—it was fantastic. Sarah even came away with a jar of gold dust of her own.

I have to confess that I was never very strict with Sarah, and spoiled her at every opportunity. I wasn't very good at telling her off, and just left that to her mother. But when Sarah came to me one day and asked if she could have a rat as a pet, I immediately said, "Of course not! Nobody keeps a rat as a pet." She kept on about it for weeks, saying they were special rats that you bought in a pet shop. I'd never heard of such a thing, so I took her to the shop that specialised in unusual pets and there they were. They were called "fancy rats", bred as domestic pets and we bought a dark brown rat, which Sarah, for some unknown reason, called Tartan. It wasn't at all what I expected - it was intelligent, clean and affectionate. I became very attached to this rodent and he would sit on my shoulder while I watched TV. His cage was kept in the small room at the back of the house, but he was out running around most of the time. Sarah felt sorry for Tartan being on his own, so we got another one to keep him company, a white one this time.

Davie Paton and I had kept in touch regularly, and he called to say he had been talking to Davey Johnstone, the guitarist with Elton John's band. He said Davey had a house in Edinburgh, which he had bought for his mother, but as she had died recently he wanted to sell it. He suggested that I have a look at it.

Davey Johnstone was originally an Edinburgh guy who was brought up in the Sighthill area, and he got his first break when he joined the British folk group Magna Carta, and then met the producer, Gus Dudgeon, who asked him to play on Bernie Taupin's 1970 solo album, resulting in a meeting with Elton John. Davey was asked to play on Elton's 1971 album *Madman Across The Water* and later he joined Elton's band fulltime. (Davey has been with Elton John ever since and is now his musical director.)

Davie Paton had also been in Elton John's band for a world tour, after playing bass as a session musician on the song *Nikita*.

So we went out to see the house that Davey Johnstone was selling. It was situated in a quiet spot called West Craigs, off the Turnhouse Road near Edinburgh Airport. It was a large bungalow on a corner site with a huge garden to the front and rear. It also had an area to the side with trees and shrubs. We loved it. It turned out that Elton John had visited the house at Christmas a number of times when Davey came to see his mother. Davey Johnstone was now living in California, so I called him and we did the deal over the phone. It was that simple.

We now had to sell our house at Drum Brae, and we put it on the market immediately. With Sheila and I both working, it was a mad rush to get home and clean up the house for the Thursday evening open-viewing. We got the place looking respectable, then sat down waiting for people to arrive.

Suddenly I realised, "Oh my God, the rats are still loose in the back room!" I ran through and grabbed them, put them in the cage, and carried them out to put them in the garage. Sheila had a 4x4 Vauxhall Frontera, which was parked in the driveway. I put the cage on the bonnet of the car and bent down to lift up the garage door, but the cage slipped off the bonnet, hit the ground, and the top flew off.

Both rats scarpered under the car. I was shouting to Sheila and Sarah, "Help me! Help me, quick—the rats are out!" They both came running and the three of us were scrambling around chasing the rats. I managed to catch the white one and handed it to Sarah, but Tartan had climbed up into the engine. I was lying on the ground under the car, and I could just feel his tail. I shouted to Sheila, "Open the bonnet. Try and grab him from the top!" but I grabbed his tail and pulled him down, catching him from underneath. Pleased with myself, I stood up and put him on my shoulder. When I turned round, there was a young couple standing on the path, just staring at us in disbelief. I said, "Are you here to see the house?" The young woman said, "No, I don't think it's what we're looking for," and off they went.

We did eventually sell the house and moved into West Craigs.

Sarah was now ten years of age. I know every father thinks his daughter is special, but Sarah was very striking. She was tall and thin, with bright blue eyes and wavy blonde hair. Very confident, she could sing and dance, and took the lead role in all of the school plays. I was very proud of her.

My job was going well, I was making money for the company, but I wasn't getting on well with the Managing Director. When I got the offer of a manager's job in a national company, taking over their Scottish preservation operation, I jumped at it. I had six surveyors working out of offices in Edinburgh, Glasgow and Grangemouth, and around thirty operatives out in vans all around the country.

One morning, a survey enquiry came in for an address in Danube Street, the street where I'd lived as a child. I thought, "I'll take this one myself." The enquiry was for 36 Danube Street, but at that time I couldn't recall the number of the basement flat we'd lived in. I picked up a set of keys on the way and arrived at the address—it *was* the flat I grew up in!

I looked over the road to the doorway of the late Dora's brothel, and down into Mrs Kirkhope's basement flat. There was no talking budgie now, and there were no gas lamps either. These flats were very sought-after nowadays, and worth a lot of money. I slowly entered the gate and walked down the stone steps. There in front of me was the cellar under the road, which Brian had locked me in when I was only four years old. I unlocked the front door and went in.

The bedroom on the right was there, where my parent's bed had gone through the floor in the middle of the night, but the rest of the flat was different. It was modernised and mainly painted white, but I could see past all of that, to the memories of the soot and the dampness. The owners had removed walls and done away with the recess where Aunt Daisy had slept, although in my mind I could still see the old curtain she pulled across the front of the recess when she went to bed. The range had been kept in place, although it was shining black now—not smoked up like it used to be, and with no teapot sitting on the hot plate. I noticed the hook was still there at the side of the fire, where my mother hung the tin bath. I got very emotional and had to get out.

We'd only been in our new house a couple of months when I got a call. A high-pitched voice said, "It's Tam, Nobby." It was Tam Paton who I hadn't heard from for a long time. Why would he be phoning me? I couldn't imagine, but we talked for a long time, mainly about the Rollers. He kept repeating, "I didn't steal their money."

When I quizzed him on where *my* money had gone, he told me that the Rollers had never received the royalties from Bell Records or Arista. He said the whole thing had got out of control, and everybody was stealing from the band, including the accountants. He kept on asking me to go out to his house, saying I would be very welcome, but I wanted to keep my distance. I had decided a long time ago that I was not going to carry the burden of hating anybody—whatever happened in the past should stay in the past. But I did want to find out if the Rollers had been paid any money that was due to me.

Over the following months he called me quite a few times, mostly on a Sunday when his house was quiet. During these conversations he told me things that were intriguing as well as dangerous. He said he'd had six months added onto his jail sentence for possessing Super-8 films containing child pornography, but that Derek Longmuir had asked him if he could store the films in his office. Tam swore that the films belonged to Derek. He said he'd had no idea what was on them as he didn't own a projector and had no way of looking at them. I didn't want to hear any of this—I was simply interested in finding out about the missing royalties.

CHAPTER TWELVE

By 1995 I had more or less given up the music business. I hadn't performed live for some time, but I was still writing and recording songs for the enjoyment I got out of doing it. Very few people got to hear my stuff, other than a few fans around the world. My top priority was my sobriety, and I now had over nine years of total abstinence under my belt, thanks to my involvement with AA.

Out of the blue, I was contacted by Wendy Antanaitis, who introduced herself as Ian Mitchell's wife. I had never met Ian and knew only what Tam Paton and Alan Longmuir had told me about him. Ian grew up in County Down in Northern Ireland, and had been the guitarist in a band called, Rosetta Stone, which Tam Paton had also managed. He took Ian out of that band and put him into The Bay City Rollers in 1976, while they were still in their heyday.

Ian was seventeen then, and stayed with the Rollers for seven months while Alan Longmuir took time out. Ian toured round the world with the band, playing guitar, and singing on the 1976 hit album *Dedication* (and also the 1985 release *Breakout*).

Wendy had called to ask if I would be interested in appearing at a "Roller Fest" in Las Vegas. I said I would consider it, but needed more details. The Roller Fest was a gathering of fans from all over the world, where they would swap Roller memorabilia and photographs, make new friends and listen to Rollers music. They asked me if I would do a spot on my own and also perform some songs with Ian Mitchell and Pat McGlynn.

I had met Pat McGlynn a few times in the past, and even had a drink with him a couple of times when I was on the sauce. He was a pretty mixed-up kind of a guy but I got on all right with him. Pat joined the Rollers just after Ian Mitchell left, and he stayed with them for around five months during which time he toured around the world. They used his image to sell records, and he co-wrote and played on the hit single *You Made Me Believe In Magic* and the album *It's A Game.*

I was a bit reluctant to do the Fest as I had cut myself off from anything to do with the Rollers for years and didn't want to go backwards. However, it offered me the opportunity to fulfil an ambition, of going to see Las Vegas, and with all expenses paid. I started to make plans that initially included taking Sheila and Sarah with me, but as it got closer I started looking for ways to avoid taking them. I wasn't consciously aware of thinking about having a drink, but I seemed to be moving obstacles out of the way so that I could if I wanted to. This illness of alcoholism is cunning, baffling and so powerful. When I started to think that way I should immediately have spoken to someone at an AA meeting, but I didn't.

When the time came, I flew out to Los Angeles on my own and was met at the airport by Wendy and three of her friends, who were all involved in the organisation of the Fest. I got into the stretch limousine they'd provided and we drove off down to Orange County where Ian and Wendy were living. They had an afternoon barbecue organised, and there I met some of their other friends. It was a beautiful, hot sunny day and I was having a great time.

They had booked me into the Laguna Bay Hotel looking over the California hills. I stayed there overnight, and in the morning they picked me up to drive across the desert to Las Vegas. It was a fantastic trip that took about six hours. When you've driven all that way, with nothing but scorching desert all around you, it is a spectacular experience to all of a sudden see this fantasy town rising out of the sand—I was quite overwhelmed by it. None of the films, photographs or descriptions I'd seen before came anywhere near to the reality.

I knew we were staying at the Aladdin Hotel on the Strip, but I wasn't prepared for the sheer size of it. The Aladdin was the first of the giant casino hotels to be built, and it took my breath away. The Roller Fest was to be held in a room at the Aladdin, and hundreds of fans would be staying in the hotel, so we got in quickly and up to our rooms before we were seen.

The event was spread over three days, and there were fans from all over the world—Japan, Australia, America—and they had a great time. I projected photographs of the group in the early days on to a big screen and told stories of how it all came about, which they loved. Then I got up on stage with Ian and Pat and sang some songs. It was really enjoyable, up until my part in the Fest was over… that's when it started to go wrong.

I went off wandering up and down the Strip, in and out of casinos, sitting at the tables watching other people play roulette and blackjack. In the Luxor Hotel I met a lumberjack from Canada who hadn't been to bed for three days—the first day he arrived he lost $5,000 and had been chasing it ever since. They say that if you sit in a barber's chair long enough you will need a haircut. It wasn't long before my gambling addiction took over. I naïvely thought, "I'll just play a couple of hands with $10. If I lose that I'll go."

$1,500 later, I was walking down the strip saying to myself, "What the hell just happened?" and walked, in a trance, straight into the bar of the MGM Grand and asked for a Tequila Sunrise. I remember being thrown out of one bar for being drunk and abusive, but the rest is just a blur. I must have visited other casinos because, the following morning, back in my room at the Aladdin, I found that all my money was gone, including what I had put aside for the flight back to Los Angeles.

I'd become quite friendly with Cathy, one of the organisers of the Roller Fest. She was the Personal Assistant to the congressman for Nevada, and quite an influential person. She was looking for me and found me in my room. I broke down in tears—ten years of sobriety gone, just like that. I told her the whole story.

She suggested I stay in Las Vegas for an extra few days to get myself together and arranged for me to be moved from the Aladdin to the Mirage Hotel, where I was given a suite on the top floor, free of charge. She also loaned me enough money to get back to Los Angeles for my flight home. Then I did another stupid thing: I phoned home and Sarah answered. She listened to me speak for a few seconds, then passed the phone to her mother who knew immediately I'd been drinking.

Now that I had set up the compulsion to drink again I couldn't stop, and it carried on at the airport and all the way home. When I got back, Sheila was at the door and went into a complete panic when she saw the state I was in. They say in AA that if an alcoholic in recovery picks up a drink, the very best they can expect, is to pick up where they left off, but the chances are it will be ten times worse than it was before—and that turned out to be the case for me.

It didn't start off like a runaway train. I drank every day and kept booze hidden in various places, drinking only what I thought I could get away with. But my wife knew—she only had to look into my eyes and she knew. There were many mornings I needed to have a drink before going to work to get rid of the shakes. I went to the office every day in my suit and tie, and acted as if everything was just dandy, but I was picking up vibes from my work colleagues—I think they knew something wasn't right.

I went back to AA and told my story exactly as it happened. It was one of the hardest things I've done, but I just couldn't get back on the programme.

Whenever I did manage to stay off the booze, I swapped one addiction for the other and gambling took over my life instead. I'd go into the office early and work non-stop till lunchtime, keeping my head down to avoid conversation. In the afternoon I went out to meet clients, timing it so I could get to the bookmakers for the first greyhound race at seven minutes past one, and after that I would stop off at various bookmakers around the town, being careful not to spend too much time in each one, but putting a bet on every dog and horse race there was throughout the whole afternoon. I did that most days. Whenever I could get away with it, I would also go to the casino on my way home, using the excuse that I had to work late.

Most months there wasn't enough money left in the bank to pay the bills. I was thoroughly addicted and obsessed. On one occasion I walked into the casino with £200 in my pocket. When I lost that, I went to the cashline and drew out the maximum amount of £200. When I lost that, I had to wait until midnight before I could get another £200 out of the cashline. I went back in to the casino and lost that. Then I proceeded to cash three £100 cheques, which was the maximum allowed with my bankcard. When that was gone I left there and drove to another casino where I cashed another three £100 cheques and lost that too.

In my head the money had no value. It was just a means to gamble. I was brainwashed into thinking that eventually I would hit a big one and pay it all back. Sometimes I did. Once, I had about £2,500 stashed in the house from winnings that week, but within days it was all given back to the casino.

It was driving me insane and took me to the depths of despair. On my doctor's advice I went back on anti-depressants, but the side effects were horrible. I couldn't sleep, and if I did I had terrible nightmares. There was a constant buzzing in my head, I was shaky, agitated and had a dry mouth all the time. So I stopped taking them.

I self-medicated, instead, using amphetamine sulphate (speed) which worked for a while, but every so often I would have terrible comedowns and suicidal thoughts. I did everything in my power to cover it up, but I was stealing from Peter to pay Paul, as it were, and the drinking binges started again.

I wouldn't go home until late, after my daughter was in bed, and sometimes I would stay out all night. She hadn't yet seen me in an incapable, drunken state but, as it escalated, she must have been aware that something was wrong as her mother and I were fighting all the time. All the experiences of the past were repeating themselves: aggression, verbal abuse, blaming my wife for everything. The morning after, I would always be full of remorse, and self-loathing, and then I'd go and do it all again.

The only reason it didn't all fall apart completely was that I did the drinking in binges. I would consume so much alcohol in a short period that I would make myself ill and have to stop for a while, telling my wife, as usual, that I'd seek help and it wouldn't happen again. But of course it did. She got to the stage where she gave up trying. Before this, she'd pour away any alcohol she found hidden, but now she just gave up, and even bought herself a bottle of vodka and kept it in the cupboard, marking the label with her fingernail to check if the level went down—but I would top it up with water, or mark the label at a lower level, to confuse her. It was a game without any winners.

Desperately trying to stay away from alcohol, I went back on the Antibuse tablets and took it a day at a time. I managed two months of total abstinence and, with Sheila's help, everything settled down again.

During all this I was getting reports from fans of more records being released around the world with my vocals on them, and I also found out that The Bay City Rollers (being Alan and Derek Longmuir, Eric Faulkner, Stuart Wood and Les McKeown) had applied to the Supreme Court in New York to have Arista Records' bank account frozen, to allow them time to file a law suit against the company. To add to my frustration, Les McKeown appeared on a television panel show where they played my original recording of *Keep On Dancing* while he sat there with a smile on his face and made out it was him singing.

My wife's brother, Alistair, who had been trying to help me deal with my alcoholism, put me in touch with a firm of lawyers that he had dealings with. I arranged a meeting with them and explained the situation I was in: Arista was fraudulently using my vocal performances and misleading the public into believing it was Les McKeown's voice on them, with no intentions of paying me a penny, even though I'd had a recording contract with them at the time. After further investigations the lawyer wrote to the Supreme Court in 1997 and asked them to register my claim.

It was made clear an Edinburgh law firm would not be allowed to present the case in New York as they would have to engage legal representation from the state of New York. I was also informed that, in order to take the case on board and to move it forward, I would have to put up a bond of £100,000. I didn't have anything like that kind of money at my disposal and to try and borrow it would mean putting our house at risk and, as it was in joint names, there was no way that was going to happen. I didn't know what else to do.

The Roller Fest in Las Vegas had been so successful that they asked me if I would do another one in Anaheim, California on the 23rd August 1997. At first I said, "Absolutely not," but eventually I thought that if I could go there and do it without drinking this time, it's going to make me a stronger person. I asked Sheila if she wanted to come with Sarah, but she didn't want to know, so I decided to go alone.

The flight over was nerve-racking, with long periods of heavy turbulence. The Roller Fest organisers, Wendy and Tammy, had booked me into a nice hotel in Anaheim, but there was nothing much around the hotel so, as I wanted to get a suntan before going to the Fest, I took a walk out into the surrounding hills.

It was very hot but I'd walked a good two miles into the wilderness, on a path through trees and undergrowth, when I came across a sign fixed to a tree that said, "If you are confronted by a Mountain Lion do not run." What? Panicking, I read on, "If you have children, lift them on to your shoulders and walk backwards very slowly." My God! I was freaking out. The most dangerous thing you're ever likely to be confronted with in the Scottish hills is a squirrel! I grabbed the biggest stick I could find and walked very slowly at first, checking all the bushes, then ran like hell all the way back to civilisation.

I had spoken on the phone a couple of times to a guy called Wayne Coy, a very successful radio DJ and programme director. Wayne had struck up a friendship with Les McKeown when he was on tour in America, and Wayne was working on an unauthorised biography he called Bay City Babylon. When he asked me if I would contribute to his book I was hesitant at first—I'd been misquoted so many times over the years that I was now very cautious.

I met Wayne for the first time at my hotel in Anaheim the day before the Roller Fest. I accepted his offer to pick me up and show me around Los Angeles as it would be a chance to get to know each other.

We visited the Capitol Records tower, which resembles a stack of gramophone records, and I was fascinated by the building and its history. Capitol Records was originally founded by the songwriter, Johnny Mercer. Anyone not familiar with his name might still have sung along with his lyrics in *One For My Baby*, *Moon River* and *Summer Winds* amongst a whole host of other great songs. Capitol Tower is home to a number of recording studios designed by Les Paul, the same guy who created Les Paul guitars and multi-tracking. Loads of famous singers and musicians recorded there including Nat King Cole, Frank Sinatra, Judy Garland and The Beach Boys.

From there we went on to Sunset Boulevard, Chinatown and Beverley Hills—I was having a fantastic time. Wayne came along to the Roller Fest too, probably to publicise his book, but I enjoyed his company nonetheless.

On stage at the Fest I sang a few songs, then got together with Ian Mitchell and we had a question and answer session with the fans. It was all great fun but, to be honest, I really didn't get much pleasure from going back and singing old Rollers songs, although the fans enjoyed it. However, I had enjoyed seeing a bit of Los Angeles and I also had proved a point to myself that I could do it without a crutch. I returned to Scotland completely sober.

When the book *Bay City Babylon* came out I thought it was a fair record of events, but biased towards Les McKeown's account of what happened with *Saturday Night* in America, which was that they re-recorded the song after it started to take off there. That in itself would have been fraud, had it happened, but it didn't. It's one thing to re-record the voice in the studio, it's another thing to break into the process when the song is already out there, being played on all the radio stations, and football stadiums, and in the shops. The evidence now shows that it didn't happen.

I'd read in a newspaper article that The Bay City Rollers were once presented with the keys to Bay City, Michigan... I can now reveal the truth about the band's name. I told the story early on in this book that when we were in Tam Paton's bedroom we stuck a pin in the map of America and it landed beside Bay City, Michigan. Well, it didn't—it was actually myself who stuck the pin in the map, and it landed beside Bay City, Texas! The rest was made up for publicity reasons, because when we discovered that the surfing waves at Lake Michigan were called the Rollers it sounded a much better story!

I was back in Edinburgh, getting on with life and keeping things together, when I got a phone call from Wendy, Ian Mitchell's wife, saying she was coming across to Scotland in December that year and would be staying at Tam Paton's house to gather information and evidence of Ian's involvement in The Bay City Rollers. I picked her up at the airport and dropped her off at Tam's.

After three days, I got a phone call from Tam asking if she could come and stay at my house because she was causing mayhem amongst the boys who lived with him. I had to put it to Sheila, who reluctantly agreed. She was as tired as I was of hearing about The Bay City Rollers over the years. I tried to prepare my wife and daughter for Wendy's arrival. She was very American, loud and boisterous. My daughter Sarah loved it—she got to try on all Wendy's outrageous clothes and makeup—but my wife hated it.

Wendy told me that most of the paperwork at Tam's that related to the Rollers had already been sifted through, and taken, by Eric Faulkner and Derek Longmuir. She asked if I would drive her down to Ayr, on the west coast of Scotland, where Eric Faulkner was playing with his version of The Bay City Rollers. I said no at first, but she kept on at me until I gave in, so we headed off on a 150 mile round-trip to the Butlins Holiday Camp where he was playing.

I watched his live show thinking, "How ridiculous." It was a four-piece band made up of Eric Faulkner and three unknown musicians, with a girl singer who turned out to be Eric's girlfriend. They were playing all the songs that I had sung with The Rollers, including *Keep on Dancing*, *Remember*, and *Saturday Night*, none of which Eric had actually played on.

After the show, Wendy and I walked unannounced into his dressing room. The look on his face was priceless. He couldn't even look me in the eye. I confronted him right away and asked why he thought they were entitled to royalties from Arista Records for songs they didn't play on, and why were they fighting to have me excluded from the court case. All I got was stuttering and mumbling.

When I asked him where my publishing royalties for *Because I Love You* (which sold over a million copies) had gone, I got a similar non-coherent splutter, and something about it not showing up on the list. I knew through my own research that the publishing money for that song had been collected by RAK Music and paid into Bay City Music's account. Since Derek Longmuir and Eric were the signatories on the account, they had to know exactly where the money came from, and without hesitation they had spent what was rightfully mine.

While Wendy grilled him on Ian's involvement, I got talking to Eric's girlfriend. They had obviously been fighting and she seemed extremely angry. Eric was not the cleanest person I've ever met, which was borne out by her comment, "Look at him, he's had his finger in every orifice in his body." I looked over and watched him scratching himself, and I burst out laughing.

The trip may not have given me any new information but it made me even more determined to pursue legal action against them. Wendy headed back to California while I started to gather evidence of any albums released around the world that included my lead vocals, backing harmonies, or songs written by me. I was getting reports from fans about other albums that were available, and I was on their trail too.

The following were the album tracks I'd managed to get hard evidence of my vocal performances on:

Rollin' (1974):
Bye Bye Barbara, Hey C.B.

Once Upon A Star (1975):
Keep On Dancing

Wouldn't You Like It? (1975 Germany, Japan):
Wouldn't You Like It, I'd Do It Again

Bay City Rollers Early Collection (1976):
Keep On Dancing, Alright, We Can Make Music, Jenny, Mañana, Because I Love You (with writing credit), *Saturday Night, Hey C.B., Remember, Bye Bye Barbara*

The Great Lost Rollers Album (1977):
Keep On Dancing, Alright, We Can Make Music, Jenny, Mañana, Because I Love You, Hey C.B., Bye Bye Barbara

Starke Zeiten (1988, Germany):
Remember

By Request (1992):
Keep On Dancing, Saturday Night

Absolute Rollers (1980, re-released 1995):
Remember

And that was just the start.

Meanwhile, the other things in my life were going well.

My daughter, Sarah, was doing great and was at a small private school in Edinburgh called St. Serfs. All the household bills were getting paid. I was probably the happiest I had been for a long time and I had done really well in that I hadn't touched a drop of alcohol for over four months. So why would I go and spoil it? Sheila always said she could tell when I had flicked the switch, and she was just waiting for it to happen again...

The beginning of 1998 saw the start of a drinking binge that topped all of my drinking binges before, and it changed everything. Every night I came home late, drunk out of my head and gave Sheila dog's abuse. She had left me a few times before, and gone to stay with her parents or with her brother, but had always come back. But as this drinking bout got worse, she just had enough.

I staggered down the road towards my house after a full day's drinking from early in the morning, and found Sheila's brother's car parked outside my house. The front door was open and there were cases standing in the hall. I walked in and was confronted by my wife with my daughter standing at her side, crying her eyes out. Sheila said, "We're leaving for good this time. The house will have to be sold as soon as possible." I started to get aggressive in my drunken state, and was grabbing the suitcases out of her brother's hands. Sheila and Sarah ran and got into the car while I was fighting with her brother in the garden. He got away and threw the cases into the car.

I will never forget seeing my daughter's face through the car window, terrified and screaming as they drove away. I stood in the garden shouting, "You can't do this to me!" That was the last time I saw Sarah for nine years.

The house was put on the market, and I stayed on there while the estate agents went through the process. I stocked up with booze, shut the curtains and drank myself into oblivion. When the booze ran out I would go out and find a pub that opened early morning, and cower in the corner. Sometimes the shakes were so bad I couldn't lift the glass and had to try and sip it out of the side while it was on the table. It would take a good few doubles before I could function without sweating and shaking, and then I would be ready to carry on for the rest of the day.

Some mornings I would wake up to a house full of people, most of whom I didn't know. Beer cans and bottles were strewn around the place, people were sleeping in Sarah's room, my record collection was scattered across the floor, and I couldn't remember anything about it. I would throw them all out, clean the place up... then go and do it all again. I was in a living nightmare.

One morning, when I was in a really bad state and desperately needed some alcohol, I walked up to the shopping centre near where I lived. As I was walking past a house, a huge snarling dog jumped up on the wall and put its head through a hole in the fence right in line with my face. I've had a terrible fear of dogs ever since a big black mongrel attacked me when I was aged ten. I jumped back out of its reach. When I got to the supermarket I filled up the trolley with beer and bottles of spirits. I sheepishly pushed the trolley to the checkout, keeping my head down for fear of being recognised, and gave the girl my card to pay for it. She put my card in the machine, but it wouldn't go through and she was told to confiscate it by the bank—she wouldn't give me it back. It was so humiliating in front of a long line of customers. I had to walk away and leave the trolley with all the booze in it.

On the way back I picked up a large piece of wood I had found at the back of the shop and walked down to where the dog had been, and started smashing the fence while shouting and swearing, "Come on, attack me now, you fucking bastard! I'll smash your head in!" The dog wasn't there, but I saw an old man looking out the window. By the time I got to my house the police came screaming down the road and arrested me for being drunk and disorderly and for malicious damage. It turned out, it was the wrong house—the poor old man didn't even have a dog.

A few days after that I must have been upstairs, where I kept the alcohol, but I don't remember much about it. Although I was the only person in the house, I still hid the booze upstairs. I must have missed the step at the top of the stairs, and fallen all the way down and banged my head on the radiator at the bottom. I was dazed for a while and didn't know where I was. Blood was everywhere and it was pouring down my face—I had broken a blood vessel in my forehead.

There was a pool of blood on the salmon pink carpet in the hall, and it was also smeared all over the walls where I had touched them with my hands. I knew my older brother Brian was up from Bradford staying at my mother's house, so I phoned him and he came over immediately. When he saw the state I was in, he drove me to the hospital and I was kept in overnight for observation.

I had forgotten all about the arrangements I had made for the following day. I was supposed to be out the house so that my wife could get in and collect some more of her belongings. What I didn't know, until much later, was that she brought my daughter with her to collect some of her things too, and she'd walked into the house first. I can only imagine the terror she felt when she saw the blood everywhere.

I cleaned the place up and offered to do the right thing, which was to move out for good and let my wife and daughter stay there until the house was sold, but Sheila refused the offer. They were staying with Callum and Fiona who had a big house in Murrayfield.

We eventually got a buyer and I stayed at the house until it was time for it to change hands. I was in such a drunken state the day before I was to move out that I hadn't done anything about packing. All the furniture was still in the house, the garage was full to the roof and I couldn't cope.

I had to be out by twelve noon the following day, so I made some phone calls to people, including my younger brother, Norman, and some people I hadn't seen for a long time, such as Jim, my best man who had let me down at the last minute, and the only neighbour I got on with and thought of as a friend. I was desperate.

Early next morning, people arrived in their cars and my brother came with a trailer. There was furniture all over the garden and stuff was being dragged out of the garage—it was mayhem! I had been topping up during the night, and had polished off the rest of a bottle of vodka that morning, so I was in no fit state to organise things. Some of the furniture went to my brother's garage. Some of the smaller stuff went to Jim's house in Bathgate. And some other stuff had to be dumped. But, worst of all, a lot of valuable items went missing.

A few days later, when I tried to put together some kind of inventory, nobody seemed to know where certain items had gone. I went back over to the house two weeks later to speak to my neighbour, but he wasn't in, so I took a look round the back of his garage and found my daughter's mountain bike and a black, lacquered bureau worth around £1,000 with all its contents. I took these back, but I never did find some antique figures and paintings, rare LP's out of my collection, and an autograph book with all of The Beatles autographs in it.

CHAPTER THIRTEEN

I needed somewhere to stay and an old friend of mine organised a room for me in a shared flat in Tollcross. There were four students staying there and I had a room in the attic. We shared the kitchen and bathroom but I saw them very rarely, just isolating myself in my room and drowning my sorrows.

I would occasionally go down to Bennet's bar and sit drinking in the corner. I was sitting there one day, shaking really badly, when this older guy I had never seen before came across and put a large whisky down in front of me saying, "I think you could use that."

His name was Norrie, and we eventually became good friends. He offered me a room in his house, which he shared with his partner Jan. They were an older couple who'd been living together for many years. He said to me, "Jan will look after you," and she really did. Jan was a wonderful cook and fed me well, and tried to keep me off the drink too, but failed in the end.

While I stayed with Jan and Norrie, I had great difficulty finding parking for my car. The authorities couldn't issue me with a parking permit because I wasn't paying council tax, and I managed to run up over £600 in parking tickets.

The last straw was when they lifted my car and impounded it. I ran after the traffic warden and pulled her up. I was so angry, I was shouting at her in the middle of Tollcross, and she took out her radio saying, "I'm going to call the police." I said, "No you won't, I'll call them," and put my hand out to grab her radio, but she pulled backwards and fell right on her back, her hat flying off. It would have been really funny, had I not been arrested and charged with assault.

So I started a campaign against Edinburgh Council's parking policy. The newspapers were very keen to cover the story, and a young female reporter from the Daily Record came to interview me. At the time, we had some traffic wardens who were employed by the council –they wore yellow round their hats to identify them—and some wardens who were employed by private companies—they had blue round their hats. The latter were on commission and took no prisoners, they were the ones who had issued most of my tickets.

In the interview with the paper I called them "The Blue Meanies". The young reporter got quite excited when I used that term, and I saw her making a separate note of it. When the story came out it had my photograph as well as a caption on the front page with the heading "The Blue Meanies," and a full two-page spread in the middle of the paper.

A few weeks later, a bus passed me in the street and on the back it had a poster that was advertising Blue Meanie Car Insurance. The young reporter would have had no idea that it was John Lennon who came up with it first, and she took all the credit.

Jan and Norrie were invited to a party by one of his buddies from Bennet's bar and they wanted me to go with them. I was trying to ease myself off the drink and wasn't that keen on going, but I said I'd come for short time.

When we got to the party it was absolutely mobbed. Jan had made sausage rolls and Scotch eggs, and was asked to put them on the table in the lounge, so I just followed in behind her. It was so full of people we were struggling to get through. I'm not comfortable in crowds so was about to turn around when I caught sight of a girl sitting in the middle of a settee at the far end of the room. I only saw her for a second, when we made eye contact, before I left and went into the kitchen. I stood there leaning against the worktop on my own for maybe ten minutes. Then she came in. She was quite petite, with long, straight brown hair, and was wearing a long, black dress right down to her feet. She was talking like she knew me but I had never seen her before. She introduced herself as Sofia, and I felt quite comfortable telling her about myself. After a long conversation she asked me to put my hand out and she raised hers in a clenched fist and opened it on top of mine then took it away. I looked in my hand and there was nothing there. I said, "What is it?" She replied, "It's contentment. Go and find it," and left the room.

I left the party early. I was intrigued by what had happened and for the next few days, I asked around, trying to find out who she was, but nobody knew her or remembered seeing her at the party. I thought that was very strange.

When my house was sold, most of the money went to my wife and daughter so they could buy a place of their own. I took £12,000 and had it in a locked suitcase under my bed. It was everything I had in the world, but it was dwindling fast through gambling and drinking. I was going mad—I was so paranoid, I thought people were coming in through the window and stealing my money. I blamed Norrie for breaking into my suitcase, and I slept with a hammer under my pillow. Jan was getting extremely worried about me—I was yelling out in the middle of the night, and sometimes in the morning I couldn't make it to the toilet without her help. She would hold a can of beer to my mouth so I could get some down to stop the withdrawal symptoms. The last straw was when she found me with a tie round my neck trying to hang myself.

I was taken to the Andrew Duncan Clinic at the Royal Edinburgh Hospital and put in a psychiatric ward. It was not a pleasant place to be. The ward was divided into four sections and I shared it with three other patients, two of whom never spoke, they just wandered around all night.

The other patient, in the section opposite me, I called Jimmy The Axe Man as he'd told me he kept an axe in his fridge because the cold made it sharper. Jimmy was a very intimidating and scary person to be around. He was a skinhead, with tattoos all around his neck and he wore big heavy boots with his jeans tucked into them, and walked around staring at people in a very aggressive manner.

Us patients were herded into a lounge area during the day where we could be observed. Jimmy would hold court there and loved it when everyone was sitting round listening to his stories, but he got very angry if he was being ignored.

His stories were hilarious. He had everybody in fits of laughter when he told a story about trying to rob a bank in London. He'd walked in with a note saying: "I've got a gun—fill up the bag with money." But they pressed the alarm and chased him down the street. The next time he went into another bank with the note and handed it over. This time he got the money, but they chased him down the street and caught him again. He did a stretch in prison and when he came out he went to rob another bank. I said to him, "Did you take the note?" he laughed and said, "No. I never bothered because I knew I was going to get caught." He demanded the money, but the teller set off the alarm again and the police chased him all through the streets and into a church. He said it was like Benny Hill running up and down and through the pews, with the police chasing him, until eventually he climbed onto the pulpit and the police grabbed him and put the handcuffs on. He looked down and the minister was standing in front of him in the aisle. Jimmy looked at him and said, "I've not done anything. I'm innocent. Is this absolutely necessary?" The minister stood before him with his hands clasped in front and said, "I'm afraid so, my son" and off Jimmy went to do a two-year prison sentence.

You had to be on your guard the whole time in the hospital. There was an office at the end of the corridor, beside the door to the lounge. It had a large window on either side to enable the nurse to see everything that was going on. I was sitting quietly, reading a book, when I heard a scream. A very large female patient had picked up a hot cup of tea and thrown it into the face of a young girl, then she picked up a chair and smashed it through the office window. She was wrestled to the floor and taken to her room.

They weren't allowed to lock any of the bedroom doors, so you never knew what was going to happen next. When I thought it was all quiet, I went through to the small lounge where we could smoke, and there I was sitting, deep in thought, when the door burst open and the very large, angry woman came storming in with a big plastic waste bucket from the corridor, and emptied it right over my head. I was sat there with old food and tea dripping down my face. She was taken away and I never saw her again after that.

Often it was very sad too. I watched a young girl of about sixteen or seventeen come in with her parents. They signed some papers at the office and just left her. She looked absolutely terrified. I was in the small lounge on my own when she came in and stood up against the wall. She was very thin, anorexic-looking, but an attractive girl. She just stared at me. I said quietly, "Hello, I'm Gordon," but she didn't respond so I carried on reading. Then about ten minutes later she said, "Gordon. Are you really there."

My younger sister, Margaret, came in to see me. We were very close but as she lived up in Perth I hadn't seen very much of her over the last two years. When she saw the kind of place I was in she said, "I've got to get you out of here," and started on the long road to finding the right place that would give me the help I needed.

I got out of the clinic after six weeks and a lot of medication… and went straight to the pub and had a drink. I was back at Jan's house for a time, but she had her own problems, and I felt I had overstayed my welcome. So I packed up my things and asked if I could leave them with her until I got something sorted out. I took a shoulder bag with some clothes in it, and half a dozen cans of beer, and jumped on the first bus that came along. I didn't know where it was going or even cared. I just sat on the top deck in a daze and was startled by the driver coming up the stairs shouting, "This is as far as we go!"

I got off and found myself looking out to the sea at Joppa, on the east side of Edinburgh. There was a bench right on the sea front and I sat there with a can of beer in my hand, staring out at the tranquil sea, not really thinking about anything, when suddenly Sofia (from the party) walked right in front of me, and came and sat down. We talked for quite a while, then she left saying, "Someone needs to look after you."

I was confused, and not in a good place. I got up and headed back towards the town. I threw my mobile phone over a wall and jumped on the first bus going anywhere, ending up in Melrose, in the Scottish Borders.

I really was at the end of the line, and I had more on my plate than I had the strength to deal with. I wasn't even able to go and stay at my mother's, where I'd usually spent my Sundays, because my family had barred me from going to see her in case I turned up drunk and upset her. I couldn't blame them for that, because she was diagnosed with early signs of Alzheimers and she didn't need to be worrying about me. When she inquired where I was, they just said I was ill again and she knew what they meant.

I booked into a country house hotel just outside Melrose, then wandered into town and went round every chemist shop, buying as many paracetamol tablets as they would allow me to buy, but I needed more. So, the following morning, I jumped on a bus to Galashiels, went round as many chemist shops as I could find and bought another load of paracetamol then headed back to the hotel.

There was a very strange, sinister-looking, Victorian conservatory on the back of the hotel that had vines growing horizontally along the window panels. There was no furniture in here other than one long wooden seat. It was a stormy night and, looking out from there, through the darkness at the trees and bushes moving in the wind, it was strange and eerie.

I sat there with a bottle of whisky and started swallowing the paracetamol, packet by packet, then went to my room and swallowed some more. I don't know exactly how many, but it was a lot. I lay on the bed, finished off the whisky, and waited for a couple of hours for the paracetamol to get into my system. Then, for some reason, I phoned my younger brother Norman, and told him I didn't want to live like this anymore and it was time to put an end to it. I then told him what I had done, but wouldn't tell him where I was. But I had called him from the hotel phone, so he was able to trace the number and he phoned for an ambulance.

I don't remember much about the next part but, when I sobered up, I was lying on a bed in intensive care at the Borders General Hospital, and I was connected to all sorts of machinery. A lady consultant came in and stood in front of me holding a clipboard in her hands. She said, "Well, if you want to kill yourself there are better ways to do it. We're trying to flush the paracetamol out of your system but, if it doesn't work, it could result in liver failure and I'm sorry to say, a very painful death." My answer to that was, "Good. It's nothing more than I deserve."

My brother and his wife arrived, having driven down from Edinburgh. Most of the paracetamol was flushed out of my system. I was told some people had a greater tolerance to it than others, and that in some cases it only takes going over the maximum stated dose to cause problems. The doctor said I was very lucky they caught it in time.

They wanted to send me back to the Andrew Duncan Clinic in Edinburgh, but I said I wouldn't go back there, so instead I was taken to Dingleton Psychiatric Hospital in Melrose, where I stayed for six weeks.

Built as a lunatic asylum in the 1850s, Dingleton was one of the first psychiatric hospitals to experiment with electric shock treatment. Doctors would come from all around the world to watch the experiments being carried out, and to observe the results. Luckily that was a long time ago.

Up on a hill, amongst the trees, looking down over the town, the building was just as you would imagine an asylum to be: starkly built in solid stone, with large oak doors and dark windows. Inside, it had long, cold hallways, high vaulted ceilings and big heavy doors with large, ornate architraves.

I knew I wasn't crazy, and I felt a bit of a fraud when I saw patients there with serious mental illnesses. But I needed the help to sort myself out.

The first week was the worst, going through withdrawal, albeit with the help of medication. I was given a lot of question and answer forms to fill in, and literature to read, but I knew this was not going to be the place to deal with my alcoholism.

At night it was creepy with a lot of weird noises going on, and I didn't get much sleep at first. Once I got used to the surroundings it wasn't quite so bad. At meal times I shared a table with people who had some very strange habits: one girl would only eat her food from the inside out. Many of the patients were unable to hold any sort of conversation.

As I started to feel better, I realised that I had really let myself go and looked terrible. My hair was long and straggly, but I discovered that a hairdresser came into the hospital two days a week and had a makeshift salon in the basement. I got permission to go and get my hair cut. As it turned out, the hairdresser recognised me. June had been a Rollers fan in the days when we played at dances in the border towns, and was quite excited about cutting my hair.

When I got back up to ward I was looking a lot better and everybody was commenting on it. But one woman, who I would say was in her mid-thirties, really took an interest. I had been told she was manic-depressive, and that would certainly describe her behaviour. I've never seen anyone go from being so overenthusiastic and excited about something quite trivial, down to the depths of despair in such a very short time. She cried a lot, and I felt so sorry for her. I liked her very much and I felt she needed a friend, so she sort of clung on to me. The doctors were trying out new medications on her to see if they could balance things out, but she said they were making her worse.

She liked to be called Sue, and she sat beside me with a pile of fashion magazines, showing me the hairstyles that she liked, and asking me if she would suit her hair like this one or that one. It was quite obvious that her appearance had not been a priority in her life for some time, but she was an attractive woman. Then she asked me if I could get the hairdresser to do her hair. At first I was reluctant, thinking I was getting too involved here, but she kept on at me so I said I would ask for her.

I went down to the basement and spoke to June, who immediately said, "No. I would get into trouble if you brought her down here. Sue's not allowed out of the ward without being accompanied by one of the nurses." I begged June to do it, promising, "I'll take the blame if anything happens, and you can tell them that I said Sue had permission." June said, quite nervously, "Okay, bring her down and I'll see what I can do—but make it quick!" I ran upstairs and told Sue if we went right now she would do it.

We waited till everything was quiet. "Just follow me," I said as we left the ward and went down a long, dark hallway. About halfway along I heard footsteps in a side corridor and pushed Sue into a doorway. We stood there quietly until the footsteps went away, then ran the rest of the way to the stairs leading down to the basement. I got her into the hairdressing room and sat her down, I could see she was getting anxious and shaky. We got out the hairstyle magazines, but Sue was picking out styles that were way beyond what was possible. Eventually, June showed Sue a more simple, bob style that she quite liked, so June got started saying, "You'll get me sacked for this."

She made a fabulous job of Sue's hair, and it transformed her appearance. I hadn't really thought it out properly, though, as it was going to be rather obvious what had happened when the nurses saw her! I did get severely reprimanded, but Sue's trans-formation was incredible. She was happy and bouncy and get-ting attention, and she was like an entirely different person. She started dressing differently and caring about her appearance.

The following weekend, Sue's husband came in to visit. They went out for a walk together in the grounds, and when they came back her husband came over to me and shook my hand. He was smiling and said, "I don't know what you've done, but she's a different person. Maybe I'll be able to take her home soon." I hadn't really done much, but what I had must have raised her self-esteem and make her feel important again.

My younger brother and his wife visited me a few times, and my estranged wife Sheila also came in to see me. It was a chance to find out how my daughter was, how she was getting on at school and coping with everything. I asked if there was any chance Sarah would speak to me but the answer was, "She's not ready for that yet—it'll take time."

My sister, Margaret, had kept in touch by phone, telling me she was making progress getting funding for me to go to Castle Craig Clinic in Blyth Bridge near Peebles. It was a residential treatment centre for alcohol and drug addiction and it was not easy to get funding from the NHS and the Social Work Department. But my sister was very persistent—she wouldn't take no for an answer. My doctor told me, much later on, that he wished he had a sister like mine.

One of the patients in Dingleton was a young guy, Gary. He had been in and out of psychiatric hospitals for years and he didn't cope very well with living out in the real world. The love in his life was playing guitar and so we spent most of our time together talking about music. I would look out of the window every morning at the beautiful countryside surrounding the hospital, and the hill dominating the skyline, thinking, "I'm going to climb that before I leave here." I mentioned this plan to Gary, who said, "I'm going to do it with you!" We were both very unfit, so I suggested we go out for a run round the grounds every morning to build up to it, and that's what we did for an hour or so every morning for a week. It was hard work to start with, but every day we got better.

After being in the hospital for five weeks, I was assessed and told I would be discharged the following week, and I was to make arrangements for going back to Edinburgh. That was frightening. I had nowhere to go. But my sister had been speaking to Jan and Norrie to keep them informed about me, and Jan had said that if I was going to get into Castle Craig Clinic I could stay with them until the admission date.

My last week went very quickly. Sue left before I did. She was so happy and had new medication that seemed to be working. Her husband even said, "We're talking about having a baby." I was so happy for her I broke down in tears.

It was time to tackle that hill. We got up in the morning and had breakfast. The sun was shining, it was the perfect day. Gary and I set off on the long walk to the hill, through the pine trees, along dirt tracks and had a rest before tackling the steep climb to the top. Some of it was more of a walk than a climb, but some of it was quite treacherous. Gary was younger and fitter than me and I was struggling. Each time I thought we were nearly there another, even steeper, hill would appear. I had to take a rest every so often, but I kept saying to myself, "I'm going to make it." Gary ran up the last bit to the top, and shouted, "Come on! We're there!" My legs were aching, but I forced myself up the last section and I found myself standing on the top. We hugged each other and then I threw my arms in the air shouting, "We've done it!" and stood there for a while taking it all in. We came down a lot quicker that we went up, and ran all the way back to the hospital. It was an incredibly fulfilling sense of achievement.

The day I left Dingleton, I walked out of the hospital, down the hill to Melrose and straight into a pub and had a drink. It was almost robotic.

I wasn't drunk when I arrived back at Jan's house, but I'm sure she knew I had been drinking. It was a couple of weeks before Margaret called to arrange to pick me up and take me to Castle Craig Clinic, and by that time I was back on the booze as bad as ever.

The morning she arrived I had my bag packed and waiting in the hall beside my guitar and small amplifier, and I had consumed the best part of a bottle of vodka. I also had a carrier bag full of alcohol. Nothing was said, they just got me into her car and off we went.

CHAPTER FOURTEEN

The nearest village to Castle Craig is Blyth Bridge, which is about an hour's drive from Edinburgh. Approximately ten miles from Peebles, the castle itself is in the midst of the countryside surrounded by hills. The entrance to Castle Craig was through large gates with a small stone building on either side, and a long driveway wound around a wooded hill, mostly in the shade of the trees, until it opened up and I saw the beautiful country estate for the first time. Then the castle came into view.

It was more of a mansion than a castle, but very impressive, with sprawling lawns down to the road on the right-hand side, and to the left a stream running through the woods. The driveway split into two and there were other old stone buildings down to the left. My thoughts were all about sitting on the lawn with my guitar and writing songs, and rambling about in the countryside.

I arrived at the main entrance and was greeted by two female nurses who straight away took my guitar and amplifier saying, "You won't be getting these back until you leave." They also confiscated the alcohol and then led me into the building. I said goodbye to my sister and was taken up to the medical ward on the first floor, for assessment and tests. There they gave me a breathalyser to see how much alcohol was in my system, then turned their attention to taking blood samples, urine tests and blood pressure. Next I was told that Dr McCann would be up to see me shortly, so I should wait in the hallway. By this time I needed a drink and I was getting agitated. I said angrily, "Not another fucking doctor."

Dr Margaret Ann McCann was the owner of Castle Craig, along with her husband. It had been given hospital status for the residential treatment of alcohol and drug addiction and rehabilitation, and was based on the Twelve-Step programme of Alcoholics Anonymous, which I was very familiar with.

Dr McCann approached me and I was calmed down just by her appearance. I didn't expect to be confronted by a beautiful woman. She was soft-spoken and very well educated. We talked for a while and, when she left, I was taken down to the main lounge area and asked to wait there.

I discovered later that there had been discussions about refusing to admit me due to the fact I was under the influence of alcohol, and also because of my aggressive behaviour. Luckily for me, the senior therapist was Gordon H. whom I knew from AA meetings over the years, and had become friendly with. He argued my case and asked Dr McCann to give me a chance. Normally the procedure would be to go through detox in the medical ward before starting on the programme. But I had so much alcohol in my system that I had to wait two days before they would give me any medication.

Neil was one of the first guys I met in the lounge. He was a patient being treated for heroin addiction. He was sitting very close to me, and making me feel uncomfortable, until he told me he just liked the smell of alcohol on my breath.

After four days of detox, I was introduced to the community at the weekly meeting where all of the residents were brought up to date with any changes, and allowed to express their grievances or complaints about anyone who wasn't pulling their weight. It was all new to me, so I was just an observer, absorbing as much information as I could.

I soon learned that this whole programme was going to be hard work. All residents were given chores to do, which they would carry out for a week, then move on to different ones the following week. Some of the chores were harder than others, but it was done in rotation to make it fair.

On my first week I was put on dishwashing duty with another five patients. Other duties were: the cleaning and vacuuming of the lounge; raising of the flag at seven o'clock in the morning and lowering it at five o'clock at night; banging the gong exactly on time for breakfast, lunch and dinner; getting everyone up in the morning; collecting the laundry; setting the tables at meal times and clearing up afterwards; making coffee and tea; and cleaning the ashtrays.

Each day started with getting up at seven o'clock, then we had an hour to get washed and clean our rooms, before an hour of meditation in the library where we would read, out loud, sections from the AA's little black book: *Just For Today*.

Breakfast was at nine, and was followed by a half hour of relaxation; a group therapy session at half past ten (that could last between an hour and an hour and a half), then reading till lunch time at half past twelve.

The afternoons were filled with individual sessions with our therapists, and preparing peer assessments (in other words, making judgement on the others in your group as to whether you thought they were being honest, or not following the programme). These would be collected daily and read out at the weekly community meeting. Later in the afternoon we would have a presentation and discussion group. The remaining time before dinner was filled with more paperwork.

There was nowhere to hide in this place. It was forbidden to have sweets, chocolate, magazines, newspapers, television, radio, music (except on a Friday night, and it was chosen by the therapists), telephone calls (except when arranged, and with a therapist present). No training or exercising allowed. No visitors for the first four weeks, except direct family members. No wearing of T-shirts or clothing with slogans or messages on them. And do not leave the grounds of the estate.

All of the patients (or "peers") in Castle Craig were there because their lives had been destroyed by alcoholism or drug addiction, and they had reached rock bottom. The addicted person has no structure in his or her life—it is completely chaotic. This was the start of putting it back together, and I felt very grateful to be there. I had to expose everything in my life and face up to the terrible effect my alcoholism and behaviour had on my family and friends, especially my wife and daughter.

I asked my therapist, Tom, for a private moment with him. I needed some advice about how best to deal with the situation regarding Sarah, my daughter. It was breaking my heart that she was too frightened to talk to me. Tom suggested that I write a nice letter to her. So I did. Without getting too heavy, I just told her what it was like in the Castle, how I was doing, and also asked about her and how she was getting on at school. I wrote to her every single week and kept her informed of my progress and some of the funny things that had happened. I never got a reply, but her mother assured me she was reading them and that was enough.

I was sitting in the lounge one afternoon, catching up with paperwork, when a new patient came in. He was dressed only in a vest and jeans and I could see he was a strongly built guy, tall and broad. He had a skinhead, his front teeth were missing, one eye was half-closed and the other was wide open. Every time I looked over he was staring at me with an angry expression on his face. I felt quite unnerved by it. I tried to avoid him but he ended up in my peer group. Maybe I was picking up the wrong vibes, but he didn't seem to like me.

It was coming up to springtime of 1999 and Matty, the general maintenance man and driver for the estate, needed a hand in the garden so I volunteered. Dr McCann was so impressed with what I did that she asked me to do gardening work in other parts of the estate as well, and would pay me £4 for every hour I worked. She even asked me to look after the gardens around her own house, and gave me special dispensation from certain other formal activities, like my chores. I saved up every penny that I made and sent it to my daughter along with my regular letters.

Then some heavier work was suggested. They asked if I would prepare some plots and plant potatoes and other vegetables in them for the kitchen. I liked the sound of that and said, "I'd be delighted, but I'll need a hand."

I approached Gordon (the new guy I was so wary of) and asked him if he fancied giving me a hand doing the gardening, and he would get paid for it. He accepted and the two of us worked together. He was quiet at first but once he got to know me better he wouldn't shut up. He told me everything about himself and we became close friends. We even got to go to garden centres with Dr McCann to pick plants. I think she saw it as being good for our treatment.

It concerned me that I'd been quick to make such a judgement on this guy, just by the way he looked. When I got closer to him I realised that he was just as scared of life as I was. He was in for heroin addiction, and he told me stories about what he'd had to do to get his fix, and it was quite horrific. Most of his life seemed to be an endless cycle of prison and drugs.

He told me that when his wife left him he was sure she was with another man, and he went to her house in the dark, high on drugs. She was standing at the kitchen sink in front of the window when Gordon leapt off the wall, right through the glass, and grabbed her by the neck. He got quite emotional when he told me the story. I think that was the turning point that got him to come here.

He was from Aberdeen, which was a long way for his family to come so he hadn't had any visitors yet, but the next weekend his brother came down to see him. On the Monday after, Gordon was no longer in the castle. His brother had brought in some cannabis and they were caught smoking it. A month after that, I was told Gordon had died of a heroin overdose.

A nurse from the medical ward came up to me one day and said, "I know you, you're Nobby Clark. I used to come and see you with The Bay City Rollers." The senior therapist Gordon H. also knew about my background, and it soon got around that I was a singer.

Friday night was the one time in the week we had off, and allowed to have Coke and lemonade. You could stay in your room, or go down to the lounge and listen to music. I was constantly getting jibed about singing and being asked to give them a song, so I said, "Tell you what—I'll sing the first one if someone else sings their favourite song," and that's how it started. The following Friday I asked if we could go into the meeting room, so that anyone who didn't want to join in would have peace in the lounge. They agreed.

There were about ten of us that night. I started it off with a song, then passed it round. Some people preferred just to listen, but others sang. They'd start off a song and then let everyone join in. It was wonderful. The next Friday we had over twenty people who wanted to join in. We had people who had been in gangs, been in prison, been prostitutes and drug dealers, and they were all singing together.

I struck up a friendship with another young heroin addict, called Andy. He'd come along on the Friday nights but never joined in. Eventually I said, "Come on Andy, it's your turn," fully expecting him to say, "I'm just going to listen," but suddenly he started singing: "*Cheer up sleepy Jean... Oh, what can it mean ?*" Soon everybody joined in! I found out that some of the nurses and other members of staff were sitting in the adjoining room, listening.

In the Scottish Borders each year they have what's known as The Common Ridings. They celebrate each border town's history and traditions, and also commemorate the capturing of a flag from the English Army in 1514. The town's folk decorate tractors and vehicles in bright colours (known as floats) and drive in a procession through the towns.

Matty, the maintenance man, had got wind that I had carpentry experience and asked me if I would help him construct a float for the procession in my spare time. I told him, "I don't have any spare time, but I could maybe put in a couple of hours in the evening if they let me." I got the clearance to do it, as long as it didn't get in the way of my programme.

Matty was a big, overweight, farmer-type. I never, ever saw him without his blue overalls and cap on. He had a big, black beard and spoke with a very broad Borders accent. He was very serious about everything and also did an awful lot of moaning and complaining. On the TV at that time was a programme called Neighbours From Hell, and Matty had picked this as the subject for the float and just said, "See what you can do with it."

As is usual with me, I take the attitude that if a job's worth doing, it's worth doing well. Matty simply dropped off the stuff and walked away, so I got a couple of people to help me.

To start with, I boxed in the tractor with plywood in the shape of a small house. I painted it pink and gave it a grey tiled roof—I even had smoke coming out of the chimney! I painted on windows with floral curtains, and around the bottom of the house I painted flowers, plants and a white picket fence with a blackbird sitting on it.

Then the trailer behind the tractor was boxed in around the sides, and painted black. I made a frame and fixed plywood, standing upright, across the middle of the trailer and painted that black too. Next I painted red and yellow flames from the bottom of the trailer all the way up through the central boards, In between the flames I painted **Neighbours from Hell** in big letters—it was very impressive. I thought it looked great and would make people smile.

Matty drove along in the procession, which passed through all the border towns, and at the end the organisers held a competition. Matty won 1st prize for best float! The winner got a cheque for £200 and a certificate from the Lord Provost. He was going around bragging about it and taking all the credit, and I got nothing.

However, I soon found out that six months earlier Matty had a dispute with his neighbour over a tree hanging into his garden. Matty had taken a chainsaw, climbed over the fence and cut it down. The neighbour had come out raging, and kicked Matty so hard in the goolies that he ended up in hospital with a rupture. This was Matty's revenge on his neighbour. I couldn't stop laughing when I heard about it.

Most nights after dinner, I went down to the small chapel in the basement for some peace and quiet. I liked the atmosphere—it was absolutely silent. The chapel had light oak seats around the walls and a beautifully carved lectern with a very old bible on it. Every piece of oak furniture in there had been designed and created by Robert Thomson from Kilburn, North Yorkshire, and if you looked carefully, you could find a carved mouse somewhere on every piece. This tradition started when one of Thomson's colleagues made a comment about being as poor as a church mouse. From then on he carved it into every piece he made, and became known as Mousy Thomson.

At first I went down and sat in the chapel on my own. Soon Angie followed me down the stairs. She followed me everywhere, in fact, and it was becoming a bit of a problem. She had some serious issues other than alcohol and drugs… one day she lifted up her T-shirt to show me scars, all over her body, where she had cut herself with knives. Everywhere I went Angie was right there beside me and it was becoming a bit creepy, so I spoke to my therapist about it. I was told that before she came to the Castle, she had been in a psychiatric hospital after smashing her kitchen window, picking up a shard of glass and slicing her arms with it, in front of her four-year-old daughter.

Other peers started to come down to the chapel after dinner too, and we had quite a gathering. I thought it might be fun to go up to the bible, open it randomly and read whatever story was on the page. To start with it was quite funny—we laughed when the first one or two took turns to stand behind the lectern and read something out, and then looked so shocked at how it seemed to relate to them. But then it got serious. Every person who went up and opened the bible at a random page found they were reading a story with names or events that related directly to them. Some were in tears, and one girl slammed the bible shut and said, "I don't like this. I'm getting out of here!" It was very strange and unnerving, so I stopped it.

Religion has always been a problem to me. When I was a young boy my mother sent me to Sunday school saying, "I want you to learn about the bible so you can make up your own mind." At every Alcoholics Anonymous meeting you will see signs on the walls relating to God and a belief in a higher power. I've always struggled with that because I don't believe in the God that the bible refers to, and I have strong feelings about religious organisations. It troubled me to be told that, in order to stay sober, it was necessary to hand over my life to the will of God.

I asked to see the chaplain at Castle Craig on a one-to-one basis, and we sat in the chapel while he listened to my concerns. There was a pause for a few moments, before he said this to me, "I get up at five thirty every morning, and talk to God and read from the bible. Then I go and do God's work for most of the day. In the late afternoon I talk to God again, and read from the bible, and in the evening I go and do God's work and finish the day in prayer. In all the years I've been doing that, I have never felt a presence."

I wasn't sure what to take from that. It left me even more confused.

I was doing really well at Castle Craig. I had worked very hard on my honesty, and myself. The intensive therapy had resulted in the stripping away of all the defensive layers I had built up over the years and I was feeling very vulnerable and lost. I was having difficulty recognising myself when I was that exposed. My therapist arranged a family therapy session and invited my brothers and sisters, and my wife, to attend. My wife declined, my sister Margaret couldn't make it down from Perth, and my older brother was in Bradford. However, my brother Norman, his wife, and my sister Rosemary all came for the session and were told by Tom, my therapist, to be as honest as possible.

We sat together in a room, and they began by telling me about the times I'd turned up at their doors in the middle of the night, drunk and giving them abuse. Then they talked about the late-night phone calls, when I would be swearing and shouting down the phone. They said they'd not put up with that ever again. They wanted me to get well and would do anything to help, but they had had enough of my behaviour. I didn't say anything—I just felt stupid and dejected.

The way it worked at Castle Craig was a four to eight week programme of intense therapy up in the main house (the Castle as it was called), depending on how you were doing. After this you would be moved to the Extended Care Unit on another part of the estate, where you could take more responsibility, and have a bit more freedom, but still attend therapy sessions, peer group meetings and assessments. Once a week you'd be driven up to Edinburgh, in a minibus, to attend an AA meeting.

I had been in the Castle for nearly six weeks, so far, and had been moved up to a room in the attic, awaiting funding from the social work department so I could move down to the extended care unit.

I was now allowed to have visitors, but not before they were given a briefing by my therapist. My two closest friends, Davie Paton and John Turner came to see me. It was really good to see them and go for a walk in the grounds, but just talking about other things for a while made me realise I was nowhere near ready to face normal life yet.

There was an open meeting the same evening for the whole community, and any friends and family who wanted to attend. I had been asked to share my story at the meeting, and Davie and

John stayed for the meeting, hearing me speak for the first time about my alcoholism. Both of them had tried to help me when I was in a bad way, but I don't think they realised just how bad it was. I was very grateful to them for coming.

I hadn't seen my guitar since the day I arrived at Craig Castle, so I was taken by surprise when Phil (the youngest of the therapists) asked me if I would do a little concert for everyone. I had to think about it for a while because I hadn't played for some time. I agreed to do it if I was allowed to involve some of the other patients. I knew of one guy who played a bit of guitar, and another guy from Glasgow who played the penny whistle. I also put out a general invitation for anyone who wanted to join in, and recruited some singers from our Friday night get togethers. Phil came to me and said, "Could you try and fit Veronica in there somewhere. She says she can play a song on the recorder."

Veronica, or Ronnie as she liked to be called, was a lovely young girl. Just eighteen, she was open and bubbly, but vulnerable, because, on top of everything else, she had a serious sex addiction, and was being pestered by some of the guys in the place. Neil, the very first guy I met when I arrived, had persuaded her to have sex with him down in the chapel and was now running around asking everyone if they had a condom. I was raging, and pulled him aside saying, "You shouldn't be taking advantage of her when she's trying to deal with her problem." He wasn't deterred, and I was about to speak to the therapist about it when one of the older girls, who'd been looking after Ronnie, beat me to it.

The concert would take place the following Friday night in the library. I had very little time to organise it or rehearse the songs, so I just threw everyone in at the deep end. We had the whole community sitting round in a big circle with therapists, nurses and staff all standing at the back. Phil had brought in his Fender guitar for me to use, and plugged into my small amplifier. I had George strumming acoustic guitar on my right and Ian playing whistle on my left. Veronica, who was terrified, sat in amongst the crowd, clinging on to her recorder for dear life, looking down at the floor, nervously waiting for her cue.

I sang through my list of songs with the help of the singers, and some wonderful accompaniment from George and Ian. Then Ian played some jigs on the whistle and it all went down a storm. But the highlight of the evening was when I introduced Veronica and she played her little tune on the recorder, accompanied by me on guitar, and the whole community just went mad, cheering her and clapping—there wasn't a dry eye in the place. It was one of the most heart-warming experiences I have ever had.

Each month, the therapists appointed a Community Leader. I was approached and asked if I wanted to take on the job and I agreed. I was to be responsible for dealing with any grievances and disputes among the patients, make sure that everyone was carrying out their duties properly, collect and distribute all paperwork, and chair and organise the weekly community meetings.

One of the first requests I received after being appointed was from Andy, the spokesman for a number of young heroin addicts. They had previously requested a football and been refused. They obviously hoped I could argue the case for them, which I did, and permission was granted on the condition it would only be for two hours on a Saturday, when there were no groups or therapy sessions, and the ball would have to be locked up the rest of the time. They were like little happy schoolboys again, jumping on each other's backs and fooling around. Some of them had a history of playing football, with quite successful clubs, before becoming involved in drugs, and they thought they could just pick up where they left off.

There was a level grassed area, surrounded by tress, at the top of the hill to the east side of the Castle. It was ideal. To start with, there were about eight who wanted to play, but ten or twelve turned up, and then some of the girls wanted to join in but that was a no go—the boys were taking it very seriously.

We got up on the hill and started enthusiastically kicking the ball around. Most of the community had come to spectate. Then, as I had expected, there were arguments about who was going to play on what team. I had to intervene and draw straws. Being one of the oldest, I had already booked my place as goalkeeper. We set up makeshift goalposts and the game got underway.

For the first ten minutes they were running up and down like fit young things and showing off to the crowd. Then the angry exchanges started with handbags at dawn, pushing and shoving, and I had to pull them apart and ended up acting as referee as well as goalkeeper. It would be hard to describe it as football, since there was more falling down and running into each other than actually kicking the ball. I wasn't any good to anybody because I was doubled up laughing. Twenty minutes in, and half of them were in the bushes throwing up while the rest were lyng on the ground gasping for breath—it was hilarious. The game was abandoned and that was the end of football.

My time came to move down to the extended care unit, or ECU as it was known. I knew all the people there already, so I was quite looking forward to it. The unit was down at the bottom of the estate and was made up of converted farm cottages and outhouses. There was a walled garden and a disused swimming pool, in which Matty kept live trout and would net them when he needed them for his dinner.

All the cottages had a number, and I was moved into house six. Some houses were female only but we all shared the laundry room and the common lounge. I really liked it there, it was right in amongst the woods, with countryside and hills as far as you could see.

Many restrictions were removed when you got to ECU. We could make phone calls, read papers and magazines, listen to music, and have coffee that wasn't decaf. I was even allowed to have my guitar. There was a lot more freedom. This was to prepare you for going out into the real world, but the thought of that terrified me, so I put it to the back of my mind.

I continued to send my letters to Sarah every week, along with the money I made, but I never got a reply.

However, it was still very strict down at ECU. We had a stringent programme to work to, and all the peers looked out for each other. If there were any signs that you were going off the rails it was soon dealt with. We still went up to the Castle to eat and go to meetings, where we were expected to encourage, and show an example to, the newer patients.

I carried on as Community Leader while staying at the ECU, and a lot of the younger peers seemed to respect me in that role, as they came to me with problems they didn't want to discuss with their therapist. I carried on with the gardening too, on my own mainly, but I would recruit other guys when there was heavy digging to do. We were now growing potatoes, broad beans, carrots, turnips, onions, cabbages and lettuce—all being used in the kitchen. It was very satisfying.

The girls in one of the cottages had a drying green at the back of their house, and would hang their washing out to dry overnight. One morning they complained that clothes and underwear had been going missing off the line. There was a lot of joking about with the guys, and finger pointing in fun, but it happened more than once so I reported it.

In the laundry room at ECU there were four washing machines which were constantly in use, so I would usually go in there early in the day to grab one. This particular morning it was busy, and four of the girls were standing about chatting, either waiting to use a machine or waiting for their load to finish.

When my stuff was ready, I lifted all of my damp washing out of the machine and onto the table in front of the girls, and a pair of pink and white, lacy knickers was right on top of my washing pile. One of the girls saw them and shouted, "So you're the knicker nicker!" The other girls burst out laughing. Oh my God, I didn't know where to look, I was so embarrassed! My mind was trying, and failing, to think of a reason why they were in my washing. Then it dawned on me that they must have been left in the machine before I put my clothes in it. I was going to be in for a right ribbing...

I had to chair the next community meeting and wasn't looking forward to it. The knicker story had spread through the whole community by then. I had to put up with the jokes like, "What colour are you wearing today?" and, "I know what to buy you for your birthday now." Even the therapist at the meeting was having a good laugh. I just had to take it in good humour.

It was over four months since I first walked through the door of the Castle. I was feeling quite raw and maybe slightly institutionalised. This had been my home and my sanctuary. It was a frightening prospect thinking I would have to leave soon. I had nothing to go back to, nowhere to live, no money and no belongings. I was fifty years old, and the thought of starting off all over again just filled me with dread. So much so, that I came up with a scheme. The two small gatehouses down at the entrance to the estate were derelict. I put forward the suggestion that I could renovate them and stay in one of them as the gatekeeper and gardener. All they would have to do is feed and water me.

Of course it was only a pipe dream. My therapist, Tom, told me I would have to start preparing for going back out into the real world, with their support behind me.

I had a visit from the social worker allocated to my case to discuss what my options were for housing and benefits until I got back on my feet. We filled in the forms for social housing and off she went.

I didn't see her again until the day I was leaving. She came in her car to take me back to Edinburgh after five months in Castle Craig. On the way back in the car, she told me all the things she had been doing on my behalf. I would get unemployment benefit and income support as soon as I had an address.

She had applied for a place for me in a homeless hostel, but wouldn't know until later that day if I would get in. I got the call saying they had a room for me and I moved into the hostel. I stayed there for six months, during which time I had to put up with fighting, stealing, drug dealing, and lots of alcohol around me, but I kept myself to myself and avoided it all as much as possible.

My social worker then got me moved to a halfway house run by the Church of Scotland. It was a really nice flat that I shared with two other men. I lived very quietly and kept out of trouble and went to an AA meeting almost every day. I had homeless and medical priority on the council's housing list and, after six weeks in the halfway house, I was offered a one-bedroom flat.

That was fifteen years ago and I haven't touched a drop since.

CHAPTER FIFTEEN

I had to start earning some money.

I had been back in touch with an old friend and he said he needed some locks changed in his house. So I borrowed some tools, put them in a bag, and got on the bus to the other side of town. I did the work and made £30. He passed the word onto someone else and I picked up some more work. I was also still in touch with the man who ran the homeless hostel and he gave me some joinery work to do—this got me off the ground and gave me back some self-respect. It was hard, but I just had to get on with it.

I was told many times in AA that if I stayed sober everything would get better. They were right. The people there were very helpful and generous, especially my friend Anne. I'd met her in Castle Craig and we got on like a house on fire. She was a great character—very old-fashioned, a bit of a snob, liked a bit of gossip, but we had some good laughs. She drove me round looking for second-hand furniture and a fire for my living room. She knew I didn't have much money, so she bought me plates and pots and utensils for my kitchen. She said, "You can pay me back when your boat comes in." It's amazing how much these things meant to me without being worth much in monetary terms. I had learned a whole new value system.

A year went by really quickly. I no longer had a driving licence and had previously been told by the DVLA medical division that, because I had been convicted three times, and was a registered alcoholic, I would not be allowed to hold a licence. It was now three and a half years since my last driving conviction, so I took a chance and wrote to the DVLA again about a new licence. I got a letter back from their Medical Officer stating that if I could give them proof in another year's time that I was still abstinent from alcohol, they would reconsider my case. I did as they asked, with the help of my doctor and Castle Craig, and so they issued me with a one-year licence. At the end of that year I had to have a Ministry of Transport medical before they would issue me with another year's licence. This went on for three years before they allowed me to hold a full licence again.

I still wrote to my daughter every week or so, and still didn't get any reply, but I was in touch with her mother and got reports on how she was doing. Sheila had to take Sarah out of St Serf's private school, which had 160 pupils, and put her into Craigmount School which had over 2,000 pupils. That must have been a difficult transition for Sarah.

Then I got the worst possible news. My sister Margaret was diagnosed with cancer. The doctors said at first that it was operable, and she was very positive about it, and up for the fight, but they did further tests to make sure. These tests showed that it had spread, meaning an operation wouldn't be possible. Margaret was amazing the way she handled it—it was the family who went crazy. How could they build her hopes up and give her the wrong prognosis? We went to see the consultant and had some angry exchanges, but it was too late. They offered her chemotherapy, which she gave some consideration, but decided she would rather spend the time she had with her family.

Margaret had two daughters, Michelle and Alison, and a beautiful granddaughter, Dannielle, whom she adored. My youngest sister, Rosemary, suggested having a family holiday while Margaret was still strong enough to go. I put forward the idea of going to Disneyland, Paris and everyone agreed. It was good to have all the family together but I couldn't say I enjoyed it. I didn't handle it very well and I'm sorry for that. I went up to Perth to see her as much as I could but within a few months she was gone.

The family decided it would be better not to tell my mother, who had been ill for a while and diagnosed with Alzheimers disease. I still spent every Sunday afternoon with her at her house, but I could see that she was no longer coping. Sometimes I would arrive and smell gas... she would have put on a pot of tea, turned the gas down too low and it would blow out. I would find food in the fridge that was mouldy and out of date. She wasn't capable of looking after herself.

It broke my heart when she asked me, one day, if I would come back and stay with her. But I was too frightened I would drink again. My flat was my safe house. I had my life in order and under control. My sister and I discussed it and decided to get Mum more help, and split up the week between us so she would have a visitor every day, but we knew it was getting near the time when she would have to go into a nursing home.

I had saved up some money and bought an old banger of a car for £300. Sometimes, when I was in the area I would drive by Sarah's school, or sit outside the gates for a while, in the hope of seeing her, but I never did. I asked her mother if she had a mobile phone and, if so, would she let me text her? She asked Sarah and she said yes. I did text regularly, but still didn't get any reply.

Then it happened, I was up a ladder, fixing windows, when my phone rang and a voice on the other end said, "It's me, Dad." I nearly fell off the ladder! I was holding back the tears. We talked for ages then I asked her if I could call her sometime. She said, "No. I'll call you." I was walking on air for days with a big smile on my face. We had quite a number of conversations on the phone before I made the suggestion that maybe, sometime when she was ready, we could meet up. She said she would think about it.

I hadn't been told, for probably the right reasons, that Sarah had been through a terrible time with eating disorders and self-harming. She had agoraphobia too, and hadn't been out of the house for the last two years. She also suffered from migraines and panic attacks.

When her mother told me all this it tore me apart. I took the blame fully on my shoulders and knew I had to put this right as soon as possible. I kept reminding Sarah to think about meeting up, but every time she said she wasn't ready. Then, at long last, the call came that I had been waiting for—Sarah agreed to meet me at her mother's house.

I was so nervous, walking up to the door, my heart was racing. I rang the bell and I could hear movement on the inside. I waited for a while then heard her voice. She said, "Dad, I'm too scared to open the door." So we had a conversation through the letterbox, with her sitting on the floor inside and me on the step outside.

I had suggested to her that if she moved into a flat with people her own age it might help her. She was quite open to the idea and so I started to look for the right situation. I had a very good friend whom I trusted, whose son was taking on a ground floor flat in a nice part of town, and was looking for another two people to share.

I managed to set it all up, and then her mother drove Sarah and her belongings, to the flat and she moved in. Unfortunately, though, she stayed in and didn't leave the place. But her flat-mates were fantastic, and understood her problems.

She said she would like to learn to play the guitar, and I asked my close friend Rab Howat, a renowned guitar player, if he would teach her. Every week he gave her a guitar lesson, which also gave me the opportunity to find out from Rab how she was getting on. It was all going the right way. She told me that she had even ventured out a couple of times with her flatmates.

But I still hadn't seen her yet.

When I first came out of Castle Craig, I wrote some songs that were very personal, and my friend Davie Paton arranged, produced, and recorded them for me. I had no intentions of letting anyone else hear them, but Davie eventually persuaded me to put them on an album, and I called it *If Only*. Because of this, I met some of the closest friends I still have today.

Davie played my songs to some people in the studio, and I met Kenny Herbert who encouraged me to perform the songs live with Rab Howat, who was one of the best live guitar players I had come across.

Davie had been working with an American guy called Kirk Kiester who had designed his website and was working on promoting Davie's new music. He introduced me to him and I asked if he would do the same for me.

Kirk lived in Atlanta, Georgia. He was a big Pilot fan and had been following Davie's career over the years. He liked my album and wanted to help promote it. We spoke on the phone many times as I was passing information to him for my website. But it was difficult to explain to him on the phone exactly what I wanted, so he suggested that I fly over to Atlanta for a holiday and combine it with working on the website together. The deal was if I could pay for the flights he would put me up when I got there, and I could do some work on his house as repayment.

As usual when it came to flying, just talking about it triggered a sense of panic and anxiety. It was going to be a long flight and I wasn't looking forward to it. I flew out on the 9th September 2001 and was due to arrive on my birthday, 10th September. It was a wide-bodied jet with three seats on either side, and four in the middle. I was sitting in the middle section. I had watched the movies, eaten dinner, and read the magazines poking out of the pocket of the seat in front for the third or fourth time. I always get disorientated on these long flights. I was thinking, "We're nearly there. Just four hours to go. I'll close my eyes and take a rest," when I heard a commotion up at the front of the cabin.

Two air stewards were wrestling with a scruffy-looking man, and another steward was moving fast up the aisle towards them. The man broke free and ran at the third steward, punching him in face. Then two large men, who turned out to be off-duty security guards, jumped on him and dragged him to the floor. They pulled him to the front of the plane and tied him down with the seat belts.

An announcement came over the speaker a few minutes later, "This is your captain. Remain in your seats, everything is under control." I could see the two heavy men sitting on either side of this crazy man. It all settled down for about an hour then kicked off again when the man somehow managed to get free, and it took four of five of them to subdue him this time.

After he was secured again all was quiet until we landed. They wouldn't let any of the passengers leave the plane until the airport police had come on board and taken the guy off. Only then did everyone start talking, and I could see the relief on everyone's faces—it had been extremely stressful. I never did find out what it was all about.

Kirk was there at the airport to pick me up, and we drove straight to his house on a private estate in the suburbs of Atlanta. Kirk's interest in music was part time. During the day he worked for the U.S. Government and had taken a few days off to spend time with me.

He had a beautiful big house, set in its own grounds, that he shared with his wife Anita, their two boys, Fox and Colin, and their brand new baby girl, Caroline. Anita's mother, Helga, also lived with them in a large apartment in the basement, that she kindly vacated so that I could stay there. They couldn't have made me feel more welcome. They were such a lovely family, and also very religious—it had been a long time since I'd said grace at the dinner table. By the time I got settled in and had dinner and a chat, I was nearly falling asleep so headed down stairs for an early night.

We were all up early the next day, the 11th September, and I was playing with the boys in the living room with the television on. Kirk suddenly came through from the kitchen and switched the television over to the live news channel, just as they showed the first aircraft crashing into the World Trade Centre. We both looked at each other. I'd thought it was a trailer for a film, but when the second plane crashed into the tower, and we were watching it live, I saw Kirk's face go white. Then Anita came running through shouting, "Oh my god, what's happened?" We all stared at the screen in disbelief.

More news was coming in as the events unfolded. We stood there and watched the towers collapse, one after the other, live on the screen. Nobody moved—we were rooted to the spot and all in shock. When they announced that a third plane had crashed into the Pentagon, it was even worse for Kirk because he worked there and knew a lot of people. I'm struggling to find the right words to describe the feeling in the house that day. Hardly a word was spoken.

Kirk and Anita had to act as normally as they could for the next few days for the sake of the children. Kirk drove into his office in Atlanta to find out more about his work colleagues at the Pentagon, while I got on with fixing things around their house. I was due to fly home in a few days but all flights were grounded. I couldn't get any information on when it would be cleared to fly again and, to be honest, I wasn't relishing the thought of getting on a plane anyway.

We managed to do some work on the website, and we also had a trip down to southern Georgia, where I had my first taste of boiled peanuts from a vendor at the side of the road. We all tried to keep our minds off the terrible events that had happened.

Kirk and Anita took me to their church the following Sunday. It was nothing like any church I had ever been to. I'm not religious, in the sense that I don't believe in the God of the bible, nor burning bushes and voices from above—that's all nonsense to me. The God that they forced upon me when I was a young boy is just the manifestation of human inability to accept death as the finality of life. I believe that all human beings need a code of conduct, but my higher power comes from somewhere else. I don't need fear and threats to tell me when I'm doing wrong.

I'm only being honest, and expressing my opinion, when I describe what I saw at that church. We drove up to a very large, spread-out building of modern construction with a high, imposing bell tower. There were to be two services that Sunday, one in the afternoon and one early evening. The car parking area was enormous—it reminded me of a large shopping centre—and there must have been thousands of cars parked all around the church. We dropped off Fox and Colin, at something like our Sunday School in Scotland, then parked the car and walked into the church.

The church could hold 2,500 people, and it was full that morning. The subject of the sermon was chosen because so many people had been asking the same thing—why God allowed such terrible things to happen in the world? The minister's answer to that was: "God is a non-interventionist God." It seems to me that religious people just move the goal posts to suit their requirements.

At the end of the sermon a group of young musicians got on the stage with guitars, drums and keyboard, and sang songs of love and peace. The congregation were on their feet singing along and dancing. That part I got. There was a real community spirit, but near the end they passed round a large box and everyone put money and cheques into it—over the whole day there would have been approximately 5,000 people all writing out cheques or putting money in the box.

I found out that the minister of the church owned a number of mansions, and other properties across America, and yet no one was questioning the use of the money they were donating. It all seemed wrong to me. I thought it was about love and charity and being kind to your fellow man and woman. I kind of felt sorry for some of the people I met because they seemed like genuinely nice people, but doing what they were told for fear of being outcast.

I had been there over a week now, and needed to try and find an AA meeting. It wasn't difficult—we just phoned a central number and were guided to an address in Atlanta. Kirk was kind enough to take me to the meeting and leave me there for a couple of hours before picking me up again. It doesn't matter where you are in the world, AA is never far away and the message is always the same.

I stayed in Atlanta a week longer than I had planned, until the authorities allowed the planes to take to the skies again, and I landed back in my home country safe and sound.

It was time to decide whether I could handle performing live again. In the past I had suffered from stage fright that made me physically sick beforehand, but once I'd got on stage all the nerves disappeared—so I knew I could do it. On the album I had arranged and sung some quite complicated vocal harmonies, and had no idea how I could reproduce that live. The thought of singing in front of a paying audience was terrifying.

I got in touch with Gus Boyd who I hadn't seen him for many years, not since we'd put a band together and played some gigs for fun. He was a good bass player but, more importantly, he had a great harmony falsetto voice.

Gus had contacts in the Edinburgh Festival Fringe where he had performed with his Eagles tribute band, at the Spiegeltent.

With his help I arranged a date and advertised it in the Fringe programme. I put a band together with Rab Howat on guitar and vocals, Martin Wykes on drums, Dougie Coulter on keyboards and vocals, and Gus Boyd on bass and vocals. I got posters printed and put up all over the town saying, "Nobby Clark and Friends appearing at the Spiegeltent at the Edinburgh Festival Fringe."

There were two main reasons why I wanted to do it: I needed to prove to myself that I could get on stage and sing live, and I also wanted Sarah to come and hear me sing, which was what motivated me more than anything else.

The band was just fantastic. We played every song off the album and it went down a storm. My wife had told me Sarah wanted to come, and was going to try and make it. When the gig finished I ran out to the bar and saw my wife, Sheila, standing talking with a crowd of people.

I asked her if Sarah was here, but she said, "No, she backed out at the last minute." I was so disappointed.

It was to take a long time.

CHAPTER SIXTEEN

Sarah had been twelve when I'd last seen her, and when we eventually met up again she was twenty-one. We had to start a whole new relationship, very slowly at first, with her mother present, just gradually building up the trust. I couldn't have been more proud of her. She was a beautiful young woman, who came across as being full of confidence and flair, but I could detect the fear and vulnerability that her illness had instilled. Controlling everything in her life was her coping mechanism.

We talked a lot. Well, she did—I could hardly get a word in edgeways! She told me everything, including how she had been bullied at school by one particular boy who would sit behind her on the bus and make a fool of her in front of his pals. One morning he even poured a can of Coke over her head, and the worst thing of all had been when he and his gang pulled her round the back of the school building, wrapped her in cling film and left her there.

I was seething with rage when she told me all this, and wanted to go and find him, but she was the one who said, "He's not worth it. I bumped into him a few years later and he was pathetic—he was still living with his mother, with no job and no friends. When I confronted him he just said, 'I did it because I liked you.' " Sarah had missed a lot of days at school because of him, but she was bright and intelligent, it wasn't going to be a problem.

We built up our relationship, bit by bit, and Sarah and I became the best of friends again. By this time I had a good building business going and was in a position to help her financially.

Meanwhile though, my mum's health was deteriorating. She'd had a bad fall but didn't tell anyone. She didn't like to make a fuss. It was only when we saw her flinching as she tried to stand up that we realised she was in pain. The doctor who examined her found she had a fractured hip, and he thought it had been that way for a while.

We had no choice—it was time to find the right nursing home for her. It was a horrible decision to have to make but she needed full-time care now. The next two months Rosemary and I went round all the nursing homes that we thought might be suitable. We trekked far and wide, and ended up back in Drum Brae where my mum lived! The home was fine and we liked the people who ran it, but I think it was more of an emotional decision—she would be in an area that was familiar to her, and when we took her out for the day she would recognise the surroundings. The whole family agreed it was the right thing to do.

Taking her there was hard enough, but leaving her there was heartbreaking. She didn't understand that this was going to be her new home. What a horrible thing to go through. I felt guilty—I hadn't done enough to help her over the years and now when she needed me I was leaving her with strangers.

Rosemary, Norman and I took turns visiting her each day until she got settled. Rosemary's children, Kerry and Keith, made regular visits too. My older brother Brian must have felt helpless and left out. He was a professor at Bradford University and needed to travel a lot round the world, but he came up as often as he could. Eventually I was relieved to see that she seemed to quite like having people around her in the home, and I got back into my routine of spending Sundays with her.

Now that I had my alcoholism under control I knew that I would never be cured, but I could arrest it, and hopefully stay sober for the rest of my life by staying on the AA programme.

But I was still gambling on a regular basis and felt helpless to stop it. I had a particularly bad run of so-called luck and lost quite a lot of my hard-earned cash. Walking the streets depressed I came across a shop at the top corner of Cockburn Street, just off the Royal Mile.

The shop was called Body and Mind, and there were displays of crystals in the window. I walked in to have a look and

217

while I was looking around, the owner came up to me and asked what my birth sign was. I told him I was a Virgo and he said, "I know what you need." I didn't know this person—I had never seen him in my life—but off he went down to the basement and brought up a large piece of rock he called fluorite. He took a small hammer, cracked off a piece, and handed it to me saying, "Carry this with you all the time."

I walked out of the shop and took that crystal with me everywhere I went, and I have not been in a bookies shop or a casino since. That was ten years ago. I have no idea why that happened, and I don't need to know.

When I'd left Castle Craig I decided it would be best if I didn't get into a relationship. I had a few liaisons, but was closed to getting too involved. Then I met Geraldine.

My guitar-playing friend, Rab Howat, had a regular Saturday afternoon gig in a pub called The Cas Rock. I didn't know him then but I had seen him play there a few times. The place was always mobbed and almost impossible to get to the bar for a soft drink. While I was standing waiting for a space, this woman came up and stood beside me. I was immediately attracted to her so I tried to make conversation but she wasn't forthcoming. She was there with her daughter and I asked her if she wanted a drink. We stood and had a conversation while her mother made her way to the back of the bar. The daughter's name was Jenny and I said to her, "Your mother's a bit standoffish." "Yeah," she replied, "she's off men just now, just split up with somebody." So I left it at that.

A couple of months later, The Rab Howat Band had moved from The Cas Rock to a new venue called Bannerman's. I walked in and there was a friend of mine, Sheena, standing at the bar with the woman I had met at The Cas Rock.

This time we did have a conversation—in fact, I missed most of the band's set. I found out that she knew me when I was a teenager as she lived almost directly behind my mother's house. She said, "Everybody in Drum Brae knew who Nobby Clark was, because all the Bay City Rollers fans used to gather outside your house. You even spoke to me once when we passed in the street!" When she told me who her brother was, I remembered him from my schooldays because he was roughly the same age as me. It was quite a coincidence. But I resisted asking her out because I was still in my no-relationship mode.

A couple of weeks later I saw her in Bannerman's again and we had a brief conversation while watching the band. As she left, she handed me a piece of paper with her phone number on it. I called her and asked her out. That was in 2005 and we've been in a relationship ever since.

I completed and released my second album *Going Home*, produced and arranged by Davie Paton again, and I was occasionally performing live, at small venues.

Meanwhile, my daughter, Sarah, was gradually getting better. She could go out now, as long as she was with someone. Her biggest problems were panic attacks and the fear of having a migraine when she was on her own. I've been a migraine sufferer since I was eight or nine, and have had some bad ones, but Sarah's migraines were very severe. She could lose all feeling in her arms and legs, become disorientated, and her eyesight would become completely distorted. Her doctor had started her on medication designed to alleviate the problem but she still got them, albeit less frequently.

I took her in to see her Granny whom she hadn't seen for over ten years. Sarah was so delighted to see her, and sat holding her hand, and talking to her. She only had to meet the rest of her cousins and aunts and uncles now and the circle would be complete, so we set up a family gathering at Geraldine's flat. I even picked up my mum from the nursing home and took her over to see everyone for a short time. It was so good, I just sat back and let them all get on with it. Sarah regularly came with me to see her Granny after that.

I loved going to see my mum. When she saw me from the far end of the room her face would light up. Although she was confused, there was nothing wrong with her long-term memory—it was her short-term memory that was fading fast. I said, jokingly, to one of the care workers, "It's great for her... every time I go out of the room and come back in again she thinks I've just arrived—she gets about five visits a day!"

In her more lucid moments she would ask if I had seen Margaret (my late sister). I felt it was better to pass over it and not upset or confuse her any more than necessary.

Geraldine and I were getting along just fine. She was a very stabilising influence and, whenever my over-eager enthusiasm clouded my judgement, she brought me down to earth. She understood that my sobriety was the top priority in my life. We often went out to revisit places from our past, and I told her the story about Clermiston House and the statue.

For all these years, it was in the back of my mind. Why did they destroy such a magical place and where did the statue go? I wanted to do some research and find out more. Geraldine was very good at searching for historical documents and family history, so the two of us got stuck in.

The obvious place to start was Corstorphine Trust. We found out that the trust was given permission to take over Dower House in St. Margaret's Park in Corstorphine village. Dower House was built in 1587 and was the oldest inhabited building in Edinburgh. It was derelict when the Trust took it over, but thanks to grants from Historic Scotland and the Lottery Fund it is now a thriving centre of the community.

I was hoping they would hold some records of Clermiston House and the family history that went with it, and we were given permission to look through their documents, old books and photographs. It was fascinating, and took a while, but then on the turn of a page there it was, a photograph of Clermiston House with the stone statue standing proud in the foreground. The photograph even showed the stone balusters along the top of the front wall. We discovered Clermiston House had been built by James Ingles, in 1792. He had originally lived in Dower House, but found it was too small for his needs, so he built Clermiston House instead. It was James Ingles who commissioned the stone statue, sculpted by Robert Forest, depicting King James V (the last King of Scotland and father of Mary, Queen of Scots), on horseback, being attacked by a band of gypsy robbers at Cramond Brig in 1532.

I always sensed that the statue was of some importance, even when I was a young boy. We read that Robert Forest carved it in 1833 out of stone from Craigleith Quarry. The stone block weighing 14 tons had to be drawn on a wagon by eight powerful horses, all the way to Calton Hill, where it was dragged up the hill by sixty quarrymen to where Forest had set up his studio. The monumental task of transporting the massive piece of rock along Princes Street, in the centre of Edinburgh, on its journey to Calton Hill, attracted a great crowd who followed it all the way to its destination.

At last I'd found what I was looking for—but where was it now? The only lead I had was that at one time it had been stored safely in a warehouse, the address being kept secret for fear of vandalism.

Meanwhile, I was given the name of a man, Bill Scott, who was writing a book about Buttercup Dairy Farm, which surrounded Clermiston House, and he was looking for people who might have some information on it. When I contacted Bill he told me that as a young boy he'd lived in one of the cottages on the farm, and had vivid memories of the place. He knew fascinating details about its owner and creator Andrew Ewing, who had started modestly and gradually expanded his farm, to the extent that the roads around his hen huts were over five miles long. He opened shops all over Scotland, and in the north of England too, selling his farm produce. They were known as Buttercup Dairy Co. shops and would have live chicks in the window displays.

Andrew Ewing amassed a vast fortune and quietly gave it away in his desire to die a poor man. He donated 100,000 eggs to local hospitals and charities during the depression of the early 1930s, and bought cars and houses for his loyal workforce, and did indeed die a poor man. Today the only thing left standing as a reminder of this fascinating man, is the big white house that he built for himself at the bottom of the tree-lined drive which took you down into Buttercup Dairy Farm.

I had many conversations with Bill Scott, but the last time we spoke he told me of a woman who had contacted him looking for information about Clermiston House. He said she had lived there as a child, before her family moved to Ireland, and could he pass on my phone number to her? "Of course," I said, "maybe we can help each other."

Three or four weeks passed before I got a call from the woman. She told me her family had lived in the house for many years but had left there when she was eight, and moved over to Ireland. She said she loved the house and the estate, and remembered, too, the statue, the sunken gardens and the orchard. She had been trying for years to find someone who could tell her what had happened to the house since they left. I was excited to hear her sharing her memories and went on to tell her all about my experiences as a young boy in this place I had fallen in love with.

I told her the story of going upstairs from the basement into the main house and runnng up the grand staircase onto the first floor landing, looking through the empty rooms which sent a chill through me. Further up the staircase, on the top landing, I'd seen two big empty rooms. One led through to the other, with a double open doorway between them, and I was looking up at the two great chandeliers hanging from the ceiling when I heard a noise like something dragging along the floor. Suddenly, a woman appeared in a long black dress with a white lace outline. She was looking down at a book that she held with both hands, and she walked slowly to the middle of the doorway then stopped and slowly turned her head towards me. She looked at me for a second, then looked back down at her book and walked out of sight. I was so terrified I ran down the stairs and out of there as quickly as I could.

The woman from Ireland asked me to describe what the woman I saw looked like. I did and then the phone went silent for a few seconds. In a trembling voice she said, "That was my grandmother." The woman seemed genuinely shaken by what I had told her and said she would phone me back, but she never did.

The trail of the statue went cold, but I wasn't giving up. I would keep searching.

The area where I had my little hideaway flat was on the outskirts of a housing scheme, called Dumbiedykes, just two hundred yards or so from the Scottish Parliament building. Despite its location there were problems in the scheme with drugs, gangs and anti-social behaviour. A mob of young thugs was kicking a ball against my window, and I did something that turned out to not be in my best interest—I confronted them. For weeks I put up with their verbal abuse and threats. I had stones thrown at my windows nightly and they kicked in the windows of the stair door every weekend. This gang was running riot on the estate and terrifying some of the older folk. I spoke to many of the residents about it, and thought people shouldn't have to live like this, frightened to come out of their front door, living in horrible surroundings with concrete everywhere.

I made contact with a senior officer at Edinburgh Council. We had a few meetings and between us we formed a group, called the Dumbiedykes Environmental Group, and we set about trying to make a difference.

Carol, from Edinburgh Council, and I had similar ideas. We wanted to involve the police in cleaning up the estate and rooting out the drug dealers, and to break up the gang who had been terrorising the residents. We also wanted to dig up the concrete that surrounded the buildings. I wanted to put in gardens so that people could grow things and make friends with their neighbours. I felt that if we could get people talking to each other, and give them some pride in where they lived, they would take back ownership of it.

There were 1,200 people living in 660 flats, and the first thing we did was to encourage other residents to join the group. We then prepared a constitution to register with Edinburgh Council. I took up the position of chairman and we also appointed a treasurer (Liz Mulligan) and a secretary (Linda Ellison). Together we prepared the mission statement, clearly setting out the purpose of the group and its aims for the future.

We set up weekly meetings and spent hours discussing exactly how to go about it. It was going to be a massive task, and it was going to take a lot of money—we would need to put together a master plan for the whole estate. In it we would design gardens which could be leased to the tenants who wanted to take them on; create green spaces with trees and shrubs across the whole estate; re-route the pathways for easier access; create seating areas where people could come out of their flats and sit in nice surroundings.

All these plans would require the services of a professional landscape architect. We knew that if we took the whole plan to the powers that be, the sums of money involved would have made it a non-starter. So we split the master plan into manageable areas and broke it down into smaller components. The idea was to take the plan to the top people at Edinburgh Council, including the director of housing, and apply for funding.

However, we were informed that an experiment was in the making: the council wanted to set up Area Boards across the city, with the aim of encouraging residents to get involved and have a say in where money should be spent in their area. A budget would be allocated to each board for environmental improvements.

The timing could not have been better—we joined the South Central Area Board and put forward our proposal. It turned out that we had some strong support from powerful people in the council who liked our plan. The budget for the first year of the South Central Area Board was £660,000. Dumbiedykes Environmental Group applied for £175,000 of that budget, and not only did we get what we asked for, they said they would fund the landscape architect out of a different budget. We were off and running.

It was important that we did this right, and so we found an architect who would understand what it was we were trying to achieve. We set up interviews and met Annie Pollock, who was perfect—she understood exactly what we were trying to do. Annie had worked on some large-scale landscape projects for councils across the south of Scotland. She incorporated our ideas into a master plan, which went beyond anything we had imagined. She came up with a design for fencing to be made by a blacksmith, which would be unique to Dumbiedykes and would set the standard for the whole estate.

It took five years to roll out the plan and, to date, a sum of around £750,000 has been raised and well spent. The work is still ongoing but the results are there for all to see... gardens are beautifully looked after by the residents who are growing flowers and vegetables; there are trees and shrubs and stone sculptures; there's a grassed area for children to play on with toadstools and a small train and carriages carved out of wood. We even persuaded the council to put in new street lighting so residents would feel safer walking home at night. The gangs are gone. People feel safer. And it warms my heart to see families out in their garden having barbecues.

To cap it all, our Dumbiedykes Environmental Group, which included Annie Pollock, the landscape architect, and Carol Duncan from Edinburgh Council, were given a BURA (British Urban Regeneration Award) for services to the community, presented to us at the House of Lords in London.

I was enjoying doing live performances again, and also released my third solo album, entitled *On The Inside*. As before, it was produced by my good friend Davie.

Unfortunately my mum's health was deteriorating—her dementia was becoming a lot worse. Sometimes I would go to see her and she would think I was my dad, or get me mixed up with someone else. It was heartbreaking. I still took her out for a run in the car, sometimes, past our old house where she brought us all up, but she didn't remember it. Or I would take her out for a walk in the grounds, but it became harder to persuade her to do that now. Rosemary, Norman, and I all stepped up our visits.

She started to pick up infections, which hit her hard and she was in and out of the hospital. Eventually a phone call came that said she was very ill and had been taken to the Western General Hospital. The doctor told us she probably wouldn't make it through the night. She was in the Accident and Emergency's observation ward because there wasn't a bed available anywhere else. I was angry and brokenhearted at the same time. All night they were bringing in drunks who were shouting and swearing, and there were emergency patients being moved about on rattling trollies.

It was like a parallel world going on around us while my mother was taking her last breaths behind a curtain that was our only privacy. My sister and I sat with her to the end. After she passed away, all they offered us was the use of a small room to grieve in. It was disgraceful.

She died on the 10th February 2010.

It's funny how life works sometimes. Not long after my mum died I got a phone call from Sarah asking if I could go and see her, as she wanted to tell me something. Before I got there I knew what she was going to say. She stood in the middle of the floor looking nervous, but excited, and told me she was pregnant. I was over the moon.

But her relationship was unstable and her financial situation wasn't great either. I told her we would work it out—everything would be fine. Mia was born on 26th September 2010 and was just adorable. To think I could have lost all of that.

CHAPTER SEVENTEEN

However, it seemed that I was going to be haunted by the ugly monster of The Bay City Rollers all my life. No matter how hard I tried, it wouldn't go away.

I'd had a message from Ian Mitchell and Wendy saying that the Rollers were proceeding with their lawsuit against Arista Records for unpaid royalties. Ian had a lawyer, Bill Buus, in California he wanted me to speak to, so I set up a time to call him. He had taken on a case for Ian Mitchell when he was touring his band around America and had suddenly been stopped from using the name Bay City Rollers. It turned out that someone, with no connection to the Rollers, had registered the name in America and had the rights to its use. Bill fought the case in court and finally won the right for Ian to go out as Ian Mitchell's Bay City Rollers. But it had taken a lot of money to fight it and Ian was still paying back the costs.

During the phone call, Bill informed me that they had also approached Pat McGlynn, who was interested in fighting his case. Bill said he would not take the case on a contingency (no win, no fee) basis, he would only take it on if two of the parties paid him hourly. Since he and Ian already had their own arrangement, it meant Pat and I would have to pay his legal fees.

Neither Pat nor Ian had any contractual agreement with The Bay City Rollers or Arista Records, but they claimed that there was a verbal agreement to share royalties with them. In my case I had a recording contract signed in 1971. Bill said it was going to be a difficult case because of the time lapse, so we would have to find a way around the Statute of Limitations.

It wasn't exactly the ideal situation I was looking for, but it was the best deal on the table, so I agreed on one condition: that Bill would be taking on three separate clients and fight each case on its merits, and would agree to that in writing. He also informed me that because his practice was outside of New York he would have to appoint a New York lawyer to sponsor him and that would mean more money.

Meanwhile, the Rollers had filed their own lawsuit under the name of "Faulkner et al", and it cited Eric Faulkner, Stuart Wood, Alan Longmuir, Derek Longmuir and Les McKeown as the claimants, along with Duncan Faure. That really surprised me—Duncan had joined the band as lead singer when it was on its last legs and, as far as I was aware, hadn't sung on anything that sold any copies. But, his signature was on a new agreement amongst the band set up in 1981.

Previously, I had asked Tam Paton if I could come out to his house to see him. I wanted to ask him to write out a statement confirming that I was the lead vocalist on all of the early recordings. He had been quite happy to do it, and we'd sat down at the table and gone through the list of song titles, with him writing it all down and signing the statement. Tam had health issues. He'd had a heart attack a couple of years before, and a mild stroke, so it was best to get his statement now, in case anything more happened.

While I was at the house, Ray Cotter (Tam's ex-partner) came over from his static caravan that stood in Tam's vast garden at the rear of the house. Ray was living in a caravan, while Tam was living in his mansion—guarded by a ten-foot fence, multiple CCTV cameras, and two massive Rottweiler dogs.

Tam was showing off in front of Ray and said, "Tell Nobby about my mother's house in Prestonpans." Tam's mother had died in a nursing home and they were clearing her stuff from the house. Ray laughed and said, "Yeah, we pulled the fire out and found over £100,000 pounds stashed in the fireplace." I was a bit suspicious—his mother wasn't that well off. Where did the money come from? He wasn't going to tell me.

Another time I'd heard an interesting story about Tam… it was said he'd had £375,000 in a bank account on the Isle of Man, which was a tax haven, and he couldn't bring the money into the UK without paying tax. He approached a guy by the name of Colin Archibald (I knew Colin Archibald and he was as crooked as they come) and told him about his predicament. Colin put him onto an accountant friend of his who said he would be able to launder the cash and get it into the country tax-free, so Tam gave him access to the bank account and arranged to meet him off the ferry at Liverpool. The ferry came in—but the accountant was gone, and so was all the money!

Three months after seeing Tam I got a very early morning phone call from one of the boys at his house, telling me Tam had died from a massive heart attack while sitting in his Jacuzzi hot tub. Tam died, age 70, at his home in Edinburgh, Little Keller-stain, on the 8th April 2009.

There must have been three or four hundred people at his funeral. Tam had mixed with a lot of very heavy characters, and I'd met some of them at his house over the last few years. As some of these more colourful acquaintances arrived, they saw me and gathered round. I could see the paparazzi up on the hill with cameras pointing in my direction, and I was grabbed by a number of reporters who asked why I was the only one from The Bay City Rollers at the funeral. I replied, "I can't speak for anyone else—but I'm here to remember and celebrate the good times we had when we were young men on an adventure, start-ing off in the music business. No matter what happened later on, these were the best times and I wouldn't change it for the world."

Tam's estate was valued at approximately £4.5 million. His nephew stood up at the funeral and gave a short eulogy, at the end of which he said, "I've been asked to announce the contents of Tam's will: there will be no human benefactor—all the money has been left to animal charities." There was a big sigh from the congregation. I laughed and said, "Selfish to the end." I'm sure he did that to try to improve his image and his legacy, to coun-teract all the bad publicity he had over the years, but it didn't work. There were a lot of people who helped Tam when things weren't so good, and I felt sorry for them.

Back with the legal proceedings, the first thing Ian, Pat and I needed to do was to intervene in the Rollers case, which meant our lawyer filing an intervention with the District Court in New York to allow us to be included in the "Faulkner et al" lawsuit. Their lawyers fought that rigorously, and we had to wait nine months for the ruling.

The judge ruled that we could not intervene in their case because we were not a party to the 1981 agreement, but it was left open for us to sue either the Rollers for a share of any recovered royalties, or Arista directly for unpaid royalties.

At this point I was convinced that we should split the case— I should sue Arista Records for my contractual rights, while Ian and Pat should proceed in suing the Rollers—but Bill persuaded me we were stronger together. He also asked for another $10,000 each from Pat and I, on top of the $10,000 we had each put in to kick the case off.

We had started this off at the beginning of 2009, and it took to the end of the 2010 to bring the case against the Rollers. It was certainly a Rollercoaster ride! One week we were full of confidence we could win, the next we were losing our argument, then Bill would score a few more points. It was up and down, all the time. The game was, no doubt, for the lawyers to do everything in their power to keep it out of court, in order to rack up as much time on it as possible.

Just when we thought we were getting somewhere, Arista filed a motion to have us all dismissed on the grounds of the Statute of Limitations.

The Statute of Limitations was set up to protect defendants (in this case, Arista Records) by stating that plaintiffs (in this case, us) with a good cause of action should pursue their claim with reasonable diligence. In other words, within a six-year period in America.

Our lawyers were trying to prove that Arista Records had a judicial duty to the group, and therefore the statute should not apply. Meaning, as it had been a long-term relationship over many years, and as they had not submitted any accounts or statements to us over many years, they were in breach of contract. (This was one of the reasons why I'd had no idea they were releasing all the songs I had recorded with the band.) We were going to have to wait a long time for that ruling—Bill reckoned it could take nine months to a year.

During this time I was doing a lot of research to find other Rollers albums with my vocals on them and was building up a long list. During this process I came across some other albums which had all my songs on them, but they had been re-recorded individually by Les McKeown and Eric Faulkner. I listened to them and thought, "These guys have no substance or pride. They are chucking out self-made albums—badly produced, badly played, and badly sung—just to milk their fans for money!"

It was nine months before the ruling came through. The judge removed the Statute of Limitations, in part, and allowed the case to continue. The next stage of the proceedings was the depositions. It would take months to sort these out, so I got on with other things.

Earlier in the year we'd all heard about the earthquake disaster in Haiti on 12th January, 2010. Everyone was shocked by its magnitude and devastating effect and I got together with a friend of mine, Liz MacEwan, to organise a concert to raise money for the Haiti appeal. Liz in her own right was a well-known jazz and blues singer in and around Edinburgh, but had also sung backing vocals with Tam White. She came up with the idea of calling the gig "Edinburgh Bands Together" and we invited some of the most talented musicians and singers from the Edinburgh area. The event was held in the Queen's Hall on the 6th March 2010.

I had known Tam White since I was a teenager, when I went to see his group, The Boston Dexters, in a tiny wee club called The Green Light. The drummer in their group was a guy called Toto McNaughton, who was widely thought of as one of Scotland's finest and most versatile drummers. In the early 1960s he had been the drummer in Tam Paton's band, The Edinburgh Crusaders.

Tam White was proud of the fact that he was a time-served stonemason, and he worked for many years in the trade. I often bumped into him on building sites around the town, but he became well known as a blues singer. Tam had a bumpy ride on the London music scene in his early days, when they tried to mould him into something he was not. He was the first artist to sing live on Top Of The Pops, with his version of the Jack Scott song *What In The World's Come Over You*. He hosted his own TV show on Scottish Television, too, but ended up back cutting stones for a living.

There were various reincarnations of The Boston Dexters before Tam got together with Neil Warden, Fraser Speirs and Boz Burrell and formed The Shoestring Band. It was no secret that Tam liked a drink, but he kicked it into touch in the early 1980s. An acting career then took off in 1990 after he was cast in the television production The Wreck On The Highway. There followed a string of film and TV appearances over the years, from roles in the films Braveheart, Orphans, and Man Dancin' through to parts in TV programmes such as Taggart, Eastenders and River City.

We managed to persuade Tam White to perform at the Queen's Hall for the Haiti appeal, and he brought the house down with his last song, a heartfelt performance of *The Water Is Wide*. It was his last live performance before his sudden death on 21st June 2010.

Our second venture with Edinburgh Bands Together took place at The Jam House in Queen Street on the 6th March the following year. This time it was to raise funds for a new building to house St. Columba's Hospice.

In the weeks leading up to the event I started to feel unwell. I had been having some problems with my breathing, especially during the night, when I was struggling to breath. My doctor prescribed an inhaler and suspected I had asthma, but, even with the inhaler, I was getting worse. One night I awoke gasping for air—I tried the inhaler but it didn't make much difference, so I phoned for an ambulance and was taken into the Royal Infirmary. They discovered I had a severe chest infection, which in turn had brought on an asthma attack. The tests also revealed that I had COPD (Chronic Obstructive Pulmonary Disease), and they kept me in the high dependency unit for a week to get it under control.

I came out of hospital the week before our charity event and, although I wasn't feeling great, I still wanted to be there to perform, and to make sure it ran smoothly. We had invited twelve different acts to appear on stage that night—including Davie Paton, whom I'd persuaded to make a very rare appearance, singing his own hit songs *Magic* and *January*. The whole night was a feast of music, and the place was packed with appreciative music lovers. Our contribution to the funds took St. Columba's Hospice total to over £300,000.

I really had plenty to take my mind off the royalties court case, as I was now doing a lot of singing with some fabulous musicians.

I made an album with Mr Crow, a group of musicians with the great John Bruce on guitar. John had been at school with a guy called Jimmy Brown and they'd become best mates. Both of them played guitar in various bands before getting together and forming Mr Crow. Jimmy was a great singer, songwriter and guitar player, and the combination of Jimmy and John was just amazing. They used to come into the studio up at West Savile Terrace when I was there, and rehearse and record their songs.

Tragically, Jimmy died suddenly and John was heartbroken. As a tribute to Jimmy, and to let people hear the fantastic songs they wrote together, John wanted to make an album of all the songs they did as Mr Crow and asked me if I would sing on some of them.

The nucleus of the musicians who played on the album were Safehouse Blues Band: John Bruce on guitar; Andrew Stirling on bass; Ali Petrie on keyboards; and Shaun Scott on drums. Their lead singer, Chris Peebles, performed some of the songs and I did some of the others. It also features a track by Kenny Herbert. The album was released under the band's name, Safehouse & Friends, and the album title is *Mr Crow*. It's well worth a listen.

Earlier on that year, I had a very interesting call from an old friend of mine, Ash Gupta. Ash was the guitarist in a group, way back in the 60s, called The Images—the same group we stole Keith Norman (the Rollers keyboard player) from. I had dropped into his "Jamming at the Voodoo Rooms" nights a few times. These were jamming sessions with, mainly, blues guitar but laced with all other styles of music in between, and they were held once a month. I would go along and grab a few musicians and get up on stage and sing a few songs.

Ash told me that he had been speaking to James Burton (the world-famous guitar player) about coming over to Edinburgh to do a one-off gig. Would I be interested in singing with him? It was a no-brainer!

James Burton started off in the music business in the 50s. His skills on the guitar were recognised very early when he met Dale Hawkins, and he co-wrote and played the guitar riff on his 1957 hit *Susie Q*. He became very close friends with Ricky Nelson and played on all of his songs between 1958 and 1967 including *Travelin' Man* and *Hello Mary Lou*. James Burton developed a playing style that he called Chicken Pickin' and he was known as the Telecaster Master. It's been said that he was the greatest player ever to touch the fret board.

He was in great demand collaborating with a host of great stars, ranging from Emmylou Harris and John Denver, to The Beach Boys and Jerry Lee Lewis to name just a very few. He even had to turn down an offer to join Bob Dylan's first touring band but, in 1969, Elvis Presley asked him to join his Las Vegas show and Burton organised the T.C.B. Band for him (it stood for Taking Care of Business), staying with Elvis until his death in 1977.

He is also in the Musicians Hall of Fame in Nashville, and a member of the Rock and Roll Hall of Fame—his induction speech given by his long-time fan, Keith Richards.

Many times I've watched my copy of the concert *Roy Orbison and Friends: A Black and White Night*. In it, Roy Orbison's backing band was an all-star ensemble: backing singers were Jackson Browne, Bonnie Raitt, K.D. Lang, and Jennifer Warnes; musicians included Bruce Springsteen, Tom Waits, Elvis Costello, T-Bone Burnett and, of course, James Burton. Interviewed as he came off the stage, Bruce Springsteen says, "You don't always get the chance to sing with the great Roy Orbison and play guitar with James Burton."

So this guy was ***immense*** in the music world, and I was really looking forward to getting on stage with him. He specifically asked me to sing *Travelin' Man* and *Hello Mary Lou*, which he'd recorded with Ricky Nelson, and I asked him if we could also do *Susie Q* and one of my all-time favourites he had recorded with Emmylou Harris, called *Till I Gain Control Again*, written by Rodney Crowell.

The event took place at the Voodoo Rooms above the Café Royal in Edinburgh, to a sell-out crowd of, mainly, guitar players and musicians. I had been asked to put a band together behind James Burton, and on stage I had Kevin Dorian on drums, Colin Hepburn on keyboards, Rod Kinnaird on bass and John Bruce on guitar. It was just fantastic and when I sang *Till I Gain Control Again* James Burton played the most beautiful guitar solo that brought the house down.

I put forward a friend of mine Davie Scott, or Davie Sloane as he's known when fronting his band The Rattlers, to do a few songs at the James Burton gig. He got up and did Elvis and Orbison as only he can. Davie had played for me at both the Queen's Hall and Jam House charity gigs and is a very obliging guy. He's a songwriter of note and a singer of substance. I've produced three of his songs so far, with more to come for a future album, and I've sung with him many times since, doing evenings of close harmony vocals and songs from our favourite artists—it's a lot of fun.

It was just after this that I met Flora. I had been asked by Kenny Powrie, a guitar virtuoso friend of mine, if I could help her with something at her house. Flora had been involved in the jazz scene, promoting many gigs in Edinburgh and around, as well as helping her close friend Tam White to promote his live gigs. She had recently suffered from a short but debilitating illness, which thankfully she was recovering from. Our friendship blossomed from the first time I met her. She liked my songs and encouraged me to continue, and complete this book which I first started over ten years ago, but had put away for fear of facing up to my past.

She had a connection, and close bond, with an American jazz band she knew and loved in the 1990s when they were young and just out of music college. She'd seen the very talented, young jazz trumpeter, Rob Mazurek, playing trumpet on stage with an actor pal doing a one-man show. Rob is a lovely guy, warm and friendly, and he often sat in and played with local musicians at their gigs. He and Flora became big buddies over a few malts, and when he was leaving for America he asked Flora if it might be possible to bring his college pals to gig at the Edinburgh Fringe the following year.

All five of them arrived the next year—all young, very talented and enthusiastic. She had found a venue for them at The Tron Jazz Cellar and did the promotion for the gigs there. They were hugely successful, so much so that, for the next five years the band crowded into her house every August while she cooked meals for them, introduced them to Islay malts, did all the publicity for the gigs and even sold the tickets on the door.

Everyone loved Rob Mazurek, including a girl he met at one of their Fringe gigs, Roselis, from Brazil. He fell under her spell, married her and three years later took off to Brazil to make music and paint. They were all so very sad to lose him. So the Robert Mazurek Quintet became The Eric Alexander Quartet. Eric played sax with the band and loved Edinburgh. He too met a girl (Spanish this time) at one of his Edinburgh Fringe gigs. They married and now live happily in New York with two young teenage sons. The band's piano player, Randy Tressler also met a girl (American this time) while in Edinburgh! They married and now live in Chicago.

Flora explained all this background story to me because, after an absence of many years,

The Eric Alexander Quartet were coming to town again! With Harold Maybern on piano this time, as well as original members from the 1990s: John Webber on bass; Joe Farnsworth on drums and, of course, Eric Alexander on sax.

Now, this is not something I admit lightly, I know there may be consequences—but I didn't know who Harold Maybern was. I hadn't followed jazz music. Most of it had gone right over my head. But the more I learned about him, the more respectful I became. He was up there amongst the very best of jazz pianists.

Flora told me about how great a saxophone player Eric Alexander was, and that he had been a student at William Paterson University, New Jersey, and was taught by Harold Maybern, a frequent instructor at the Stanford Jazz Workshop. Flora, when she had been feeling unwell, told John Webber, the bass player, that she would love them to visit Edinburgh one more time, before she fell off the perch. The band had a couple of gigs coming up in Europe so they managed to change their itinerary and fly via Edinburgh on their route back from Dusseldorf to New York.

In Edinburgh they played two truly wonderful, sell-out gigs at the Edinburgh Jazz Bar. Flora made a quick recovery when she managed to get them to Edinburgh, and she insisted I go along to the gig too. I sat the whole night absolutely gobsmacked— they just blew me away. Harold Maybern, who was now in his late seventies, got up from his piano about halfway through the set and introduced the members of the quartet, "The wonderful John Webber on bass and Joe Farnsworth on drums," and then said, "This young man here, Eric Alexander, is the best Jazz and Blues saxophonist you will hear on this planet!"

I'm out of my depth commenting on jazz, but I know when I'm listening to something special, and I thought it was out of this world. Flora kept saying to me, "You and Eric should do something together," and I thought, "These two worlds will not collide."

One year later Eric Alexander came back to Edinburgh while on tour with his old mate, and former band member, the trumpet player Jim Rotondi, who was now based in Europe.

When Flora told Jim that I was in litigation in the New York courts with Arista/Sony and The Bay City Rollers, Jim started dancing around and singing "*S-A-T-U-R-D-A-Y... NIGHT!*" He said when he was at music college, in 1976, my original version of *Saturday Night* was always the first song on the jukebox at lunchtime in the cafeteria.

The day after the band arrived, Flora invited me over for a late lunch to meet the band. I was introduced to Eric Alexander first, and he introduced Jim Rotondi, who played the trumpet

237

and flugelhorn, Bern Reiter who was the drummer, and Renatto Chicco who would be playing keyboards. I've been in and around music for the best part of my life and I've met a lot of people but I'm still in awe of great musicians.

Eric and I got talking. He was a fair bit younger than me, and a very handsome guy - "great front man" was my immediate thought. I expressed my feelings about the last time I saw him with Harold Maybern and how I'd loved it, in particular his arrangement of the Michael Jackson song, *You're Out Of My Life*. Eric's words nearly knocked me off my feet: "Why don't you come up and sing it with us tonight?" What do you do in a situation like that? You can say, "No I'm not prepared for that."... Or you can say, "I'd love to, but I'm not even sure of the lyrics!" which is what I did say. So Eric wrote them down on the back of an envelope and I sang it to him. He said, smiling, "Do it just like that." But I really didn't feel ready, so I excused myself saying, "I'll see you all at the club," and I went back to my flat and spent an hour and a half getting familiar with the song so I could move it around a little.

That night I arrived at the club, which was full to the brim with musicians and jazz enthusiasts. I can tell you, I was more nervous getting up for one song with these guys than I would have been getting up to do a one-hour set on my own. These guys are amongst the very best in the jazz world.

I couldn't get a seat and was standing at the bar when Flora came down the stairs on the arm of her son, David. She had a certain presence about her—it was like being in a film set in a dark nightclub when someone with class walks in and lights up the room. She got the attention she deserved and I picked up immediately the respect and love the guys in the band had for her. She had the natural attraction of an open, honest, generous and warm-hearted person. She was also very determined and could make things happen. We were shown straight to the front of the stage where two seats were placed at a table for us.

The band played a tremendous first set and, towards the end of it, Jim Rotondi introduced me onto the stage saying enthusiastically, "We have with us tonight a wonderful vocalist—most of you will already know him, he's sold millions of records around the world." And I'm saying to myself, "No, no... Please play it down, don't talk up their expectations." Then I heard, "Ladies and gentlemen—Nobby Clark!" I got up on stage and, as usual, after the first word was gone, so were the nerves. To sing in front of top musicians is the greatest buzz a singer can get. I loved it and I hope I did a good job.

Kenny Herbert and Rab Howat had been friends of mine for a long time now. Rab Howat's history goes away back to The Incredible String Band, when he played guitar on their first album. Originally from Glasgow, he was the guitarist in The Chris McClure Section for five or six years, before going on to join Frankie Miller and play guitar on *Caledonia*. Following that success he joined Davie Valentine's group R.A.F. on guitar and backing vocals, and also recorded sessions with Runrig.

Kenny writes and records solo albums, and in 2012 was nominated for the second time for the Frankie Miller Songwriter of the Year award. He and Rab started singing live and writing songs together many years ago, making albums entitled *Famous Faces On A Bar Room Wall*, *Songs Of Our Lives* and *The Last Song At Abbey Road*. As the music developed, so did their band, and they became The Apple Beggars.

I sang harmonies on some of their album tracks and recorded with them at Abbey Road Studios, and I've also written some songs with Rab—including *Pandora*, which will appear on my next album, planned for release in 2014.

Kenny and Rab were playing at The Jam House in Edinburgh, so I went along to hear them. Before the gig started I was casually chatting to Rab, when all of a sudden he collapsed on top of me. At first I thought he was just having a dizzy spell, and I lifted his head to make sure he could breathe, but when I saw his eyes rolling I knew it was more serious. We got him out to the reception area and called an ambulance. He was rushed into hospital and found to have had a stroke.

When I first went in to see him he was still dazed and confused, but his main concern was "Will I be able to play the guitar?" His ex-wife, Pam, took his acoustic guitar into his room at the hospital and propped it up against the wall. He told the nurses that he was a guitarist but he was too frightened to pick it up in case he couldn't play as he didn't have full control of his left arm. After a couple of weeks, the guitar was still standing against the wall and hadn't been touched. I was getting really concerned about him—Rab told me that if he couldn't play the guitar, life would not be worth living.

One day, when he was on his own, he plucked up the courage to pick it up and play. When he looked round, all the nurses were looking through the window, cheering and clapping—everything was going to be alright. It took him over a year to get back on track, and although he still has some concentration problems he is back playing and singing as well as ever. I'll be eternally grateful to Rab for helping Sarah during difficult times, when he taught her to play the guitar.

CHAPTER EIGHTEEN

I got word from Bill Buus that the depositions would be happening soon in the United States. In litigation cases, a deposition is the oral testimony of a witness, taken under oath, which will later be used in court. It is usually held in the offices of the council for the defendants. To ensure an accurate record of the statement is made, a court recorder or stenographer is present, and they make audio and video recordings of the statement.

They sent out the schedule via my lawyer, and I discovered that my deposition, along with those of Alan Longmuir, Stuart Wood, and the Rollers representative Mark St. John, would all be taken in New York. I protested to this on the grounds of financial difficulties, and my fear of flying, but they forced me to go.

Duncan Faure and Ian Mitchell were to have their testimonies taken in Los Angeles (although Ian was recovering from a very serious illness and was unable to go) while Les McKeown, Eric Faulkner and Derek Longmuir would all have theirs taken in London.

The date for my deposition was set for the 30th March 2012. When I told my girlfriend Geraldine about it, she got quite excited and said, "Let's make a holiday of it. We could go for a week." I had never been into the State of New York before, I had only changed flights at Newark Airport. I got quite excited myself, but the thought of flying that distance put a damper on it.

My fear of flying had developed over the years from a nervous hesitation to a massive phobia. I would much prefer not to do it, but the alternative is to stay at home. The fear would start up as soon as I agreed to go somewhere, and stay in my mind until I got back. It's just not right to have hundreds of people in a tin can, high in the sky, with no escape route! On the plane I'd get claustrophobic and panicky—I didn't like being enclosed in that small space—and every bump and noise would be exaggerated by my heightened awareness. I was on a flight once when an announcement came over the speakers saying, "Ladies and gentlemen, I'm afraid we have a serious problem..." At that point I was unbuckling my seat belt and looking for the exit... "Someone has forgotten to bring water on board, so we won't be able to serve coffee." I could have strangled him!

I fell in love with New York. Geraldine and I had arranged to arrive there two days before my appointment, and we'd booked into a small boutique hotel called The Metro on West 35th St. between 5th and 6th Avenues, in the shade of the Empire State building and close to Times Square where my deposition was to be taken.

We did the whole tourist trip—the Empire State building; the Rockefeller Centre (where I had to smile when I saw the businessmen, in suits and ties, skating round the open air ice rink); Pier 17 at South Street Seaport, in view of the Brooklyn Bridge; the John Lennon Memorial in Central Park; and, of course, no trip to New York would be complete without taking a ferryboat to Liberty Island, in the rain, to see the faded outline of the Statue of Liberty appear through the mist and spray thrown up by the freezing cold March wind.

But one of my most lasting memories is of getting off the ferry, and walking along with hundreds of other people in the same direction, to the site of Ground Zero where the World Trade Center once stood. It was like something out of a science fiction movie. As we approached the site, the sound of the construction work seemed out of place and imposed upon the thoughts and reflections of the visitors. It was noisy and dusty but as you reached the memorial, set in the footprints of the towers, it was eerily silent—just the sound of the waterfalls cascading down into the dark depths of the wells. It took me back to that moment on the 11th September 2001, when I was in Atlanta, seeing the attacks in real time.

My other lasting memory was going to the Waldorf Astoria on Park Avenue as it was like stepping back in time—the absolutely stunning interior was preserved in all its luxurious Art Deco glory. As well as inventing the Waldorf Salad, of course, and playing host to many famous names down the years (Lucky Luciano, Marilyn Monroe, Al Pacino, Franklin D. Roosevelt, etc.) what interested me most was that Cole Porter, the composer of great songs such as *I've Got You Under My Skin, I Get A Kick Out Of You, Night And Day*, and possibly my favourite, *Every Time We Say Goodbye*, had lived there in an apartment in the Waldorf Towers. I got such a buzz sitting at his Steinway piano on display in the lobby of the hotel!

On the day of my deposition I was quite nervous. I didn't know what to expect—my lawyer's short briefing told me just to answer the questions and not give too much away, which seemed strange to me since this was going to be my testimony.

I left Geraldine to do some more sightseeing and walked along 6th Avenue to Times Square. I had been told by Davie Paton (who was a New York veteran) that I would get a sore neck looking up at the skyscrapers all the time and that's what happened. I reached the offices of Manatt, Phelps and Philips at No.7 Times Square, too early as usual. (I'm always early for everything these days. My friends used to call me "the late Nobby Clark" until I realised it was disrespectful to keep people waiting, and now I set my watch and my clocks at home ten minutes fast and I try to work to that time.) I had half an hour to spare and found myself looking in the window of a television studio where they were filming a live morning show, in front of a crowd of onlookers desperately trying to see the celebrity presenters, whom I had never heard of.

My asthma had flared up, probably due to stress and the exhaust fumes of the rush hour traffic, so I was wheezing and having to use my inhaler by the time I met Bill Buus at the entrance to the offices. We signed in, put on visitor badges, passed through the security barrier and got the lift up to the fifth floor. All I was thinking was, "This must be costing Arista Records a fortune. It would be cheaper just to pay us!" Bill and I had a quiet talk in a side room before I went in for the grilling.

We walked into what looked like a boardroom, with a long table in the centre, where a video camera was being set up and a lot of shuffling was going on, by a lot of official-looking people who were pulling papers out of briefcases and sorting them out on the table. Each one of them had a laptop set up at their chosen position.

I was asked to sit at the head of the table and they fitted me with a microphone. I took the oath: Are you Gordon Clark? "Yes." Do you swear to tell the truth, the whole truth, and nothing but the truth, so help you God? "I do." It was like getting married. "Just answer 'Yes' to the camera," she advised me, like a schoolteacher. The woman lawyer who was conducting the proceedings, and also representing Arista, was being very nice to me... but I remembered Bill saying, "Don't be fooled. If they are being nice to you it's to get you to say something they can use against you in court."

Before it went any further, everyone round the table introduced themselves for the record, starting with counsel for Arista, then the lawyer representing Sony Music, the stenographer, the cameraman, the counsel for The Bay City Rollers, and finally Bill Buus, my lawyer. I wasn't so much intimidated by it all, just rather uncomfortable in such an alien environment. We started at ten a.m. and, after a break for lunch, went on until five p.m.

During the proceedings I was presented with every letter and document that had changed hands since 1971, including my contract with Bell Records (a subsidiary of Arista).

I was asked why I left the group:

I told them that my concerns started with the recording contract in which we were being offered 4% of record sales. Not 4% of a 100 %, but 4% of 90%. This had seemed like a rip-off to me, so I'd refused to sign it. A meeting had then been called by Dick Leahy, the managing director of Bell Records in London, to discuss the deal. We'd read through the contract and when we got to the clause stating the percentages, Dick said, "I didn't think you would be happy with that." He had then gone on to say, "We will increase that after the first year to 5%."

I'm no genius, but I knew it was a rip-off. The contract had also left it wide open for Bell Records to spend as much as they liked on promotion and expenses and charge these sums to our account. But Tam Paton, our manager, had bullied us into signing it.

I told them that any trust in them, went out the window when the advance of £5,000, mentioned in the agreement, was handed to our producer and we didn't see a penny of it. I also told them that at that time I had been unhappy with the direction the record company were taking the band—we were just puppets in their minstrel show. I also told them how members of the group had been treated like rent boys by our manager, Tam Paton, and the arguments between Tam and I had become unbearable.

They asked me to tell them why I thought I was due money from record sales:

I went through the list of songs I'd recorded while I was in the band: *Keep On Dancing, We Can Make Music, Mañana, Saturday Night*, and *Remember* were all single releases. I listed all the songs I had done the lead vocals on, and also those I did the backing vocals on (which can still be heard on later versions by Les McKeown).

The lawyer for Arista asked me if I knew what the sales of these records were and I replied, "Since Bell Records didn't release any accounts or statements, as they should have done legally as it was written into the contract, it was very difficult to know.

"What I do know, is that *Keep On Dancing* reached No. 9 in the charts; *We Can Make Music* was a minor hit in the U.K. but was also released in other countries; *Mañana* was a major hit in Europe and had my composition, *Because I Love You*, on the B-side and the last verbal update I got from Dick Leahy was that it had sold over 1 million copies; *Remember* got to No. 6 in the U.K. charts and was a hit in other European countries; and *Saturday Night* got to No. 1 in America."

I told them I had also identified 24 albums released around the world, from 1974 onwards, which included my compositions as well as the singles, the B-sides, and the other songs that I'd recorded with the group. The last one on the list was The Rollers

Anthology released in 2011, which contained twelve tracks of mine and, so far, I had not received one single penny in royalties or had any statements or accounts.

When I told them all this, I saw the lawyer representing Sony Music throw his head back, as if to say, "That's unbelievable."

I stated that none of the other members of The Bay City Rollers played on any of these songs, as they were all recorded using session musicians. And I also told them of the time Alan Longmuir had called me to say, "You better get in touch with your lawyer—*Saturday Night* has just gone to No.1 in America with your voice on it."

All throughout these proceedings I was saying to myself, "There cannot be a judge in the land who would allow this to happen." They even showed me a copy of the letter that I had sent to my lawyer, the one written by Tam Paton and signed by him, verifying that I was the singer on all of these songs.

It was left to the counsel for The Bay City Rollers to complete my deposition. He was a young guy and seemed to me to be inexperienced and a bit flaky. He started asking me questions which had already been asked, then stuttered his way into other questions which he never finished and jumped from one thing to another, finally giving up and saying, "I have nothing more for Mr Clark."

I met Bill later that evening in a restaurant and the general consensus of opinion was that it went very well. He mentioned that Mark St John (the Rollers representative) approached him after his deposition and said, "I want you to know I have nothing against your clients, it's just business." I hate when people say that! I've heard it so many times from company executives—they are simply trying to justify stealing from others. Someone makes all the decisions, they don't just happen.

Bill was also informed that they had filed a motion to have me dismissed from the case under the Statute of Limitations—but this was something I was kept in the dark about until almost 2 months later.

In the meantime, I was beginning to feel a bit more confident about my chances in the case, now that things were coming out into the open. But we still had Eric Faulkner, Derek Long-muir and Les McKeown's depositions to come in London. They were scheduled for sometime in May, and Bill had informed me that anyone involved with the case had the legal right to attend the deposition of any witness. He suggested that I attend Les McKeown's, as I might find it enlightening.

I made arrangements to take the train down from Edinburgh to London (instead of flying), stay at a cheap hotel overnight and catch the last train home the following night. Pat McGlynn had decided he wanted to attend both Les McKeown's and Eric Faulkner's depositions. All the lawyers and all their assistants for all of the parties were flown over to London and put up in top class hotels for two weeks. I was paying a share of these costs from my own pocket, and money was starting to run out. All the savings I had worked hard for were disappearing fast.

It was a warm, sunny morning when I set off towards the lawyer's offices where Les McKeown's deposition would be taken. I was there far too early, again, so I wandered around people-watching as they frantically jostled around on their way to work, and when I spotted Bill sitting in a café adjacent to the lawyer's offices I joined him for a coffee.

I didn't know Les McKeown at all, personally, as I had only met him on one occasion many years ago, and we were civil to each other. I had absolutely nothing against him, or the other members of the band, and certainly was not out to cause them harm. It wasn't Les's fault that I was in this position. I left the band and gave him the opportunity that led to his success, so he could have been more gracious about that—rather than slagging me off in the press and at his live concerts. In all these years I had never said a bad word about him. All I was doing by attending his deposition was trying to get at the truth so that I could get paid for my recordings. Why he took that as a personal attack I've never understood. He had done enough in his own right after joining the band, without falsely claiming it was his voice on my recordings.

Bill and I walked into the lawyer's offices in London and found it was almost exactly the same set up as it had been in New York, only this time the vacant seat at the head of the table was reserved for Les. The setting up and testing of the camera and microphone, and the milling about of the various parties, was a familiar sight.

Although I did have the legal right to be there I was uncomfortable with it, like a gate-crasher at a party. It felt like I had made the wrong decision, and that Les McKeown might think I was there to harass him.

In walked Les, accompanied by his lawyer, and took his place at the head of the table. He never made eye contact with me. The proceedings were conducted by Robert Jacobs, a partner from the Los Angeles office of Manatt, Phelps, Phillips. He was assisted by the female attorney who had taken my deposition in New York.

Just as the process was about to start, Pat McGlynn walked in with his friend from London. Pat shouted across, "How's it going Les?" and they exchanged a few words. Robert Jacobs approached them and told Pat that as his friend was not a party in the case he would have to leave. That seemed to cause a few problems because Pat was staying at his house and had no idea how to get back there.

Again, things got underway about 10 a.m. with a barrage of questions to which Les pleaded ignorance, giving an implausible explanation: "I was pretty much out my head that whole time." The more it went on the more obvious it became that he had been primed not to say anything.

Jacobs presented him with some papers asking, "Have you ever seen this document before?" There was a short spell of silence as Les flicked through the first two or three pages then looked up and replied, "Nah. I've never seen it before." "Turn to the second last page," Les was instructed, which he did very slowly. "Is that your signature at the bottom of the page?" to which Les replied, "Yeah, I suppose it is. I don't remember signing that." "What does it say above your signature—will you read it out?" Jacobs asked. Les read "One million, two hundred thousand dollars in full and final settlement of royalties."

Jacobs then presented him with another document, and went through exactly the same process with Les replying, "Nah.

Never seen it before." "Can you turn to the second last page—is that your signature?" "Yeah. I suppose it is." "What does it say above your signature—can you read it out?" "One million, seven hundred thousand dollars in full and final settlement of royalties."

They repeated the same questions and got the same answers, document after document. At the end of it, Robert Jacobs, with a slight smirk, and holding his pen between his two hands in front of him said, "All of these signed documents amount to the sum of approximately **seven million, five hundred thousand dollars** and yet you say that you haven't received any royalties?" To which Les replied, "Not that I know of."

With every question Jacobs put, Les's lawyer put in an objection, whilst Les denied any knowledge. I could see it was beginning to get to Jacobs. To the next question he asked, Les's lawyer put in yet another objection—Jacobs finally lost his rag, stood up and shouted, "If you continue like this I will phone Judge Preska and tell her you are deliberately disrupting proceedings with no good reason!"

I was sitting at the other end of the long table, directly opposite Les McKeown and watching his reactions. He was cocky, confident, and quite funny at times. He was asked if there was any verbal agreement between the group and Ian Mitchell to share royalties. Les replied, "It was never discussed."

Pat, who was sitting next to me, said under his breath (but loud enough for everyone to hear), "You fucking liar." When Les was then asked if there was any verbal agreement with Pat McGlynn for a share of royalties, he said, "There was no verbal agreement." Pat was getting more agitated, and said more loudly this time, "He's a fucking liar!" Robert Jacobs came quickly over to Bill and said, "You need to keep your client under control, or else he'll be asked to leave."

Hours were spent presenting letters and documents. The lawyers even challenged Les to explain certain paragraphs in his biography *Shang-A-Lang*. To which Les again denied any knowledge, saying, "Maybe I should have read my own book." I was thinking: maybe you should have *written* your own book.

249

It was all becoming a mockery—the less responsive Les became, the more determined and demanding Mr Jacobs became—and it was going to take a lot longer than anticipated. I had to leave at five o'clock to make my way over to King's Cross station for the train back to Scotland, and by that time my lawyer hadn't been given the chance to question Les.

The deposition went on till 7.30pm and Bill was given his opportunity towards the end. He confronted him with the list of the songs I had sung on, which other members of the group had admitted were released commercially. He responded by saying, "We re-recorded some of them later on." Bill then brought up the subject of *Saturday Night* and told him that other members of the group had admitted it was Nobby Clark's voice on the record when it reached No.1 in the U.S. charts. Les got annoyed at that and said, "It was a bit stupid for the record company to release the song with the original singer's voice on it."

That was a bit of a result.

I didn't attend Eric Faulkner's or Derek Longmuir's depositions, but the report was that Eric Faulkner was a nervous wreck, sweating profusely, and Derek Longmuir was non-committal, but he did admit it was my voice on the recordings.

At the end of the month came the bombshell: Faulkner et al. had filed a motion to have Pat McGlynn, Ian Mitchell and myself dismissed from the case under the Statute of Limitations. When I eventually received the documents, I noticed that the motion had been filed with the court in New York back on the 3rd April 2012, but it was not until the end of May 2012 that I was informed of its existence. This meant that my lawyer had known about it, but for some reason had decided not to tell me.

We now had to oppose and prepare an argument against the enforcement of the Statute of Limitations. Our best defence was to claim Unjust Enrichment, meaning Faulkner et al. would be unjustly enriched if they accrued any royalties from recordings containing my vocal performance.

The judgement finally came through on the 15th January 2013, some ten months since the start of the depositions. The judge upheld the Statute of Limitations, and dismissed Ian Mitchell and Pat McGlynn and myself from the case.

Bill Buus called it "an erroneous and legally-flawed decision" and strongly urged me to appeal, but I was running out of money and told him I could not afford to pay him anymore. He offered to take it forward on a contingency basis (no win, no fee) for 33% of any monies recovered. That sort of percentage might be acceptable from the start of a case, where the lawyer has to absorb all the costs along the way, but I had been paying his legal fees and all expenses up until now, which had cost me many thousands of pounds. I told him it wouldn't be acceptable under the circumstances, and offered him 25%, but he had me in a corner and we eventually settled on 30%.

We lodged an appeal in writing and in due course we would be given the opportunity to present our verbal argument in front of three appeal judges—but, again, it would take months for a court date. It was going on and on, and I didn't really hold out much hope of having the decision overturned. I was quite anxious about the appeal. It was the last gasp, and if it went against me I would never see again the thousands and thousands of pounds I had put into fighting the case. It had gone on for so long now that I just wanted it over with.

The appeal date was upon us. Present in the court were the counsel for Faulkner et al., the counsel for Arista Records, and my lawyer Bill Buus. After all the arguments were presented to the three judges, they retired to consider their verdict. Bill said his reading of their reactions was that one judge was in our favour, one judge was against us, and one judge said nothing. It might take months before we heard the judges' decision.

The judgement came through the following week—they upheld Judge Preska's original decision and enforced the Statute of Limitations, dismissing us from the case. But The Bay City Rollers (Faulkner et al.) had got around the Statute—the one reason for this was they had a sent a letter in early 1980s claiming unpaid royalties, and Arista had responded to that letter. I didn't have such a letter.

I was pulling my hair out. Why are they stopping me from presenting *my* case in court? They're releasing records, downloads and CDs all over the world right now with my voice on them—it's a nightmare—why will nobody listen? The law really is an ass.

Immediately the announcement was made, The Bay City Rollers were in the papers and on their blogs saying: "We've got rid of the hangers-on," and "We're going to get a pay out of $30 million." Part of their settlement deal was a contract to record a new album and to do a World Tour with the original members (the "classic" line-up, as they called it) of Les, Eric, Alan, Derek and Woody. But Alan Longmuir had had a heart attack in 1995, and a stroke in 1997, after which he lost the use of one arm for a long time, while Derek had actually left the band in 1981, and had been convicted of possessing child pornography in 2000.

Les McKeown spoke about me on his Twitter page in very derogatory terms. I won't even repeat the words he used because they are an insult to people with learning difficulties. I'm way above that school playground mentality. Alan Longmuir even used the term "hanger-on" when referring to me in a newspaper interview. I just thought, "Greed will eat itself."

My last conversation with Bill Buus was when he advised me that my only course of action was to sue Arista records directly. He said that the 1975 and 1981 agreements, between the then members of the group and Arista, did not remove any of my rights under my 1971 contract. Bill also added that I would find it difficult to get a lawyer to take it on a contingency agreement. He wouldn't do it because he had taken a big financial hit and, due to my financial position, I would be best to take on the case myself. This would mean that I would have to present the case in court in New York, which was a daunting prospect. He said he would speak to Robert Jacobs to see if they were willing to offer a settlement, but he didn't hold out much hope. Neither did I, but I awaited their response.

It wasn't long before it came through: Arista said they had no intentions of paying me any royalties and had no legal obligation to do so under my contract, and would fight me rigorously.

Basically, I didn't have a snowball's chance in hell. Jacobs also felt it necessary to remind me that if I took them on and lost, I would be responsible for all legal and court costs which could amount to hundreds of thousands of dollars.

That got my back up. I sent them my response:

Dear Mr Jacobs,

I received your reply from Bill Buus. I want to inform you that Bill will not be representing me any further in this case. I already have the documents you sent and have studied them and discussed them with Bill previously.

The 1975 agreement was between the then members of the Bay City Rollers and Arista and has nothing to do with me. I was not party to that agreement. It does not remove any of my rights. Some of my rights may well be determined by the Statute of Limitations, but I intend to sue Arista for albums they have released commercially onto the market that contain my vocal performances from the time my claim was registered and up to the present day, and in the future, for which they have no intention of paying me a penny.

It is my belief that Arista's executive (Clive Davis) and Bell Records managing director (Dick Leahy) were complicit in the cover-up, and deliberately misled the public into believing that Les McKeown was the vocalist on the songs which I had recorded and released before he took over as lead singer, and that includes Saturday Night (No. 1 in America) which, I have been informed by the writer of that song, sold over twenty million copies.

Neither you nor I know how many contained my voice but you have paid out someone else on the strength of it.

The difference between you and me is that everything is not about the money. I will fight for my rights and principles with all I have.

I have attached the album list prepared and verified by me.

Your bully boy tactics only serve to strengthen my resolve and determination that Arista Records will not benefit any further financially from my vocal performances without an agreement to pay me a fair and just amount.

Please forward any further correspondence directly to me. I am ready for the long haul and I am looking forward to it.

At the bottom of the letter I added:

Small dog takes on pack of wolves (Press release)

The Bay City Rollers

The Band originated in the late 1960s, and in the beginning were called **The Saxons,** formed by **Derek Longmuir** (drums) and his brother **Alan Longmuir** (bass guitar) together with **Nobby Clark** on lead vocals. The name **Bay City Rollers** came about when **Nobby, Alan** and **Derek** decided that they needed an American-sounding name, and literally stuck a pin in a map of the USA. The nearest town was **Bay City**, and after tagging various words such as Stompers and Strollers, they eventually settled on **The Bay City Rollers.** They were unaware at the time that the name **Bay City Rollers** was already well known in the area, as it referred to the waves used by surfers in the bay.

After many years of performing in nightclubs and dance halls throughout Scotland and England, the band built up a huge following, even before they had made any recordings. **Nobby Clark** performed lead vocals and harmonies on all the early **Bay City Rollers** hits: *Keep On Dancing*, *We Can Make Music*, *Mañana, Remember* and *Saturday Night* (No.1 in America). **Nobby** also wrote the song *Because I Love You* which was very popular with Roller fans and appeared on the B-side of *Mañana,* a massive hit all over Europe following the Rollers success in the Luxembourg Grand Prix. Unhappy with the musical direction and hype that surrounded the band, **Nobby** left the band in 1974 to pursue a solo career as a performer and songwriter. The following albums were released with Nobby Clark's lead and backing vocals on all the listed tracks:

Album releases with lead and backing vocals by Nobby Clark

1974
Artist   Bay City Rollers
Title   *ROLLIN'*
Release Year/Country   1974/Germany
Lead vocals and backing vocals by Nobby Clark:
1. *Bye Bye Barbara*
2. *Hey C.B.*

1975
Artist   Bay City Rollers
Title   *ONCE UPON A STAR*
Lead vocals and backing vocals by Nobby Clark:
1. *Keep On Dancing*

1975
Artist   Bay City Rollers
Title   *WOULDN'T YOU LIKE IT*
Release Year/Country   1975/Germany
Lead vocals and backing vocals by Nobby Clark:
1. *Wouldn't You Like It*
2. *I'd Do It Again*

1975
Artist   Bay City Rollers
Title   *WOULDN'T YOU LIKE IT*
Release Year/Country   1975/Japan
Lead vocals and backing vocals by Nobby Clark:
1. *Wouldn't You Like It*
2. *I'd Do It Again*

1976
Artist   Bay City Rollers
Title   *EARLY COLLECTION*
Catalogue Number   IES 50011.12

Label   Arista
Release Year/Country   1976/Japan
Type/Length   Vinyl/75:25
Lead vocals and backing vocals by Nobby Clark:
1. *Keep On Dancing* (Jones/Love Shann)
2. *Alright* (King)
3. *We Can Make Music* (Josie)
4. *Jenny* (King)
5. *Mañana* (Howard/Blaikley)
6. *Because I Love You* (Clark)
7. *Saturday Night* (Martin/Coulter)
8. *Hey! C.B.* (Martin/Coulter)
9. *Remember* (Martin/Coulter)
10. *Bye Bye Barbara* (Martin/Coulter)

1977
Artist   Bay City Rollers
Title   THE GREAT LOST ROLLERS ALBUM
Catalogue Number   SYBEL 8006
Release Year/Country   1977/Taiwan
Type/Length   Vinyl/68:56
Lead vocals and backing vocals by Nobby Clark:
1. *Keep On Dancing* (Jones/Love Shann)
2. *Alrigh* (King)
3. *We Can Make Music* (Josie)
4. *Jenny* (King)
5. *Mañana* (Howard/Blaikley)
6. *Because I Love You* (Clark)
7. *Hey! C.B.* (Martin/Coulter)
8. *Bye Bye Barbara* (Martin/Coulter)

1988
Artist   Bay City Rollers
Title   STARKE ZEITEN
Catalogue Number   258850-222 (CD)
Label   Arista
Release Year/Country   1988/Germany
Type/Length   CD & Vinyl/ 53:02
Lead vocals and backing vocals by Nobby Clark:
1. *Remember*

1992
Artist   **Bay City Rollers**
Title   *BY REQUEST*
Catalogue Number   **BCVA-151**
Label   **Arista**
Release Year/Country   **1992/Japan**
Type/Length   **CD/77:09**
Lead vocals and backing vocals by Nobby Clark:
1. *Keep On Dancing*
2. *Saturday Night*

1995 (originally released 1980 then re-released 1995)
Artist   **Bay City Rollers**
Title   *ABSOLUTE ROLLERS—THE VERY*
          BEST OF...
Catalogue Number   **74321 26575 2**
Label   **BMG, Bell, Arista**
Release Year/Country   **1995/European Community**
Type/Length   **CD /68:06**
Lead vocals and backing vocals by Nobby Clark:
1. *Remember*

2000
Artist   **Bay City Rollers**
Title   *THE DEFINITIVE COLLECTION*
Lead vocals and backing vocals by Nobby Clark:
1. *Keep On Dancing*
2002
Artist   **Bay City Rollers**
Title   *GREATEST HITS*
Lead vocals and backing vocals by Nobby Clark:
1. *Keep On Dancing*
2. *Saturday Night*
3. *Remember*

2004
Artist   **Bay City Rollers**
Title   *ONCE UPON A STAR*
Lead vocals and backing vocals by Nobby Clark:
1. *Keep On Dancing*
2. *Alright*

2004
Artist   **Bay City Rollers**
Title   *WOULDN'T YOU LIKE IT*
Label   **Sony Music**
Lead vocals and backing vocals by Nobby Clark:
1. *Wouldn't You Like It*

2004
Artist   **Bay City Rollers**
Title   *THE VERY BEST OF...*
Catalogue Number   82876608192
Label   **BMG/Bell**
Type   **CD**
Lead vocals and backing vocals by Nobby Clark:
1. *Keep On Dancing*

2004
Artist   **Bay City Rollers**
Title   *BEST OF BAY CITY ROLLERS*
Lead vocals and backing vocals by Nobby Clark:
1. *Keep On Dancing*
2. *Mañana*
3. *We Can Make Music*

2004
Artist   **Bay City Rollers**
Title   *THE ONLY BAY CITY ROLLERS ALBUM
YOU'LL EVER NEED*
Lead vocals and backing vocals by Nobby Clark:
1. *Keep On Dancing*
2. *I'd Do It Again*

2005
Artist   **Bay City Rollers**
Title   *GREATEST HITS*
Lead vocals and backing vocals by Nobby Clark:
1. *Keep On Dancing*

2009
Artist   **Bay City Rollers**
Title   ***ROCK AND ROLLERS: THE BEST OF***
Lead vocals and backing vocals by Nobby Clark:
1. *Keep On Dancing*
2. *We Can Make Music*
3. *Mañana*

2010
Artist   **Bay City Rollers**
Title   ***THE GREATEST HITS***
Catalogue Number   88697770842
Label   Sony Music Entertainment LTD
Lead vocals and backing vocals by Nobby Clark:
1. *Keep on Dancing*
Backing vocals by Nobby Clark:
1. *Saturday Night*
2. *Remember*

2011
Artist   **Bay City Rollers**
Title   ***ROLLERMANIA—THE ANTHOLOGY*** (box set)
Lead vocals and backing vocals by Nobby Clark:
1. *Keep On Dancing*
2. *Alright*
3. *We Can Make Music*
4. *Jenny*
5. *Wouldn't You Like It*
6. *I'd Do It Again*
7. *Mañana*
8. *Because I Love You*
9. *Saturday Night*
10. *Hey C.B.*
11. *Remember*
12. *Bye Bye Barabara*

The list above was compiled from hard copies listened to, and verified as being my vocals. There are many more albums that contain the track titles, but I have been unable to verify the lead and backing vocals on them.

Nobby (Gordon) Clark.

So, I was on my own now. I couldn't help feeling abandoned. All the money I'd paid out to fight my corner was gone forever and I was back to square one. Most of those I spoke to said, "It's time to forget it. Put it behind you and get on with your life. You tried your best." However, my daughter Sarah said, "You should go for it. If there is any way left you should pursue it. How could you live with it when they are still doing it to you? Go for it!"

Her opinion was all I needed. I thought the same, too, but needed to hear it from her as well as Geraldine's, who has helped me so much already and gone through the pain of these decisions with me.

My next move was to try and find a sympathetic lawyer willing to advise me without wanting a fortune. I had no idea how to file a court case, and I had to find out how to prepare the documents in such a way as to comply with the law of the State of New York. Each day my mood changed—some days I was full of determination but others I was depressed, with no confidence at all and ready to give up.

My friend Flora helped to spur me on—she had absolute confidence that I am in the right. Geraldine said she will support me whatever decisions I made.

At this stage I have no idea what the outcome will be, but I know I couldn't live with giving up and allowing them to continue releasing and making money from my songs and vocal performances. There will be mountains to climb, but I'm up for the challenge!

CHAPTER NINETEEN

During the time of the legal proceedings I was asked to write some jingles for Castle FM, a radio station in Edinburgh. While I was doing so, the Station Manager asked me if I would be interested in doing a radio show. At first I turned it down, then I thought about it—why not try something new, spice things up a little? It might be a chance to promote some of my own music, and to help my songwriting friends, so I said I'd do it if I had a free hand to choose my own playlist and guests. They agreed and gave me four 2-hour shows, live at Sunday lunchtimes.

I engaged the services of my friend John Glen, who had a vast knowledge and collection of 60s music. Together we compiled the playlist each week, and I researched the background of the songs and the artists in order to tell the stories of the people who put them together and I'd explain what the songs meant to me in my life. I called the show Back Tracking With Nobby Clark. Not only did I love doing it, but it was also a welcome distraction from the stress of the royalties fight. The response to the programmes was incredible—I had so many great reviews and requests to do more. Who knows? Maybe!

Geraldine and I also followed up some more leads we'd found in the search for the elusive statue of King James V from Clermiston House. According to my contacts at Corstorphine Trust, the Cramond Association had shown interest in the statue, once upon a time. I finally got in touch with a representative of the Cramond Association who had done some research and come across the credible information that, when last seen, the statue was stored in a building at Cramond Brig—but it was some time ago.

He gave me the exact location and we headed there straight away. Up a driveway, which opened out into a courtyard, there it was... standing facing me... exactly as I remembered it: the

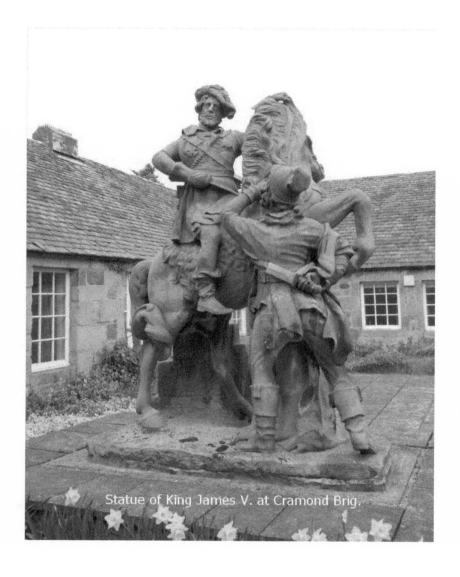

Statue of King James V. at Cramond Brig.

King on horseback, with his floppy hat, and the gypsy robber holding the horse.

The statue was safe and intact. Even more impressive than I remembered, it stood in the middle of the courtyard in the open air and I walked around it staring, just as I had done as a boy. It was strange to see it, after all these years, in a different setting—it just didn't fit. All the memories came flooding back, and something in me was finally fulfilled. I had such a connection with it that it almost felt like it belonged to me! There's something about the statue that I can't quite put my finger on— it's more than just a stone carving—and now I go down there sometimes… just to look at it.

Geraldine and I do have some fun together. She's my partner and my friend. I'm lucky she is still with me after all my mood swings and moaning.

My adorable granddaughter, Mia, is three now and rules the world. I would be with her every minute of the day if I could. She inspired me to write a song about her called *Lucky Light On Me*.

Her mother, Sarah, has conquered most of her fears and phobias, and is now working as a care worker in a nursing home, something she has wanted to do for a long time—and she loves it. I couldn't be more proud. I love and admire her so much.

I'm sober, and have been for fifteen years. And still carry my piece of fluorite crystal with me everywhere.

Now I understand my father. I'd blamed him for everything… but he was addicted, just like me, and must have been driven crazy, like I was, over the years. He probably saw a lot of himself in me. I think about him a lot these days, and I forgave him a long time ago.

There can't be a more heartbreaking experience than watching your mother being taken by Alzheimers. I remember Tam Paton saying, when we were just young guys starting off as The Bay City Rollers, "Your mother is a very beautiful woman." But I already knew that.

Writing this book has been therapy in itself. It has forced me to confront the past and deal with it. Getting sober is a process that takes time, but the freedom when you eventually let go of the rope is beyond your wildest dreams. My family and close friends are what really matters. They might be spread far and wide, but they are always with me.

The last word in my book goes to my mum.

I took her out in the car, one autumn day, from the nursing home. I drove to the seafront at Silverknowes, a place she often took us to when we were children. She had known it well, before her illness, but it didn't mean anything to her now.

There was a small teashop there looking out to sea, but as it was nearing the end of the season there weren't many people about. I helped her out of the car and into the teashop and sat her down at a corner table while I went up to order some tea. Although they were starting to close up they served me the tea, and I took it back to the table.

When I got there my mum was rummaging through her bag. I said to her, "What are you looking for?" She said, "Never you mind!" with a little smile on her face. Then she pulled something out of her bag and slid it across the table towards me, covered by her hand, and said, "Put that towards your petrol."

When she took her hand away, lying on the table was a strong mint.

Hitmakers
NOBBY CLARK